THE
GREAT WESTERN
AT WAR 1939-1945

Patrick Stephens Limited, an imprint of Haynes Publishing, has published authoritative, quality books for enthusiasts for more than a quarter of a century. During that time the company has established a reputation as one of the world's leading publishers of books on aviation, maritime, military, model-making, motor cycling, motoring, motor racing, railway and railway modelling subjects. Readers or authors with suggestions for books they would like to see published are invited to write to: The Editorial Director, Patrick Stephens Limited, Sparkford, Nr Yeovil, Somerset, BA22 7JJ.

THE
GREAT WESTERN
AT WAR 1939-1945

Tim Bryan

Patrick Stephens Limited

Dedication
For my Mother, with love and gratitude.

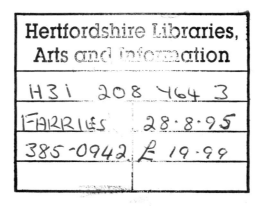
© T. F. Bryan 1995

All rights reserved. No part of this publication may be reproduced, stored in
a retrieval system or transmitted, in any form or by any means, electronic,
mechanical, photocopying, recording or otherwise, without prior permission in
writing from Patrick Stephens Limited.

First published in 1995

British Library Cataloguing-in-Publication Data:
A catalogue record for this book is available from the British Library.

ISBN 1 85260 479 4

Patrick Stephens Limited is an imprint of Haynes Publishing, Sparkford,
Nr Yeovil, Somerset BA22 7JJ

Typeset by J. H. Haynes & Co. Ltd.

Printed and bound in Great Britain by
Butler & Tanner Ltd, Frome and London

Contents

Acknowledgements

No work of this kind can be attempted without the assistance of a large number of individuals and institutions who have helped in many different ways, loaning photographs and historical information, and giving valuable advice.

Thanks are due to the staff of the Public Record Office at Kew and the Reference Library at Swindon. Further information was also supplied by the library at the National Gallery, and Bristol Reference Library.

Much material has been drawn from the collections of the Great Western Railway Museum at Swindon, and I am grateful to the Thamesdown Borough Council Leisure Officer, John Fisher, for permission to use and reproduce items in the book. Thanks are also due to other members of the Thamesdown team, including Martin Sheppard, Julia Holberry and Robert Dickinson. As usual, I am grateful for the help and support of the team at the GWR Museum, including Elizabeth Day, Marion Flanagan, Marion Robins, Neil Swatton and Christine Warren. The various wartime advertisements are reproduced courtesy of *Railway Magazine*.

A number of individuals were particularly helpful in the compilation of this book; Ian Coulson kindly allowed me access to his unpublished research on the war period and supplied a great deal of valuable information and pictorial material. David Hyde generously allowed me access to his collection, and as well as loaning material for inclusion in the book, gave valuable advice on various aspects of wartime working on the GWR. Various members of the Great Western Trust at Didcot were also very helpful, both in the loan of items and the supply of photographs and thanks are due to Amyas Crump, Peter Rance and Laurence Waters. I am also grateful to Mr Tony Brookman for permission to use material relating to his late father, who was steward on General Eisenhower's train. Michael Wyatt kindly gave me access to his collection of paperwork and ephemera, and I am grateful for his help. Finally thanks are also due to Mike Burnett and Terry Silcott of the Railway Correspondence and Travel Society and Dieter Hopkin at the National Railway Museum, York for their help.

Many other people helped in various ways, either by supplying information, or answering the awkward questions I had! I hope that the following list does not miss anyone out, and apologise in advance for any omissions. Thanks are due to: Brian Arman, David Ellis, Ken Gibbs, Jack Hayward, Tom Middlemass, Alan Parrett, Alan Peck, Mrs A. Tallboys, Roger Trayhurn and John Walter.

No list of acknowledgements would be complete without reference to the assistance of my family; thanks are due to my mother and sisters, Clare and Elizabeth, who acted as babysitters whilst I wrote and researched the book. Finally, a special thank-you must go to my wife Ann, who put up with my enforced absence as the book was written; she also read and corrected the manuscript making many valuable suggestions.

Introduction

Although numerous books have been written about the Great Western Railway, to date none has chronicled the exploits of the Company and its staff during the Second World War. It is therefore very apt that this account of the railway during those difficult years should be published during the fiftieth anniversary year of the end of hostilities.

In 1945, the 'Big Four' railway companies published a small booklet entitled *It Can Now Be Revealed*, in which they promised to lift "the veil of secrecy" which had shrouded both the achievements and problems of the war period.[1] Although some information was released to the public, much has remained secret, or difficult to discover. This book aims to lift that veil again, and to reveal something of the history and atmosphere of the period, giving the reader an impression of what it was like to both work and travel on the Great Western in the years 1939 to 1945.

Although the GWR had suffered like all the main line railways in the interwar period, struggling with increased road competition and the effects of the depression, by 1937 it was reporting its best year of trading since 1930, with revenue and passenger receipts up, enabling a dividend of 4 per cent to be paid to its shareholders.[2] The Great Western was an extremely large concern, its train services running over 9,094 miles of track. The Company owned 1,614 stations and depots and employed nearly 9,000 staff to run the operation; its locomotive fleet numbered 3,588 in 1938 and there were 8,796 passenger vehicles and 89,169 goods wagons also being on the stock list.[3]

Speaking at the Company's annual general meeting in February 1938, the Chairman, Viscount Horne, reported the good figures for the last year, but warned that, "No man would be so imprudent as to predict what troubles may emerge in the near future from the clash of rulers or the rivalries of nations".[4] The Chairman was of course referring to the continuing unrest in Europe, caused by the rise of Nazi Germany. Twelve months later, after a year of prolonged international tension, he was unable to report any such good news. The uncertainties caused by the threat of war in Europe had hit trade badly, and both passenger and freight traffic was down, with revenue reduced by almost £2 million. Commenting on the outlook for the Company in 1939, Viscount Horne was at something of a loss; "it would be a rash man who would predict anything with confidence while Europe is so unsettled", he concluded.[5] By the next GWR agm, the Company and its workforce would be facing quite a different set of problems.

IS YOUR JOURNEY REALLY NECESSARY?

TICKETS

DON'T HELP HITLER BY TRAVELLING THIS SUMMER!

RAILWAY EXECUTIVE COMMITTEE

RAIL TRANSPORT is "Half the Battle"

3 MILLION TONS OF COAL are carried by the Railways every week

BRITISH RAILWAYS
GWR · LMS   LNER · SR

CARRY THE WAR LOAD

INVASION
means more trains
for the
Fighting Forces

Give your seat to a shell!

British Railways have a double duty—to feed the factories with raw materials and to clear the factories of the finished products, the Weapons of Victory.

More factories, and still more output means more strain on Britain's lines of communication. Help the Nation and the Railways by travelling only when you must. The fewer the passenger trains, the quicker the wagon wheels will turn.

BRITISH RAILWAYS

GWR   LMS   LNER   SR

1
The Exodus

Concluding the annual general meeting of the Great Western Railway Company on 28 February 1940 Viscount Horne, the Chairman, noted that "We meet in the shadow of another Great War. Those of us who went through the four years of the last conflict have an unhappy feeling of waking up, after an interval of broken dreams, to find the war which began in 1914 still in progress".[1] He went on to remark that the threat came from the same enemy, and that although there were some detail differences, the causes for which the country was fighting were much the same.

War engulfed Europe for the second time in 25 years when on Sunday 3 September 1939, Neville Chamberlain the Prime Minister announced to the British people in a radio broadcast that Germany had been warned that if it did not withdraw from Polish territory and stop all aggressive action by 11am, Britain and Germany would be at war. At 11.15am Chamberlain told his listeners that "no such undertaking had been received and that consequently this country is at war with Germany". The sirens that sounded all over the country almost as soon as the broadcast was over sent a chilling warning of what might be to come; there had been much discussion about the course any new conflict might take, and aerial attacks were expected to be the main threat to Britain from the Nazi regime.

To some, the outbreak of war was not completely unexpected; the long build up of tension in the late 1930s had led many to believe that a war of some sort was bound to happen sooner or later. The government and the railway companies including the Great Western, had already made preparations for war, although no one could have really foreseen the extent and nature of the conflict that was to come. Numerous writers and historians have used the term 'Total War' to describe the Second War, with some justification; unlike the Great War, where the conflict was enacted in the muddy fields of Flanders, the Second World War saw the population under attack themselves. Houses, streets, factories and even railways were targets, and the British people found themselves engaged in a long and bloody struggle which was to last six years.

As Hitler's advance across Europe continued, in September 1938 the Ministry of Transport announced that railways would be taken under government control through a 'Defence of the Realm' act, if and when the country seemed to be under threat from enemy aggression. With the passing of the Munich Crisis, the immediate danger of war receded, however the statutory apparatus was in place and in the following months the members of the Railway Executive Committee met to put together various emergency plans and arrangements which could be brought into action at very short notice. The organisation was divided up into a number of smaller committees which met on a wide variety of issues, and included operating superintendents, goods managers, mechanical and electrical engineers, civil engineers and accountants amongst others. Issues such as the evacuation of the civilian population, air raid precautions, staff

Memories of lost comrades from the Great War: GWR staff at the War Memorial at Paddington 1920.

matters and a host of other potential problems had already been discussed long before war finally broke out.

For its part, the Great Western Railway had not been slow in making preparations itself; in the September 1939 issue of the *GWR Magazine*,[2] staff were advised of some of the preparations already well in hand. Amongst these were extensive air raid precautionary schemes, restricted lighting and black-outs. Also noted was the stockpiling of vital supplies such as sleepers, timber, rail and other spare parts. New breakdown trains were assembled, equipped with larger more powerful cranes; permission was given by the Locomotive Committee of the GWR for the purchase of six Cowans Sheldon cranes in early 1939. The conversion of vehicles for use as ambulance trains was mentioned, as were the arrangements for the evacuation of the civilian population from cities. The article concluded, "The necessary timetables have been printed and are stored in readiness, and the distribution by rail of emergency supplies for the population evacuated has been arranged". For those members of Great Western staff who still hoped that war could be averted, this article could not have made comfortable reading.

The headquarters of the REC were originally at Fielden House in Westminster, but as the European Crisis intensified, it was decided that for safety from air attack, its offices should be situated underground and to this end an old tube station at Down Street was converted and was ready for use by September 1939. As the situation in Europe worsened still further, the Emergency Powers Defence Act 1939 was passed which enabled the government to enact any regulations which were deemed to be 'necessary' or 'expedient' for the "efficient prosecution of the war". These regulations gave the authorities powers to take control of any undertaking or property it saw fit, and very quickly the 1939 Defence regulations appeared with sections 69 to 78 dealing with transport. Order No. 69 applied to railways most specifically, and in it the Minister of Transport was empowered to "take control of the undertakings or portions of undertakings in Great Britain wholly owned by, leased to or operated by any one or more of the following undertakings..."[3] The list included all the 'Big Four' companies, any joint committees operated by them, the East Kent Railway, the Kent & East Sussex Railway, the Kings Lynn Docks &

Railway Company, the Mersey Railway and the Shropshire & Montgomeryshire Railway. The order appointed Sir Ralph Wedgwood, formerly chairman of the London & North Eastern Railway as the Chairman of the REC, with all the general managers of the other companies, including Sir James Milne of the GWR as committee members.

As Bell notes in his history of the railways in the Second World War, what is most strange was that no public announcement was made about what was effectively the nationalisation of Britain's railway system[4]; as far as the Great Western was concerned, it was 'business as usual' with passengers and traders expected to go on dealing with the company as they had done in peace time. The GWR made no official comment about the arrangements, merely printing a bland announcement of the creation of the Railway Executive Committee in its October 1939 issue. The General Manager however, did send a personal message to the staff noting that they had "always been quick to respond to demands made on them in time of emergency" and noting that further effort would be required "in the strenuous and difficult days that are ahead".[5]

The first example of such extra effort required from the staff came two days before the declaration of war with the evacuation of children from London and other major urban areas. It was already common knowledge that the arrangements for this operation had been made in advance; the 166-page timetable printed by the company in August 1939 listed in great detail the plans for the evacuation.

There had been some debate within government circles about the danger of evacuation causing panic amongst the civilian population, and as a result, a note on the front of the booklet warned staff that "The Evacuation Train arrangements shewn in this Notice must not be circulated to more members of staff than is necessary for the smooth working of the Programme and information must not be circulated to the General Public."[6] On 31 August 1939 the Ministry of Health announced that, "It has been decided to start evacuation of the schoolchildren and other priority classes as already arranged under the government's scheme tomorrow, Friday September 1...Evacuation, which will take several days to complete, is being undertaken as a precautionary measure in view of the prolongation of the period of tension."[7]

Thus began a hectic four days during which 163 trains carried a total of 112,994 evacuees from the London area, as well as substantial numbers from the Birmingham and Liverpool areas. The government had agreed to give railway companies 24 hours notice to put the scheme into action, and thus the first train was timetabled to leave London at 8.30am on 1 September 1939. Almost all the evacuees transported left not from Paddington, but from Ealing Broadway station, which was closed for the duration of the operation. Ealing was a natural location, with its connection to the Underground system; smaller numbers of children were to be entrained at Acton and Paddington, but the numbers

In May 1940, authorisation was given for the construction of 50 of these special wagons for the carrying of aircraft propellers, a vital role as the bomber offensive continued.

The scenes at Paddington in 1938 during the Munich Crisis evacuation.

involved, around 850 per day at Paddington, and nearly 3,200 per day at Acton were small compared with Ealing, where the Great Western estimated it would move up to 46,500 each day. In the event, these estimates were a little high, some parents being reluctant to let their children go.

Many schools had practised evacuation procedures already, walking to their local station and making up lists of equipment and belongings to take with them when the time came. Some had no choice in the matter, being part of an earlier evacuation in 1938, when during the Munich Crisis, a smaller scale exercise took place. On this occasion, the Great Western ran a programme of over 200 trains, which, as well as school children included men, women, children and some hospital patients. The

company learned much from this experience, and also from having to run special troop and goods trains in connection with the mobilisation of the fleet at the same time. The return of Chamberlain from Munich with his now infamous piece of paper signed by Hitler, which he claimed would bring "peace in our time", signalled a lessening in tension, and the *GWR Magazine* reported that the following weekend the company found it necessary to provide trains "in anticipation of the return to London of these 'voluntary' refugees".[8]

Returning to the account of the "exodus" as it became known, the company had estimated that it would need 50 trains, each capable of carrying 800 passengers on each journey. No more than twelve coaches were to be used in each train, which was to be numbered, each having its number pasted to the front and rear brake vehicles. Of these trains however, eight non-corridor sets, (presumably made up of London Division suburban stock) were used for short journeys, such as the first train from Ealing, numbered 101, which departed at 8.30am and ran to Maidenhead, where it arrived at 9am. Other shorter trips included Henley-on-Thames, Slough, Banbury and Newbury. In the main however, trains ran much farther than this, into the West Country, far from any threat of bombing.

It was planned that the first two days of the operation were to be devoted to the movement of schoolchildren, with the passengers on the remaining two days consisting of mothers with children and the sick. The success of the initial stages of the operation, which was the most complicated, relied heavily on the planning that had already gone on; tickets were issued to children at the schools where they assembled. Yellow tickets were issued to schoolchildren with teachers and pink tickets to mothers with children. Schools were instructed to arrive at the station 15 minutes before the departure of their special train. Collie Knox, a journalist who witnessed much of the operation recalled how at Ealing Broadway, "children collected from every nook and cranny of London…poured out of the underground trains in a never-ending stream to change into the West of England expresses."[9]

London County Council staff assisted Great Western personnel by acting as marshals at each of the stations, especially at Ealing Broadway, where children were transferred from London Transport trains to Great Western stock. In all, 164 trains were run over the four days, which must have put an enormous strain on the resources of the company both in terms of staff and rolling stock; all the trains were marshalled at Acton and Old Oak Common, and each special was timed so that if necessary, the empty stock could be returned to London quickly after detraining its passengers. The circular urged that station masters at destinations spare no effort to ensure a quick turn around.

Once each train was loaded with its precious

Evacuees being assembled for embarkation at Paddington in 1939.

Some children were not moved far from the dangers of German bombing; this group was photographed at Maidenhead.

DAY RETURN TICKETS

FROM

PADDINGTON

ON

SUNDAYS,
December 10th and 17th

FOR

RELATIVES AND FRIENDS WISHING TO VISIT EVACUEES

For particulars of Train Times and Fares on each date, see pages 2 and 3.

cargo, it was timed to run non-stop at express speeds if possible; staff were told not to "divulge any information to the public as to the destination of an Evacuation Special", an instruction which must have been particularly upsetting to many anxious parents waving off their loved ones at the station. Once on the journey, to avoid confusion or delay caused by evacuees getting off trains at the wrong destination, it was arranged for trains to have, if possible, a clear run through platform lines and not to be halted at signals at platforms. On departure, a telegram was sent to the receiving station, advising the number of passengers, the actual departure time, and the train number. Once at their allotted destinations, station masters were instructed to hand over 'refugees', as the emergency timetable called them, to the local reception officer who was then to arrange accommodation for the children. Members of staff with St John Ambulance experience were provided at each station where evacuees departed and arrived.

The total number of evacuees transported was actually less than originally estimated; statistics

A handbill issued by the GWR in December 1939.

2

DAY RETURN TICKETS FROM
PADDINGTON

SUNDAY, DECEMBER 10th.

Outward Times. Departure From Paddington.	Arrival.	To	Return Fares. Third Class. s. d.	Departure.	Ealing Broadway.	Paddington.
a.m. 8 55	p.m. 12A40	AXBRIDGE	12/-	p.m. 6E15	p.m. 10 10	p.m. 10 25
8 55	a.m. 11 40	BATH	11/6	7 25	10 10	10 25
8 55	p.m. 1 0	BRIDGWATER	12/6	6 0	10 10	10 25
9 30	1B 5	BRIDPORT	12/6	6F 5	9 35	9 50
8 55	12A50	CHEDDAR	12/-	6E10	10 10	10 25
8 55	a.m. 11 20	CHIPPENHAM	11/-	7 50	10 10	10 25
9 5	p.m. 12C 5	CIRENCESTER	11/-	7G20	—	10 14
8 55	12A35	CLEVEDON	12/-	6E30	10 10	10 25
9 30	12 55	DORCHESTER	12/6	6 25	9 35	9 50
8 55	12 50	HIGHBRIDGE	12/6	6 10	10 10	10 25
9 30	12 40	MAIDEN NEWTON	12/6	6 40	9 35	9 50
8 55	a.m. 11D40	MELKSHAM	11/-	7H25	10 10	10 25
8 55	10 50	SWINDON	10/3	8 20	10 10	10 25
8 55	10 30	UFFINGTON	8/10	8 40	10 10	10 25
8 55	10 20	WANTAGE ROAD	8/-	8 50	10 10	10 25
8 55	p.m. 12 35	WESTON-SUPER-MARE	12/-	6 25	10 10	10 25
9 30	1 10	WEYMOUTH	12/6	6 10	9 35	9 50
8 55	a.m. 11 0	WOOTTON BASSETT	10/6	8 5	10 10	10 25

A—Change at Yatton and proceed at 12.23 p.m.
B—Change at Maiden Newton and proceed at 12.45 p.m.
C—Change at Swindon and proceed at 11.20 a.m. also change at Kemble and proceed at 11.57 a.m.
D—Change at Chippenham and proceed at 11.25 a.m.
E—Change at Yatton and proceed at 6.40 p.m.
F—Change at Maiden Newton and proceed at 6.40 p.m.
G—Change at Kemble and proceed at 7.43 p.m.
H—Change at Chippenham and proceed at 7.50 p.m.

3

DAY RETURN TICKETS FROM
PADDINGTON

SUNDAY, DECEMBER 17th.

Outward Times. Departure From Paddington.	Arrival.	To	Return Fares. Third Class. s. d.	Departure.	Ealing Broadway.	Paddington.
a.m. 9 30	p.m. 12 50	BRUTON	11/6	p.m. 7 0	p.m. 10 15	p.m. 10 25
9 30	a.m. 11 35	DEVIZES	10/6	8 15	10 15	10 25
9 30	p.m. 1 15	LANGPORT EAST	12/-	6 30	10 15	10 25
9 30	a.m. 11 5	SAVERNAKE (Low Level)	9/3	8 45	10 15	10 25
9 30	p.m. 1K 5	SHEPTON MALLET	11/6	6P15	10 15	10 25
9 30	a.m. 10 25	THEALE	5/6	9 25	10 15	10 25
9 30	noon 12 0	TROWBRIDGE	11/-	7 45	10 15	10 25
9 30	p.m. 12N38	WARMINSTER	11/6	7Q15	10 15	10 25
9 30	1K15	WELLS	12/-	6P25	10 15	10 25
9 30	12 35	WITHAM	11/6	7 10	10 15	10 25

K—Change at Witham and proceed at 12.40 p.m.
N—Change at Westbury and proceed at 12.29 p.m.
P—Change at Witham and proceed at 7.10 p.m.
Q—Change at Westbury and proceed at 7.35 p.m.

Tickets at the fares shewn will be issued only at the Booking Offices at Paddington Station on surrender of vouchers which can be obtained from the London County Council Schools.

CONDITIONS OF ISSUE.

The Tickets are issued subject to the conditions applicable to tickets of this description as shewn in the Company's Time Tables.

Children under three years of age, Free; three years and under fourteen, Half-fares.

Any further information may be obtained from the Divisional Superintendent, Paddington Station, W.2, or from the Superintendent of the Line, Paddington Station, W.2. 'Phone, Paddington 7000, Extension "Enquiries" (8.0 a.m. to 10.0 p.m.).

showed that on the first day 58 trains ran rather than the timetabled 64, carrying a total number of 44,032 passengers, reducing to the fourth and final day when only 28 trains operated, carrying 17,796 evacuees, which although less than estimated, was still a large number of passengers. Although fewer evacuees were transported than was originally thought, it was still an emotional time for the children's parents and GWR staff. Few can fail to be moved by the evocative photographs of children, some of whom, although smiling for the camera, were bravely holding back the tears. The tears and anxious expressions of parents tell their own story too.

A further complication for the Great Western was that the operation took place over a weekend, involving extra staffing arrangements to be made on the Sunday. Added to this was the not inconsiderable number of 'unofficial evacuees' who had decided to leave the capital of their own accord. These passengers put extra pressure on a system already working to a severely limited timetable. Knox reported that the luggage of these evacuees "ranged from beds to kettles and saucepans, and to all that goes to make up a home, even to the parrot and the kitchen stove though mercifully a ban was put on furniture."[10] No figures have ever been collated as to how many of these people actually fled to the West Country in the early stages of the war; one estimate is that it could have been up to two million.[11]

Even today, the operation still rates as one of the smoothest and most efficient movements of

passengers ever carried out by the railways of this country; in all 1,334,358 children, parents and teachers were transported by railways from not only London, but also industrial areas all over Britain as far North as Glasgow. In a radio broadcast on 4 September, Captain Euan Wallace, Minister of Transport, praised the work of the railways concluding that "Transport men are entitled to be proud of the blow they have already struck in the country's cause".[12]

At the same time as the London operation, the Great Western also carried out an evacuation from the Birmingham area. On the 1st and 2nd of September a total of 22,379 passengers were moved out of the West Midlands by 64 special trains which took evacuees south into Wales and Gloucestershire. Further specials were run in the following days, moving another 35,606 evacuees from the Liverpool and Birkenhead area.

Most accounts of the arrangements for the evacuation conclude by noting that the whole operation went without a hitch which is not completely true, as a circular issued by the Chief Mechanical Engineer at Swindon, C. B. Collett, in October 1939 reveals. Writing to divisional superintendents, Collett noted that after trains used for evacuating children had been broken up and distributed throughout the line, "serious complaints were received from the travelling public that verminous children had travelled in the vehicles".[13] Cleaners and train examiners were urged to furnish particulars of any coaches in this condition, and send them to Swindon for disinfection. A special disinfection plant had been installed at the works some years before, and it was brought into use to remove any unwanted "passengers" left by the children who had last used the carriage.

A less well-publicised evacuation took place at around the same time as the one already described; the Great Western took drastic steps to move its own administrative offices into the country, well away from any possible danger of bombing. As the international situation had deteriorated, officers at Paddington had made contingency plans which led in July 1939 to contracts being let for the construction of a purpose-built headquarters at Aldermaston in Berkshire. Six steel framed and brick panelled buildings were planned, and construction was complete by 18 December, when the first offices were occupied by staff. In the meantime, the Company had the use of a number

One of the tickets issued to evacuees; these are now extremely rare. (Mike Wyatt Collection)

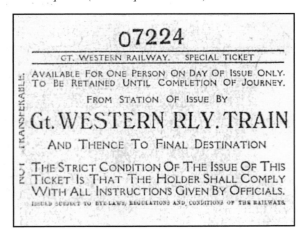

An interior view one of the offices at Beenham Grange. (D. J. Hyde Collection)

of country houses in the Thames Valley, each of which was occupied by particular departments. By far the largest was at Beenham Grange, at Aldermaston, which initially provided accommodation for the General Manager, the secretary, and the company solicitor.

Also used were Crookham House, Thatcham, (chief goods manager), Hyde End House, Midgham (chief accountant), Wasing Place, Midgham (further accounts staff), Wharf House, Padworth (the surveyor), and The Gables, Cholsey (Registration Office). Before the war, Crookham House had been the residence of a Major Tull, who was often seen by staff threading his way through the desks and trestle tables in his old home, making his way out towards the greenhouses and fruit gardens, which were strictly out of bounds to railway employees. In the early stages of the war, sidings at Newbury Racecourse station were requisitioned for use by Paddington staff, who used restaurant cars as accommodation until more permanent accommodation could be found.

The Company first gave notice of these large scale evacuations in the *GWR Magazine* in October 1939, and in an article entitled 'Somewhere in the Country' it noted that "an excellent spirit prevailed in among the various office staffs, and grumbles were few and half hearted".[14] Once "The Huts", as they became known by staff, were opened, further staff from locations such as South Lambeth, Smithfield and the engineers office moved into the complex. Two trains brought staff from London, arriving between 9 and 9.30am each morning, although if bombing had been heavy the previous night, the train was often late, and a number of staff were usually absent, having been bombed out in the previous night's raid. On one occasion a lone German aircraft machine-gunned the long crocodile of neatly dressed staff making their way from the station to the office, all of whom dived rapidly into a nearby ditch to the detriment of their clothing but avoiding any casualties.[15]

In an article dated April 1940, the *GWR Magazine* proudly boasted that "by means of thoughtful and painstaking assessment of actual needs, much had been accomplished".[16] Some attention was focused on the staff canteen, which was capable of seating 400 people, and which was staffed initially by

Before sufficient space was available for GWR office staff at Beenham Grange, Aldermaston, some were evacuated to a number of carriages situated at Newbury Racecourse station. (National Railway Museum)

restaurant car staff, supplemented by local female labour. The article went on to note that "a well varied menu is available every day and that prices are distinctly reasonable".[17] On one memorable occasion however, the varied menu was certainly not "distinctly reasonable", and approximately three quarters of the staff went down with food poisoning, necessitating the administering of castor oil by one particularly conscientious first aider!

During the large scale evacuations at the beginning of September 1939 a drastically reduced timetable was operated, which continued until the 24th; the circular noted that "all through carriages, slip coaches, restaurant and sleeping cars normally advertised will be withdrawn".[18] A very basic timetable operated, with all trains for the West Country running via Bristol, with departures from

Paddington at two-hourly intervals on average. The 10am from Paddington to Penzance, which replaced the "Cornish Riviera Limited", called at Reading, Didcot, Chippenham, Bath, Bristol, Taunton and Exeter and a good number of further locations, before arriving at its destination at 6.45pm. South Wales and Birmingham trains were similarly curtailed.

The Great Western Railway became the first of the Big Four companies to issue a new emergency timetable on 25 September 1939, replacing these temporary arrangements; if passengers were hoping for dramatic improvements to the service they were to be sadly disappointed, since the new timetable contained both a reduction in the number of trains run, and a severe deceleration of train speeds. *The GWR Magazine*, announcing the

Wartime photography of trains was forbidden, and thus pictures of 'ordinary' trains are rare; No. 4961 Pyrland Hall *is seen near Tilehurst in July 1941. (RCTS Collection)*

changes, argued that the timetables were "drawn up in recognition of the fact that war time necessities must take precedence over public requirements".[19] What was not mentioned, was the fact that many inside and outside government were expecting German air raids very soon after the outbreak of war, and although these had not come by the time the new timetables were put into operation, the new schedules clearly had substantial amounts of recovery time allowed in case damage from bombing raids was a factor to be considered.

As a hint of possible future trouble, the Company warned in its introductory notes to the new timetables, that they were "unable to guarantee the punctuality of trains, and cannot be responsible for any delay, loss or damage to passenger train traffic".[20] West of England trains continued to run via Bristol, and thus some of the most drastic increases in journey times were on Plymouth and Penzance services. Fear of aerial attack meant that no daytime trains used the Westbury route, and the only regular express on this line was the 1.15am from Paddington to Penzance, which ran non-stop to Taunton. Examination of some of the fastest and average

times for journeys made from Paddington before and after the outbreak of war emphasise the severity of the changes; Penzance, which in 1938 had been served by nine trains daily had this number reduced to six under the new arrange-ments, and the quickest prewar time, 6 hours 30 minutes, was increased to 8 hours 35 minutes. Bristol, served by 14 daily trains in 1938, found itself with only eight in October 1939, and the fastest journey was increased from 1 hour 45 minutes to 2 hours 35 minutes. Average journey times from the Capital were no better, with that of Penzance increasing by 2 hours 17 minutes and Bristol by 46 minutes.

Although suburban and branch line services were left relatively untouched, the timetable noted that "these arrangements will not apply to local residential services unless specially authorised",[21] while cross country and through travel were made particularly difficult. Through carriages were abolished, and the timetable warned that passengers might be required to change at junctions *en route*. All through trains from the Southern Railway, using the line from Basingstoke and Reading were discontinued, as were London & North Eastern services via Banbury, with the exception of one train to and from Swindon. To try to soften the blow for regular travellers, Great Western management attempted to maintain as many characteristics of its old timetables as possible; one example of this was the retention of some regular departure times so that South Wales trains still left Paddington at five minutes to the hour, and Birmingham expresses left at ten minutes past the hour.

Matters improved somewhat on 16 October 1939 when the Railway Executive allowed the reintroduction of restaurant cars, which were restored to a number of the more important long-distance services. As well as this improvement, which was applied to 28 weekday trains and ten on Sunday, the Great Western was also able to put on a train which amalgamated two of the company's crack expresses, the "Cornish Riviera Limited" and the "Torbay Express". This service, which left Paddington at 10.30am, the usual departure time of

the "Riviera", did use the Westbury line, and ran non-stop to Exeter. The front portion of the train was destined for Plymouth and Cornish stations beyond, and the rear was detached at Exeter for stations on the line to Torquay. On 30 October, more extra trains were announced, with two extras for the West Country, three for South Wales, and two extras to and from Birkenhead, connecting with Shrewsbury, Leamington, Birmingham and Wolverhampton.

Despite these improvements, progress could be very slow, and a correspondent in the *Railway Magazine* was prompted to write, reporting on some remarkable journeys he had experienced on both the Great Western and other lines with the introduction of the emergency timetables. The anonymous writer noted that some drivers were better at sticking to the new schedules than others; he described a journey from Bristol to London with a 'King' class locomotive in charge that arrived

The GWR assisted with the distribution of materials for air raid shelters in 1938. Here a Company crane loads up some corrugated sheeting onto a Scammell Mechanical Horse. (National Railway Museum)

at Paddington 68 minutes late on the Emergency timetable, caused by 15-minute stops at Swindon and Didcot, and a 30-minute pause at Reading for the loading of parcels. At the other end of the spectrum he described a trip from Paddington to South Wales when the driver of the 8.55am from Paddington "completely forgot there was a war on"[22] and touched 80 miles per hour at Pilning, which despite a subsequent signal check, meant that the train still arrived in Newport at 11.39am instead of 11.50am. Clearly the "funereal gait" remarked on by the correspondence was not universally popular with the locomotive crews! As the Blitz intensified however, train speeds were brought down by necessity as well as the timetable. Many of the restrictions placed on travel by the Railway Executive were done to discourage members of the public from making unnecessary journeys; there was much emphasis on allowing the armed forces, who were being mobilised in the early months of the war, the ability to travel without too much difficulty. An interesting insight into the class divisions which were to diminish as the war progressed, can be gained from correspondence between the War Office and the Ministry of Transport in September 1939; the Railway Executive Committee were asked to comment on a proposal that officers in the armed forces travelling on leave at their own expense, and those travelling to and from their home base should be granted the privilege of either obtaining a first class ticket on payment of the third class rate, or a first class season ticket at the third class rate. In a letter dated 22 September 1939, Major A. L. Mitchell of the War Office noted that since the outbreak of War, serving officers had been required to wear uniform whenever they were on duty. He further noted that "all such officers, by reason of this instruction have, in order to maintain the prestige that has always been obtained in HM Army, felt compelled to travel first class".[23] Since many of these officers were of junior rank, with only their army pay to rely on, they found travelling first class a "serious financial embarrassment". A letter from the Air Ministry which submitted a similar proposal for "sympathetic consideration" was also received, and discussed by the Passenger Superintendents committee of the Railway Executive on 3 October 1939. The social standing of the these hard pressed officers cut no ice with the committee however, who argued that if such a concession were to be made, "loss of revenue would result and on commercial grounds, the superintendents cannot recommend that the requests be acceded to".[24]

When the expected German aerial assault did not come, further relaxations of the harsh cuts in train services were introduced. The issuing of cheap day return tickets was resumed in early October, with the proviso that no tickets to the capital were valid on trains leaving before 10am, and there was also a ban on the use of these types of tickets on trains leaving London during the rush hour during the week. Passengers could purchase cheap day tickets for any trains on Sundays.

No doubt the restoration of such facilities was a relief to the parents of children evacuated to the west country in those frantic days in early September 1939. Although the railways had run a number of relief trains for relatives visiting evacuees in mid-September these had been little used, mainly because cheap fares were not available. It is clear however, that the provision of special arrangements for parents and relatives was not initially thought to be a good idea, and at a meeting of the Passenger Superintendents Committee of the REC on 19 September, the whole question was discussed in some detail.

Representatives from the Ministry of Health, the Ministry of Transport and London County Council, who had coordinated the evacuation scheme, were present and all spoke quite strongly against the idea of encouraging such a scheme. The representative from the Ministry of Health argued that it was their policy to "discourage visits from parents at the present time...such visits have a disquieting effect on the children".[25] The London County Council representative further emphasised this by adding that "any encouragement given to parents to pay these visits would reflect adversely on the Evacuation Scheme".[26] Clearly the last thing the authorities wanted was the large scale exodus of children back into the capital which was still a target, even though it had yet to be attacked by the German air force.

In view of the attitude of the government, it was decided that no special fares or arrangements for relatives visiting evacuees should be introduced for the time being, although it was left for "each company to make the best arrangements possible as regards train services, to avoid any inconvenience to the general travelling public".[27] Thus, although no special tickets were introduced at this time, the

Railway Executive Committee did consider that "where Cheap Day bookings could be rostered without giving rise to working difficulties this should be done".[28]

It was not until early December that special trains for parents of evacuees were finally run; the matter having been discussed by the GWR board of directors on 24 November, and large numbers of passengers were transported on the three Sundays before Christmas to what must have been an emotional reunion for most. The scheme started on Sunday 3 December when over 4,000 parents and relatives took advantage of the facility. Cheap tickets had to be purchased by the acquisition of a special voucher which was issued on one of the three days before the Sunday they were to travel. The *GWR Magazine* noted that if only one ticket could be afforded, it was usually purchased for the mother of the family; not surprisingly mothers outnumbered fathers on the special trains and the article continued "the first greeting to a father 'on his own' would probably be: 'Where's Mum?'"[29]

On Sunday 10 December further large numbers were conveyed to and from the West Country, mainly visiting locations in North Somerset. One train, which left at 8.55am, ran in three portions and carried 1,556 passengers. The following weekend trains were run mainly to locations in South Somerset and Wiltshire. Although the scheme was suspended over the Christmas period it resumed early in the new year. The seal of approval from the authorities was given by the Minister of Health the Right Hon. Walter Elliott, who was pictured with his wife at Paddington waving off some of the excursion trains.

Discussion of the significant changes that had overtaken the Great Western in the early stages of the war have so far centred around the effects the declaration of War had on passenger services. Freight traffic was as dramatically affected when, on 3 September 1939 the Minister of Transport, by virtue of the powers vested in him by the Defence Regulations, requisitioned all privately owned railway wagons.[30] By this action the Minister transferred over half a million wagons into the direct control of the Great Western and the other railway companies. The Chief Goods Manager of the company was quick to respond, and sent a circular to all divisional superintendents the following day, outlining the new arrangements.

A 'Common User' scheme, administered by the Railway Clearing House had already been introduced gradually and extended before the war, but running in tandem with these arrangements were all wagons owned by "Colliery Proprietors, Public Utilities, Wagon Hiring Firms and Coal Merchants".[31] Excluded were tank wagons, 'Internal User' wagons and stock set aside for special traffic. This category included wagons for carrying night soil and sewage, copperas and nitre cake. Vehicles not taken over by the government were to be fitted with a 6in x 4in enamelled plate bearing the letters 'NP' (Non Pool). The circular instructed staff that wagons taken over "may be supplied to any colliery regardless of their previous ownership".[32] Clearly this new arrangement was not universally popular with colliery owners, and for some time, caused a great deal of confusion amongst the staff; it was difficult to forget instantly what was still painted on many wagons, especially the "Return to...when empty" lettering!

In the main, the wagons which were most effected by these new regulations were those used in mineral traffic, such as the movement of coal, limestone or coke. Wagons of this type, the circular concluded, could also be used for the transportation of pit props, imported ore, slag or pitch. Within a year, a larger more general pool of freight rolling stock, which was controlled centrally was created, and the 'Common User' scheme was suspended for the duration.

Towards the end of 1939 what caused the management of the Great Western and the other main line companies the greatest anxiety was the lack of any firm resolution for the financial arrangements resulting from the taking over of the railways by the government. Under the terms of the defence regulations, no actual reference was made to the payment of compensation, although considerable debate between the railways and the government had been taking place as early as 1937, when the matter of arrangements in time of national emergency was discussed. Having considered the matter, the companies submitted proposals based on the 'Standard Revenue', a figure recognised in the Railways Act of 1921, which represented a reasonable level of income for each of the Big Four companies. In the event none of the companies ever reached this notional figure, mainly due to the encroachment of road competition in the 1930s.

This idea did not prove popular with the government however, when finally in July 1939 they revealed their own proposals. The

4200 class 2-8-0 tank No. 4212 heads a freight train near Stroud in November 1940. (RCTS Collection)

arrangement was that the companies should be given a guarantee of pre-emergency profits, with an additional amount for any extra profit earned, the rest being taken by the government. This was, not surprisingly, unpopular with the railways, which, although dependent on money earned, would not have any control over expenditure, which in wartime might be considerable. Responding to this proposition, the companies suggested an alternative which was to ask the government to guarantee a sum based on the average net revenues for an agreed period. In addition to this there were to be arrangements that allowed companies to benefit from any excessive profits over and above the amounts mentioned. The railways hoped that the years 1935, 1936 and 1937 could be used as a benchmark, avoiding 1938 which had been a disastrous year for both the railways and the British economy as a whole.

When the government finally replied to these proposals in November 1939 it was to reject them, and to add further modifications to the terms of compensation they envisaged. The most contentious issue was that the main line companies were to pool their financial interests with the London Passenger Transport Board. Viscount Horne, the Chairman of the Great Western Railway, speaking at the Company's annual general meeting on 28 February 1940 emphasised that this arrangement was flawed since "the London Passenger Transport Board were interested only in the London suburban passenger traffic, which had suffered a heavy decline".[33] What the Big Four railways were worried about was that they would be the ones to subsidise the losses of the LPTB from their freight income. The Minister of Transport was not prepared to compromise on this matter, and on 16 January 1940 he informed the railways that the inclusion of the LPTB was an essential condition of any settlement. Matters were complicated further when he stated that the financial arrangements involved in the pooling of privately owned wagon stock already described would also have to be taken account of in the agreement.

As a concession, a modified form of the companies' proposals was accepted by the government in that they were offered a guaranteed income based on their average net revenues for the years 1935 to 1937; the ceiling at which the government started to take its own slice of the railways' income was also increased. The guaranteed payments amounting to £40,000,000 were divided as follows: the LMS 34 per cent, the LNER 23 per cent, the Great Western and Southern 16 per cent each, and the London Passenger Transport Board 11 per cent. After the payment of these amounts, any balance of revenues up to the sum of £3,500,000 was again divided amongst the railways using the same formula; any further monies were then taken by the government. A further important factor was that the government agreed to guarantee an amount of £10,000,000 to the railways against any possible war damage. Any sum over and above this amount had to be found from the companies' own budgets. Although this seemed a generous amount, cynics noted that no one was really sure what any damage would cost in the long run. The agreement also confirmed the payment of a large sum by each of the railway companies for air raid precautions under an existing scheme begun in 1939.

Given the terms of this offer, the railway companies were naturally under great pressure to accept, which they did. Viscount Horne noted that the railways had "recognised that during a period of war, restrictions and obligations which in normal conditions they might strongly resist might have to be accepted in the national interest."[34] The Chairman could not resist some criticism of the government when he added that the companies felt bound to add that, "their own proposals would have provided a simple, sound and equitable basis for settlement."[35]

Although happy to accept the agreement on purely financial grounds, one recurring worry was what the role of the Railway Executive Committee actually was. The companies asked for a formula defining the functions of the committee, since, as we have already seen, few members of the public were really aware of the dramatic changes in the way Britain's railways were being run. The Minister of Transport had, Viscount Horne continued, indicated that he had no desire to interfere in the day to day management of the railways "in so far as is necessary to secure that they are carried on in such a manner as he thinks desirable for the efficient prosecution of the war".[36]

A very rare ticket issued by the Great Western's agent in Berlin, in August 1939. It is for a child, perhaps being evacuated to safety as the clouds of war darkened. (Mike Wyatt Collection)

There are indications however, that Great Western staff had been instructed not to take such assurances on face value and early in the war C. B. Collett, Chief Mechanical Engineer at Swindon, had issued a circular to all divisional superintendents warning them that "plant or property of the railway companies must not be requisitioned or otherwise removed save on the express authority of the Minister of Transport".[37] Collett went on to emphasise that any request from the services should be declined and referred to divisional superintendents or himself. Staff were however allowed to carry out necessary work for the services, so long as it did not exceed the value of £50.

The inclusion of so much detail on these fairly complicated financial agreements will hopefully have given the reader some idea of not only the complexity of moulding the Great Western and the other railways into government control, but also to show that the 'business as usual' line given by the Company was not completely true. The *Railway Gazette*, commenting on the outcome of these long and sometimes bitter negotiations argued that all in all the railways had received a fair deal, and printing the reaction of other railway sources and the national press as a whole, it would seem that most were also agreed that in the circumstances, no better arrangement could have been arrived at.

The early months of 1940 provide a useful dividing line marking the end of the first phase of the Great Western's role in the Second World War. The Company had dealt well with all the difficulties it had so far faced. Passenger services had been restored to about 80 per cent of their prewar level, although journey times and train speeds were still slow. As well as the large scale evacuation operation it had carried out in early September 1939, the GWR also ran over 3,500 special trains carrying troops and munitions, many connected with the embarkation of the British Expeditionary Force to France. Coupled with these demands, goods traffic had also increased dramatically. Ironically, because with the rationing of petrol, road transport, the bane of railway business in the years before the outbreak of war, was now severely limited. The blackout and air raid precautions seriously reduced the efficiency of the operation by making both work in stations and goods depots and yards much more difficult. In summing up his report to the shareholders Viscount Horne was in no doubt of the seriousness of the position faced; the war he noted "would be more bitter than the last. It is already more brutal."[38] In 1940 and in following years the Great Western and its staff would come to realise how chillingly true the Chairman's statement was.

2
Air Raid Precautions

In an attempt to keep up staff morale, the *GWR Magazine* reported in January 1940, that despite the war, the Company had still moved several hundred thousand Christmas trees from its station at Grange Court to locations as diverse as Aberdeen, Belfast and Penzance. Unlike today when trees often appear long before the Christmas holiday, in this period the railways helped run a quick service concentrated in the week or so preceding Christmas, enabling trees to be fresh when they were put up in homes on Christmas Eve. The magazine reported that "even this year, when the festivities in many homes were shadowed by the war, the number of trees transported by the company was not seriously reduced".[1]

Staff had just experienced one of the most difficult holiday periods dealt with by the Company for many years; despite attempting to estimate the kind of traffic they would have to face over the Christmas Holiday, a combination of factors which they had not bargained for upset all forecasts. The outbreak of the war had caused a great deal of dislocation and disturbance of the civilian population, for as well as the evacuation of children already described, there had also been large scale movement of businesses and numerous government departments to the safety of the provinces. Many of the people effected by these moves travelled back to the Capital for the holiday period; three trains to bring civil servants back from the West Country were run by the company on 21 and 23 December, with return services being run immediately after Christmas.[2] Presumably in such troubled and uncertain times, many people took the opportunity to travel, not sure when they could do so again.

On top of all this traffic, the military authorities decided to give as many service personnel as possible the chance to have leave over the Christmas period; this alone putting an incredible strain on the Great Western system, with over 62,000 men and women being transported on 143 special trains from 21 to 30 December. This figure did not include all the other military traffic that the railway carried during the period.

Things were not made any easier by the restricted services already in operation, and this led to a large number of relief trains being run, especially on the last two days before the holiday. On Friday 22 December 41 additional trains were run, and the next day a further 51 additional through trains had to be provided. As well as these extra trains, many existing services were so oversubscribed, that they had to be run in two or more parts; this in itself necessitating another 174 extra trains to be provided. Difficult though this holiday period must have been, important lessons for the future were learned, and the *GWR Magazine* concluded, the traffic was "carried safely to its destination and praise is due to all members of the staff who helped bring this very exceptional holiday period to a successful conclusion".[3]

If staff had thought that things might be easier in the early part of the New Year, then they were mistaken, since in early February the Great Western carried out another evacuation of schoolchildren from the London area. During a six-day operation, the railway moved another 102,600 evacuees to a variety of locations on the network, including Weston-super-Mare, Monmouth, Cheddar and Penzance. The company operated a special programme of trains each day, running in total 128 specials during the period.[4] The railway also had to move further valuable evacuees later in the year, this time it was not children, but paintings from the collection of the National Gallery in London; works of art were moved to Aberystwyth initially, but in 1942 the Company also helped move the pictures into even safer storage in a slate quarry in North Wales.[5]

One factor which had clearly made matters far more difficult for the staff were the air raid precautions and blackout now in place. Much attention was paid to this subject and there had been much debate and discussion at a national level

amongst politicians, civil servants and other interested parties as to the form any new war might take. Most were agreed that air power would be of great significance, and that in this war, the civilian population would not be immune from the effects of the conflict as they had been for much of the First World War. The relatively small number of bombing raids over Britain in the Great War, involving some 200 airships and 430 aircraft, brought some 4,400 casualties, almost all civilians. This total was small in comparison to the 51,509 civilians killed by bombing raids in the Second World War,[6] and there had been considerable unease amongst the population as a whole, as to the relative ease with which German bombers were able to reach their targets.

With the experience of these bombing raids in mind, much time and effort was spent in planning for the next conflict after the Great War, taking into account the effect it might have on the civilian

A purpose-built air raid shelter at Ealing with member of the staff wearing a gas mask.

One major aspect of ARP was the protection of vulnerable buildings; this impressive sandbagging could be seen at Birmingham Snow Hill station. (National Railway Museum)

public. What became known as Civil Defence had its roots in the setting up of an Air Raid Precautions Committee by Sir John Anderson in 1924. Civil servants were faced with the task of predicting what and where potential casualties might occur, and also the setting up of suitable arrangements to protect the population. This included the evacuation of high risk groups such as children and the sick, and the safeguarding of the citizens who remained; the latter involving the provision of air raid shelters, warning sirens, and the setting up of a 'fourth service' of volunteers to deal with bombs, gas, contamination, casualties and fire watching. The Great Western Railway, as a large public utility, obviously had an important role to play in this.

It was only in the late 1930s, when the fear of air attack began to really strike home in Britain, that air raid precautions began to be taken really seriously. In Parliament, Clement Attlee, leader of the opposition, argued that "another World War will mean the end of civilisation".[7] His Conservative counterpart, Stanley Baldwin, had already coined the famous phrase, "The Bomber will always get through".[8] Visions of huge civilian casualties in any new war were propounded, with estimates varying wildly from thousands to millions. The reports of

the 'Blitzkrieg' techniques used by the Nazis in the Spanish Civil War of 1938 did little to reassure many, but it was not until 1939 that any significant money was spent on Civil Defence. In 1935, when planning for air raid precautions began, a total budget of £100,000 was allocated; by 1939 this total had gone up to nearly a £1,000,000 with a further £6,000,000 for gas masks.

In tandem with governmental efforts, the railways were taking steps to introduce measures that would protect their infrastructure and keep traffic moving in war conditions. In 1937 a Railway Technical Committee on Air Raid Precautions was set up. On this committee all the 'Big Four' railways were represented as well as the Home Office, the Ministry of Transport and the London Passenger Transport Board. The Great Western's representatives were Gilbert Matthews, the Company's Superintendent of the Line, and Mr F. H. D. Page. The proposals put forward by this committee a year later formed the basis of the arrangements put into action by the GWR and the other companies. The subjects dealt with by the committee and further debated with the Ministry of Transport were discussed at a meeting of the Great Western's Board of Directors on 20 January

1939, and an account of proceedings forms a useful introduction to the Company's ARP measures. The General Manager, Sir James Milne, noted that the government was proposing "to introduce general legislation to carry out at their own cost the air raid precautionary measures which good employers might reasonably be expected to take".[9] The government he continued, "recognised that special precautionary measures would be necessary in the case of railways".[10]

From the Company's point of view, what was more important was that the government was prepared to bear the initial cost of these measures, which it was estimated would cost the 'Big Four' companies £3,250,000. This arrangement was on the understanding that if war broke out, and the railways were brought under government control, the railways would repay up to 50 per cent of the expenditure out of any surplus they might make under the compensation scheme already discussed in the previous chapter. This arrangement was accepted by the railways, on the understanding that it would not prejudice any of the discussions about compensation, which as we have already seen, were the subject of a good deal of debate and disagreement.

The board was informed of five special measures to be taken by the company, most of which were recommendations made by the Committee on Air Raid Precautions. The first was the provision of additional stores and plant for the engineering and signalling departments. The civil engineers of all the main line companies had budgeted for three month's additional reserves of material to repair damaged permanent way and bridges, and in the case of signal and telegraph reserves where it was thought that the greatest difficulties would ensue, it was hoped that a year's spares could be kept. With Britain's isolation after the fall of France in 1940, these estimates proved to be rather conservative, and as we shall see, the railways suffered badly from shortages of vital materials, and went to great lengths both to economise and to improvise with alternative materials.

The second special measure to be adopted by the government was the special protection of control centres, important signal boxes and power stations. This measure included the evacuation of key staff out of danger areas for the duration of the war, as already outlined in Chapter 1. Signal boxes, by their nature, were extremely vulnerable, and plans were set in motion to protect the more exposed locations, although by virtue of the huge number of boxes, the protection of all would have been prohibitively expensive. In fact the Committee estimated that the cost of protecting ordinary boxes worked out at £3 per lever for a brick or concrete box, and £8 6s a lever for wooden boxes. Finally, measures were also taken to protect power stations such as the one at Royal Oak, near Paddington, which were also likely targets of enemy bombing. No details were given of precisely what these measures would entail, presumably for reasons of security, although a handwritten note in the minutes reveals that the Chief Civil Engineer, Carpmael, was asked to put the work in hand on 23 February 1939, with an estimated cost of £6,000.

The third important action to be taken by the Company was the protection of the staff. Under this heading came the provision of air raid shelters and other civil defence measures such as sandbags and protective clothing. An example of this in action can be seen in an account of the construction of a new depot for electric rolling stock at Ruislip in the July 1939 *GWR Magazine*, which notes that below the canteen was situated an "ARP shelter".[11] More detail on some of the other ARP measures introduced will be given in later chapters. The fourth measure noted was the provision of emergency telephone connections with the General Post Office circuits. Although the railways all had their own telephone and telegraph networks, these connections were vital, since the government passed messages warning of possible air raid attacks through the GPO system. In this respect, the country was divided up into almost 150 areas, and initially four types of signals were sent: Yellow, which meant a preliminary caution, White, which cancelled this caution, Red, which warned of enemy action, and Green, that signalled the 'All Clear'.

The final area dealt with was that of lighting restrictions. In his report to the GWR Board, the General Manager estimated the costs of all these measures as being around £500,000. In addition he also mentioned that from the information already given by the government, further financial commitments not exceeding £200,000 would be required for the training of staff in ARP and the provision of other equipment. An example of this kind of expenditure occurred in October 1939 when the board gave permission for the purchase of 26 light trailer pumps and accessories from Sigmund Pumps (UK Ltd) at a cost of £4,326 12s

Shunting in the blackout. Not an easy task even in daylight, it became far more difficult in the darkness.

4d, and also the purchase of a Fordson motor ambulance for Swindon Works, which cost an additional £294 10s.[12] At its January 1939 meeting the board approved the steps taken, and authorised both the £500,000 expenditure on behalf of the government and the additional outlay just mentioned. The minutes note, that with regard to this expenditure, "such part of the latter amount as is not of a capital nature to be charged to the Contingency Fund".[13]

Although the General Manager asked the board for the sum of up to £200,000 for the training of staff in air raid precautions, work in this regard had already been proceeding for some considerable time. In July 1937 the General Manager issued a circular headed 'Air Raid Precautions' to all staff stating that "arrangements are in hand for the preparation of schemes for the protection etc. of the personnel and property on the Company's system during any air raids which may occur in future".[14]

The circular continued, noting that it was proposed that staff not essential to the running of the railway in an emergency would be invited to volunteer for service as air raid wardens, or other emergency groups such as first aid, decontamination or rescue. The General Manager went on to argue that because similar schemes were being prepared by local authorities, the Company felt it necessary to let staff know that although they had no objection to them enrolling in such schemes, "the enrolling authorities should be informed that they are employees of the Company, who, in the event of an emergency arising, would have prior claim on their services".[15]

This somewhat high-handed statement did not pass without some adverse comment and less than a week later, another 'circular' printed in the style of the Great Western, but by its content clearly not sanctioned by it, was distributed around the Works at Swindon. Also entitled 'Air Raid Precautions', it began: "The G.W.R. claims prior right to your services for the protection of their own property during air raids. But what is being done for the protection of your own homes, your wives and children?".[16] The handbill, which was signed Jack Jones (General Worker), continued, arguing that before discussing efforts to safeguard Company property demands for the best possible shelters, gas masks and evacuation facilities should be met. The local branch of the Communist Party which had produced the handbill, was echoing concerns amongst some, who felt that the government was not telling the whole truth about the possible dangers of air attack. Some historians have argued that in the years leading up to the Second World War, class divisions were still sharply defined, and it was thought by the establishment that under the threat of enemy bombing, the working classes "were bound to crack, run, panic, even go mad, lacking the courage and self discipline of their masters or those regimented in the forces".[17] As a result, some felt it was better to keep people in ignorance as long as possible.

Events in Spain, and the Munich Crisis in October 1938 began to harden attitudes, and many felt that it was a case of 'when' rather than 'if' as far as another war was concerned. Leaving aside the political debate behind its efforts at ARP, the Great Western Railway took further steps in 1938 to train its staff for any future air raid damage. In an extensive article in the Company magazine, it was revealed that a Great Western Railway Air Raid Precautions Committee had been set up, and as a result of thorough investigations, "plans and schemes to give effect to emergency conditions have been prepared".[18] One of the most important aspects of these arrangements the article continued, was the training of staff not only in precautionary measures against bombing raids and gas, but also to enable them to "render practical assistance to ensure the line being kept in operation as long as possible".[19]

A two-day 16-hour course of instruction was prepared and schools were set up in Bristol, Birmingham, Swindon, Cardiff, Newport and Plymouth with an additional school at Swansea planned. Each class was to consist of 25 members of staff, instructed by qualified instructors who had been trained at the Civilian Anti-Gas School at Falfield near Bristol. Much of the course concentrated on the dangers of gas attack and how to deal with and decontaminate areas effected by poison gas. The use of gas by the Germans on the Western Front in the First World War left many people convinced that they would be bound to use it on the British civilian population during air raids. The magazine article noted that although the Geneva Gas Protocol of 1925 forbade the use of poison gas in war, "there is no guarantee that gas will not in fact be used in any future conflict".[20] A great deal of time was spent dealing with the use of respirators, or gas masks as they were more commonly known. Three types of these were available: the General Civilian type, which was issued to every member of the public by the government and offered protection from gas for a limited period, and the Civilian Duty type was an improved model, and was to be issued to railwaymen whose duties would mean that they might be exposed to gas for a longer period. The final type was the Service pattern which was used by those who would be exposed to gas during emergency work such as decontamination, fire and rescue work. To assist in building confidence of staff using these respirators, special gas chambers were part of the equipment of the schools, allowing students to test their gas masks in actual gas conditions.

Further details of the air raid precautions taken by the Company were given in a 31-page booklet issued by the GWR in April 1938. In the introduction the author, George Stephens, Chief of the Railway Police, noted that "the risk of attack from the air, however remote it may be, is a risk which cannot be ignored".[21] The preparations being made, Stephens continued, assumed that "the scale of attack would greatly exceed anything which was experienced in the last war, and would involve the use of High Explosive and Incendiary Bombs".[22]

The ARP measure which caused the GWR and all the other railways the most difficulty was that of Lighting Restrictions. In 1937, yet another committee had been set up, to examine how feasible it would be to reduce lighting levels in wartime conditions, without unduly affecting the safe and efficient working of the railways. Following special tests, and as a result of a number of experimental blackouts, the committee agreed

that a total blackout was simply not workable. One such experiment took place at Paddington on the night of 28–29 January 1939, when the station, offices and other buildings were blacked-out, the scheme extending as far as Old Oak Common depot. The opportunity was taken to test out reduced lighting embracing all aspects of the Company's work; lighting within the station was either extinguished, replaced or screened with blue cloth shades. Lighting was drastically reduced in the various marshalling yards and locomotive and carriage sheds, with specially prepared blue lamps replacing the normal floodlighting, and modified forms of illumination in signal boxes were also tried.

The GWR Magazine, commenting on the January 1939 experiment, argued that in the tests carried out, "the ideal of a lighting system should be adequate to emergency conditions, but 'only just' was very nearly achieved".[23] As a result of these trials and others done elsewhere, the committee agreed a number of different specifications for lighting of stations and other railway facilities, recognising that a complete blackout would jeopardise both safety and the speed at which

An official view taken to illustrate the three types of gas masks, or respirators.

operations could be carried out. Specifications for restricted lighting were issued, the first being category B (fully restricted) which was intended to be of such a low intensity that it would not be necessary to switch it off during air raids. The specification called for lamps to be screened so that no direct light should be visible above the horizontal plane, and that the illumination of the ground should have no perceptible colour, lamps giving a light between blue and green being recommended.

Because the lighting provided under category B conditions was so dim, alternative arrangements had to be made for larger stations, marshalling yards, engine sheds and goods depots, where safety and efficiency were of paramount importance. Category C (exempted) was of a higher intensity, but although lamps were screened, the light they provided could be seen from the air at a distance of about twelve miles. As a result, lighting had to be switched off in the event of an air raid warning and to assist in this, all switches for installations of this type were grouped together at one control point. Despite this concession, conditions for staff and passengers were far from good. We shall look at

conditions for the travelling public in a later chapter, but some insight into the conditions endured by staff in goods yards can be obtained by an article which appeared in the Company magazine entitled 'A Good Word for Shunters', which quoted the *Manchester Guardian*, when it gave "welcome recognition of the importance, as well as the onerous character of war-time work on the railways".[24] The trains were made up, the article continued, almost instinctively by shunters, who had of course, been originally trained to work in brilliantly lit yards. Some further indication of the difficult conditions experienced by shunters and yard staff may be gauged from the fact that not only did they have to work with greatly diminished lighting, but their acetylene lamps were also modified by the fitting of a shade, to reduce its output.[25]

The committee also issued a specification for the lighting of passenger rolling stock which, the Ministry of Transport instructed the railway companies, should be capable of being put into force at very short notice. On 1 September, after the declaration of war, less than a month after the original instructions were issued, the Secretary of

A member of GWR staff at Bristol further illustrates blackout conditions.

State for Home Affairs issued an order, bringing them into force. Some idea of the stringency of these regulations can be obtained by a look at the way in which the Great Western implemented them; examination of the circulars sent to divisional superintendents, who were charged with a good deal of the work involved in the introduction of these measures, also shows that things did not always go to plan.

The regulations called for each compartment to be fitted with only one bulb having an output of approximately ten candle power, to be shrouded in a metal cylinder which was to have an opening of no more than ⅞ in. In practice, the Great Western with the agreement of the authorities, intended to install one 15-watt blue glass bulb in each compartment and train lavatory. In a circular issued in late September 1939, Frank Potter, the Superintendent of the Line instructed staff that "it is not necessary for blinds to be drawn, but station staff should be instructed to observe train lighting".[26] This final instruction was to ensure that no white light was showing, caused by either tampering or accidental scratching. A problem did arise however, when supplies of blue bulbs were delayed, since one of the ingredients for the blue glass had to be imported from abroad; to overcome this, the time-consuming alternative was for the Carriage & Wagon Department at Swindon Works to "dip, paint or spray with blue paint the standard train lighting bulbs".[27] The gas lighting still used in many vehicles presented further problems; in order to conform with the ARP regulations, it was necessary to blacken with black paint the whole of the outside of the gas globe, with the exception of a disc 3in in diameter at the lowest part of the globe, and a band ½in wide around the top. The interior of the globe was also to receive two coats of blue lacquer to cover the spaces where the black might have been omitted.[28]

From the foregoing it will be seen that the measures introduced in the early months of the war were strict indeed; the very dim lighting endured by passengers was not popular, and gave rise to many complaints. In an article in the *Railway Gazette*, an anonymous contributor noted that the blue bulbs fitted in carriages did not give sufficient light for reading, but did allow the passenger getting on a train to see with whom they might be sharing a compartment, and if the choice of travelling companion was not suitable, then another could be chosen. The problem was, the

article continued, that "in a dim blue light even the most amicable of us takes on the appearance of the late Count Dracula".[29] F. G. Richens, writing in the *GWR Magazine* in November 1939, gave a good impression of what travel in the blackout in this period was like. Describing the difficulties of both walking around blacked-out stations (he mistook the telegraph office for the refreshment rooms in the dark) and the fact that although the ARP lighting restrictions were effective for their main purpose, they were of no use to the travelling public.[30] Some of the perils faced by the travelling public during the blackout will be described in a later chapter, but it is interesting to note that even in the early months of the war, the hazards created by the darkness had led to the creation of a special first aid post at Paddington, which in the first three

Stemming the flow of light from locomotive fireboxes was a difficult problem; this picture shows the anti-glare screen introduced by the GWR to combat this hazard. This is 'Castle' class 4-6-0 No. 4096 Highclere Castle.

months of hostilities, treated more than 230 cases, mostly of crushed hands and fingers and sprains caused by passengers stumbling on platforms and staircases.[31]

Barraged with complaints, the government relaxed its restrictions in late 1939, and amended instructions were issued by the Great Western on 20 November. The blue bulbs were replaced by ordinary white lamps, fitted with shades; windows were to have black painted borders, to prevent light escaping past blinds, which were to be drawn during the hours of darkness.[32] Corridors and lavatories were to continue to be lit by blue lamps however, a fact reinforced by another circular on 11 December. Guards and travelling ticket collectors were made responsible for the maintenance of the blackout under these new arrangements; staff were instructed in November 1939, that any member of the public who did not cooperate in ensuring that blinds were drawn and windows shut should have their name and address taken and reported to the Divisional Superintendent.[33] The white lighting did however, have to be switched off during air raids or air raid warnings. Lighting in passenger brake vans, parcel vans and luggage compartments had been restored a month earlier due to difficulties experienced by staff in the handling of parcels, mail and luggage. To prevent any light escaping, windows, especially on brake third or composite vehicles, were painted black as necessary.[34] Although the instructions mentioned were issued towards the end of November, a report in the *Railway Gazette* reveals that the first Great Western express to be fitted with the revised white lighting was the 5.55pm Paddington to South Wales service on 10 November. This was probably an experimental run as the magazine noted that "similar lighting is to be fitted to all main-line and suburban trains as soon as it is possible to manufacture the necessary fittings".[35] Some indication of the enormous scale of the operation however, can be realised by the Company's estimate that it would need to provide 80,000 special light shades as well as alterations to blinds and curtains.

General instructions for staff on air raid precautions were issued at regular intervals, and as the war progressed, procedures were modified, especially once German bombing began to take its toll. Revised instructions were issued on 6 September 1939, and these were further altered on 16 October. After receiving a warning by

telephone, as already described, warning of an air raid was given either by the municipal siren, or on railway property, by intermittent blasts on a whistle. A piece of steel rail, suspended by wire and struck by a hammer or iron rod could also be used. The 'All Clear' was to be given by whistles sounding a continuous note, or by the ringing of hand bells. The warning of a gas attack would be given by hand rattles the circular noted, with hand bells again used to sound the 'All Clear'.

When a warning had been sounded, staff were divided into three groups; those who had volunteered for ARP duties such as fire, first aid, decontamination and rescue were to proceed to their posts, whilst staff required for what the Company called 'Essential Railway Services', were "to remain at their posts until enemy aircraft approach, when they should take shelter until the raiders have passed".[36] The third group, who were not required for such essential work, were advised to proceed at once to their allotted shelter.

With regard to the operation of services during air raids, the Company circular stated that on receipt of a warning, passenger trains were to be stopped at the first station, and passengers warned and given the chance to alight and go to the shelters if they wished. Staff were originally instructed that passengers already on the station when the raid began, were to be directed by air raid wardens, either to the nearest shelter on the premises, or to a nearby public shelter. Another circular issued on the 16 October modified these instructions, noting that passengers who were already on the premises after a warning should "be allowed to join trains about to depart if they so desire".[37] This may have been as a result of pressure from passengers, who were reluctant to miss their trains, air raid or no air raid! Staff should, the circular continued, try to advise passengers in shelters of impending departures. Those arriving at a station during a raid were however, to be sent to the nearest public shelter, and not admitted to Company premises.

Staff arriving for work during a raid were to report to the air raid warden, to ensure that they were not contaminated by poison gas. In the earlier circular, once examined, staff were instructed to proceed to the nearest shelter, however by October the Great Western had realised that they could not operate the railway if all the staff were in the shelters, so the revised arrangements stated that, providing there was no evidence of poison gas in the vicinity, "staff required for essential railway services will proceed to their duties".[38]

Lighting restrictions, as detailed earlier in this chapter, were to be supervised by a responsible member of staff who was to ensure that all the Home Office restrictions were being adhered to. To assist movement in darkened areas, the circular noted that obstructions, pillars, lamp standards and edges of platforms were to be painted with white paint or whitewash, with road curbs also painted white in one foot lengths at one foot intervals.

The problem of how to deal with passenger trains which were caught between stations when an air raid warning was given was a difficult one. A joint circular issued by the Chief Mechanical Engineer's office at Swindon, and the Superintendent of the Line's office at Paddington in October 1939, detailed the procedures to be undertaken by footplate crews and train staff in the event of an air raid warning. When a warning was received, signalmen moved all distant signals to the 'Caution' position, stopping the train at the first available station. Here, the passengers were to be advised by travelling ticket collectors or Guards that a raid was imminent and that they could make use of shelters at the station if they wished, although the train would still be proceeding. To indicate that the train crew were aware that a warning had been received, the driver was instructed to place one headlamp in the centre of the buffer beam and to extinguish all the others; tail lamps were not affected.[39]

If it was safe for the train to proceed, the signalman or station master was to instruct the driver to: "Proceed cautiously at a speed not exceeding 15 mph subject to the proper observance of signals".[40] Drivers were also warned to take extra care when approaching underbridges; distant signals were kept at 'Caution' until the 'Raiders Passed' message was received, when headlamps were returned to their correct position. These instructions were to apply both at night and during the hours of daylight, both in the event of an air raid warning or an actual raid. As shall be seen in later chapters, under actual air raid conditions, the arrangements just described were not quite as straightforward as they seemed in the relative calm of the early months of the war.

Further instructions were displayed in each carriage compartment, and in the event of an air raid warning, passengers were instructed to close all windows and ventilators and to pull down blinds as protection against flying glass. As a further

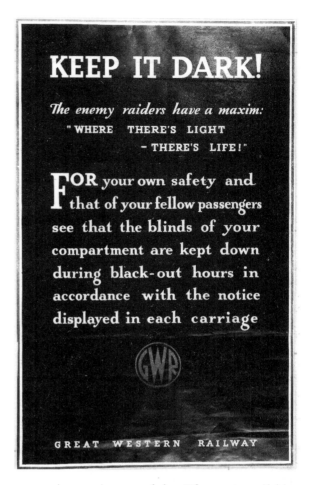

KEEP IT DARK!

The enemy raiders have a maxim:
"WHERE THERE'S LIGHT
- THERE'S LIFE!"

FOR your own safety and that of your fellow passengers see that the blinds of your compartment are kept down during black-out hours in accordance with the notice displayed in each carriage

GWR

GREAT WESTERN RAILWAY

precaution, notices stated that "if room is available, they should lie on the floor".[41] Bearing in mind the amount of floor space available in most compartments, this particular instruction did cause some amusement amongst the travelling public. F. G. Richens, whose article on travel in the blackout has already been mentioned, described a journey in a compartment already filled with five burly passengers and remarked that "one glance at the stalwart frames around me was sufficient to show that my chances of securing living space on the floor without suffering complete and final extinction in the process were negligible".[42] Although the Company experienced some considerable difficulty in adhering to the blackout regulations regarding rolling stock, they were even more troubled by the arrangements necessary to prevent the glow from locomotive fireboxes from presenting the enemy with an easy target. In the

NOTICE TO PASSENGERS

AIR RAID PRECAUTIONS

DURING AN AIR RAID :—

1. Close all windows and ventilators and pull down the blinds as a protection against flying glass.

2. If danger seems imminent, lie on the floor.

3. Never leave the train between stations unless so requested by a railway official.

4. Do not touch any outside part of a coach if a gas attack is suspected.

DURING BLACKOUT HOURS:—

1. KEEP ALL BLINDS DRAWN.

2. KEEP ALL WINDOWS SHUT except when necessary to lower them to open doors.

3. MAKE CERTAIN the train has stopped AT A PLATFORM and that you alight on the PLATFORM side.

4. WHEN LEAVING THIS COMPARTMENT, close windows, lower blinds again and close the door quickly.

A copy of one of the notices placed inside carriages warning of air raid procedures. (Author's Collection)

circular issued to footplate staff, it warned that "every precaution must be taken during firing operations to prevent firebox glow at all times during the hours of darkness".[43] Swindon Works was given the task of solving this problem, and the files of the Chief Mechanical Engineer are full of references to the various measures undertaken to combat firebox glow.

The solution was to fit each locomotive with what became known as anti-glare screens, which would prevent light from escaping. Writing to all Divisional Locomotive Superintendents on 28 August 1939,[44] C. B. Collett initially estimated that there were to be at least seven different variations on the general drawing which had been produced. This estimate soon proved to be woefully inadequate, purely due to the large number of different locomotive types operated by the GWR. The records show that there were at least 45 variations, each having a different arrangement of screens, bolts and hooks, all of which were ordered from the general stores at Swindon. On 7 September 1939 a further letter was sent to superintendents instructing that engines with

side windows in the cab "must have these windows obscured at once, either by painting the glass, or by removing the glass and replacing it with plywood or thin steel plate, if such is available on the spot".[45]

As the war progressed, most locomotives had the glass windows replaced with steel inserts, the glass being carefully stored, and reinstated after the end of hostilities. Since the operation of fitting all locomotives in the GWR fleet with anti-glare screens could obviously not be done overnight, footplate staff were told to use existing storm sheets until the material could be sent out from Swindon. The anti-glare screens, nicknamed Zeppelin Sails by some drivers, although cutting out most of the light escaping from the locomotive footplate, made the life of engine crews very difficult, particularly during warm weather. Condensation built up inside the screens, making them hot and humid, an exhausting combination for staff, especially on long journeys.

This chapter began with a brief account of the difficulties faced by the Great Western over the course of the first Christmas holiday of the war;

Signal boxes were extremely dangerous places to be in air raids, with so much glass all around. The solution was to build steel 'coffins' to which signal staff could retreat. One can be seen in the far left corner of the box.

poor weather had added to the problems faced by all the main line railways, although it was only a foretaste of further arctic conditions which were to sweep the country less than a month later. The cold and foggy weather experienced over the Christmas period was followed by intermittent snow storms, although it was not until the last week of January that heavy falls of snow coupled with arctic conditions brought widespread disruption and dislocation to railway services throughout the country. With the exception of the far west of the network, the whole of the GWR experienced falls of snow which drifted, particularly in the Midlands and North. In many places so much snow fell that it obliterated points and trackwork in yards and depots, slowing shunting and train movements. Coupled with this, the weight of ice on signal and telegraph wires

brought down the supporting poles, making communication difficult. The *GWR Magazine*[46] estimated that over 500 miles of cable were brought down, necessitating the use of time-interval or pilot working of trains in many areas where block signalling was not possible.

The chaos caused can be illustrated by the example of a serious accident at Hay Lane, near Swindon on 29 January 1940, when the 5pm Stoke Gifford to Old Oak Common goods train ran into the rear of the 6.40pm ex-Penzance mail train. The accident occurred at 4.25 in the morning, so both trains must have been badly delayed; the mail train was hit whilst waiting at a signal, and two vehicles were derailed, blocking both the up and down main lines. In the event, one coach, No. 814, was completely destroyed, and another, No. 795, was seriously damaged, while a third suffered severe

The Air Raid Control Centre at Paddington, 1942.

damage to its underframe, with one axle being bent double.

Weather conditions made it impossible to telephone either Bristol or London, and frozen points at Swindon meant that it was almost twelve hours before the line was clear. The location of the accident also meant that all South Wales trains had to be diverted via Gloucester, causing further delay and disruption. An interesting insight into wartime censorship and secrecy can be gleaned from the account of the crash which appeared in the *Swindon Evening Advertiser* later the same day. After describing the clearing up operation presumably still in progress, the report noted "although the driver and fireman of the goods train were shaken, nobody, rail or postal employee, was hurt".[47] More

The rear of a Great Western lorry carrying art treasures from the National Gallery, seen as it disappears into the Manod slate quarry in North Wales.

recent evidence has revealed that in fact 18 of the 25 Post Office employees on board the train were injured, two seriously.[48]

Frozen points and point rodding were a further hazard, with the extreme weather also leading to some wagons wheels being frozen to the track on which they stood. In some cases, even the grease in wagon axleboxes was frozen solid. Long delays were experienced by passengers travelling through this period of bad weather, and a special restricted service was run from Paddington during the worst of the weather. The Great Western and the other railways made special arrangements to have additional supplies of food on hand in station refreshment rooms to cope with the demands of hungry passengers delayed by the weather. The *Railway Gazette*, reporting on the Great Freeze-Up as it was known, quoted a statement by the Railway Executive issued on 31 January 1940 which declared that "it was the worst weather for a century; railway history records nothing like it".[49]

The difficult conditions and long hours worked by railwaymen took their toll, and it was reported that in some areas as many as 25 per cent of staff were absent through sickness.

One benefit of the bad weather was of course that it discouraged any German attack. The same edition of the *Railway Gazette* reported that Germany had also suffered badly in the cold spell, with frozen points and snow drifts having much the same effect as they had in Britain. Throughout the winter of 1939 and early 1940 there was no sign of the predicted air attack from across the Channel, and although many found the air raid precautions described here both tiresome and inconvenient, the 'Phoney' or 'Bore' war helped prepare many both psychologically and physically for the onslaught that was to come. As we have seen, the Great Western Railway had done its best to be prepared, but it would be some months before its procedures and arrangements would be tested to the full.

An atmospheric view of the Slough Fire Service vehicle, complete with trailer pump. (D. J. Hyde Collection)

3
Operation Dynamo

In the early months of the conflict, the Great Western participated in two important ventures vital to the war effort. The first of these was the provision of casualty evacuation trains, assembled for the purpose of removing wounded from urban areas, particularly to hospitals in safer parts of the country. Once again the provision of such vehicles had been at the request of the Railway Executive, and all the main line companies cooperated in providing 30 trains in total. Of these, 20 were based in the London area, six in the provinces, and a further two in Scotland. In all cases, these trains were made up of existing rolling stock which was modified by each railway in their own workshops with the Great Western providing six of the trains.

The first mention of the work done by the Company in converting these vehicles came in the form of a minute in the Locomotive Committee of the board, which noted on 5 October 1939 that the six trains, each comprising two brake thirds, and ten stretcher vans fitted with steam heating, had been converted. Initially the twelve vehicle composition was a standard feature, although in late November 1939 the *Railway Gazette* reported that at the request of the Ministry of Health, one of the stretcher vans had been replaced by an open saloon carriage for staff use. However, this was only intended as a temporary measure, with special mess and recreation vehicles being converted to replace them in due course.[1] The *GWR Magazine* reported a month later that six restaurant cars were being converted for that purpose.

The main feature of these trains was that they could be adapted easily from their peacetime purpose. The GWR decided to convert 'Siphon' bogie milk vans for the main part of the train, the stretcher vans, or ward cars. Conversion work involved the fitting of demountable brackets onto which stretchers could be supported and each van was capable of carrying 41 stretchers. The vans, normally unheated, were fitted with steam heating pipes which ran along the inside of the roof, with an operating valve to control the heat at one end. A bell push was fitted that allowed nursing staff to communicate with medical staff in the brake thirds at either end of the train. Screened electric lighting was installed and a chute in the middle of the floor was provided for the emptying of latrine buckets. All the vehicles in casualty evacuation trains remained in the liveries of the companies to which they belonged with the only identification being the painting of a yellow stripe at the end of each vehicle.

The brake third carriages were used to carry food and medical supplies, and also served as accommodation for staff; cooking facilities being provided, as well as two large tanks of 100 and 200 gallons, for the storage of hot and cold water respectively. All the windows in the vehicles were blackened, and staff worked under the dim glow of blue electric light, the only exception being in the kitchen where a shaded white light was provided. The corridor third, placed in the middle of the train, had two large saloons and was used as a rest and recreation area for staff. Here, windows were not blackened and after dark, blinds were used to maintain the blackout.

A detailed article in the 24 November 1939 issue of the *Railway Gazette*, as well as giving information on the formation and construction of the evacuation trains, also provided readers with an exhaustive list of equipment carried on the trains which ran to over 120 different items. Included in this eclectic catalogue were 30 bed pans, 12 packs of toilet paper, 600 blankets, 320 pillow slips and 100 hot water bottles. The stores carried by the train included 4lb of tea, 2lb of coffee, 20lb of sugar and two bottles of brandy.[2]

The order to fit up the trains was given at very short notice on 30 August 1939, and all the trains were ready for duty at their appointed station two days after the outbreak of war. An idea of the speed at which the work was done came in an account by R. J. Blackmore of some of the work done at Swindon Works in the early months of the war – as hostilities continued, this kind of detail would not have been permitted by the censor, but in these early months, material reproduced in the magazine was still relatively precise. Blackmore described the last days before the completion of the casualty evacuation trains as "animated and exciting".[3] One feature which tested the ingenuity of Swindon craftsmen was the fitting of the water tanks into the brake thirds. The hot tanks were heated by pipes from the train's steam heating system, and Blackmore noted that the fitters "worked each day as long as daylight lasted, until the steam hissed,

bubbled and boiled under the final tests".[4]

Once completed the trains were manned initially by staff who maintained a 24-hour watch, with locomotives being periodically attached to keep up the steam heating. The *Railway Gazette* reported that nursing staff were given regular refresher courses by local hospitals, and in the waiting hours aboard the train they also received lectures by its medical superintendent. When the expected aerial holocaust did not come, questions were asked in Parliament about the cost to the taxpayer of keeping over 30 trains, each with eight crew, standing idle. Replying to a question by Sir A. Knox on 7 December 1939, the Minister of Health stated that the number of trains 'on call' would be reduced to ten, with the others available at 24 hours notice. He added that the average weekly cost of staff for each train was around £26. Later the same month, C. B. Collett reported to the Locomotive Committee of the GWR that two of their trains had been temporarily released, and returned to normal traffic.[5]

Hard on the heels of the request by the Railway Executive Committee for the conversion of the casualty evacuation trains came a further instruction, this time issued on 30 September, to convert 136 LMSR carriages for use in ambulance trains. The Great Western contribution, the modification of 18 vehicles in total, was just a small part of what was an excellent example of how the

A general view of a Casualty Evacuation Train, January 1940.

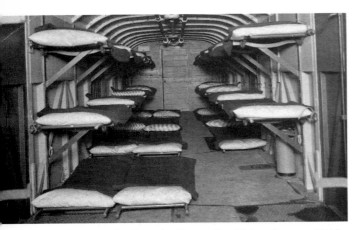

Interior of a Casualty Evacuation Train, January 1940.

main line railways worked together closely in wartime conditions. During the Great War, railway companies had produced complete ambulance trains, however, it was decided well before hostilities began in 1939 that this time each company would specialise in particular types of vehicle, these being sent subsequently to be marshalled together into trains. The detailed plans for the trains had been prepared by the LMS as early as 1937 with two types of train being assembled, one for home use, consisting of two trains each of nine vehicles, and the other for overseas use consisting of four trains, each of 16 vehicles.

As well as Swindon, six other railway works helped produce the trains: Derby and Wolverton on the LMS, Doncaster and York on the LNER, and Eastleigh and Lancing on the Southern Railway. Of the 18 vehicles the Great Western was to modify, twelve were for overseas use, and six for home service. By the time the GWR Locomotive Committee was informed of the work being undertaken on 5 October,[6] much had already been done, and the *Railway Gazette*, reporting some months later,[7] revealed that the trains had been ready by the end of the second week in October – a tremendous achievement by any standard.

The vehicles converted at Swindon for overseas use included four brake and infectious ward cars, four pharmacy cars, and four brake and stores cars. The brake and infectious ward cars were, like all the LMS vehicles received, 57ft brake thirds which were completely gutted, with seats, partitions and upholstery replaced by wards, surgeries, stores and staff quarters. Two 75 gallon water tanks were added, as well as new flooring and double doors in the attendants compartment. The pharmacy cars were converted from corridor brake third coaches and included a pharmacy, treatment room, office and store. The brake and stores cars contained both storage for meat and other items, as well as a sleeping compartment for non-commissioned officers, whilst the administrative car, in addition to containing offices, also featured a compartment for 'sick officers', another pharmacy and a dirty linen store.

All the vehicles converted for use in ambulance trains were turned out in a khaki livery, with white roofs. In the centre of each roof was a red cross, with a smaller red cross on a white background being painted on the centre of the coach body side. The red cross could only be used on vehicles carrying service casualties under the terms of the Geneva Convention, which in theory, entitled them to freedom from attack by the enemy. As a result, civilian casualty evacuation trains did not carry the red cross. Equipped with electric lighting, all the windows on ambulance train stock were painted black.

Having supplied all the drawings and specifications for the ambulance trains, as well as the rolling stock, the LMS also assumed responsibility for the supply of material to the other railway workshops. Included within this remit was the manufacture of drawgear and couplings for the Continental stock, which was fitted by Swindon; brake gear for these vehicles was also stripped out, being replaced by Westinghouse rather than vacuum equipment. One fitting which was manufactured at Swindon that seems to have caused some curiosity however, was a large bracket which resembled a steel loop. These were in fact used to hold down vehicles when they were secured to the deck of a train ferry or transport ship.

Reporting on the tremendous effort to prepare the carriages in three weeks, the *GWR Magazine* noted that quick drying paint had been used to speed up the process of conversion. It also observed that whilst work was continuing apace, time was taken by the Swindon workforce to observe "the differences in design from Great Western practice, and in debating the relative merits".[8] Knowing the partisan nature of some Swindon employees, it is probably better not to enquire any further as to what they thought of the rolling stock they were working on!

The admirable speed with which the railways delivered the ambulance trains was reported extensively in the railway press, although within a month the *Railway Gazette* had reported more sombre news, revealing that on 28 October the first two ambulance trains of the war had arrived at a "country station not far from London" bearing around 50 accident and sickness cases from France. Little further detail was given, save that 20 special motor coaches, converted into ambulances sped the patients away to hospital.[9]

Apart from a number of relatively minor attacks on mainland Britain, including the bombing of a cottage in the Bridge of Wiath near Scapa Flow in Scotland by a German raider intent on striking at nearby shipping in March 1940, and two small attacks on villages in Kent two months later, the war still seemed a distant prospect to many. In the City of London, by April 1940, over 700 firms which had fled to the country in the early months of the war had returned to the Capital. Although all around were signs of preparation against air attack, like sandbags and air raid shelters, it was reported that few felt threatened enough to carry a gas mask.[10]

Most historians agree however, that the 'Phoney War' was well and truly ended on 10 May 1940 when German forces invaded the Low Countries. The armies of Belgium and Holland were no match for the ferocious assault mounted by 200,000 troops backed by strong air support. Within a week the Germans had entered Brussels, and by 19 May it seemed likely that the British Expeditionary Force, which the Great Western had helped to transport to France in the early months of the war, could be completely surrounded, destroyed or captured. The speed at which the war moved led to plans being formulated very quickly to evacuate the British Expeditionary Force from Channel ports. Arrangements were coordinated by Bertram Ramsey, Vice-Admiral of Dover who, using meagre resources, was able to organise what became known as the 'Miracle of Dunkirk'. The Great Western both at sea and on land, played a vital part in this historic operation which was to change the course of the war dramatically. The detailed story of the evacuation has been told in numerous publications, not least in a small book published by the Great Western itself in 1946[11]. However, our survey of the role of the railway in the Second World War would not be complete without chronicling some of the exploits of both Great Western ships involved in the actual operation, and the efforts of the Railway to move troops and casualties once they were safely back in England.

The official start of the Dunkirk evacuation, known as 'Operation Dynamo' was signalled by the Admiralty at 6.57am on 26 May 1940; it ended

Administrative car No. 6204 from one of the Home Ambulance Trains; converted at the beginning of the war from an LMS 57ft corridor third.

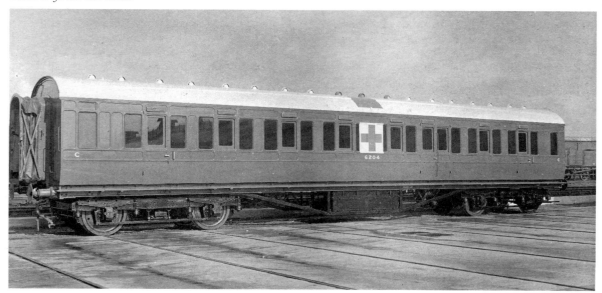

The SS St Helier *in more peaceful times; at Weymouth in August 1929. (National Railway Museum)*

some nine days later when the final ship, the destroyer HMS *Shikari* left the war-torn harbour at Dunkirk at 3.40am on Monday, 3 June 1940. Almost a week before this however, efforts were being made to move troops from elsewhere on the coast of France. The initial plans were to start by moving around 2,000 troops per day, followed by a larger operation to move up to 15,000 unit, hospital and other miscellaneous staff, or what the services called 'useless mouths'. Within a day of these plans being discussed however, the military situation had changed so quickly that the question of how large numbers of troops could be evacuated rapidly was the main item on the agenda.

With the use of passenger ferries, it was estimated that up to 30,000 men could be moved each day from the ports of Calais, Boulogne and Dunkirk and a sufficient number of ships was already available. GWR vessels were part of this operation, one being the *St Andrew* which had been requisitioned on 11 September 1939. This steamer, built in 1932, had been used extensively on the Fishguard–Rosslare route before the war. Fitted out as a hospital ship, it had been based at Southampton, serving the military hospital at

Netley. The *St Andrew* arrived at Boulogne on 20 May, spending a dangerous night moored in the port during an air raid and with shrapnel raining down, the crew had anxiously awaited the patients that they were told would be arriving at any time. It was not until the following morning however, that casualties were loaded aboard, and the ship had a quiet journey back across the Channel, arriving in Southampton at 4.30pm.

This eventful expedition was only a foretaste of what was to come; the ship then completing a trip to Cherbourg, after which she was refuelled, and put on one-hour standby. Proceeding to Dover to report to Vice-Admiral Ramsey, the *St Andrew* had a close call when she was bombed by German planes, but by 4.30am on 24 May she was sailing to Calais where heavy shelling prevented her from docking. The *St David*, requisitioned shortly after its sister ship, the *St Andrew*, was also converted as a hospital ship, but saw limited action until the actual Dunkirk operation.

The *St Helier*, more usually seen on the Channel Islands service in peacetime, was also involved in the operations around Calais, although unlike other members of the Great Western fleet already described, she was not converted as a hospital ship, but was intended as a troop transport. Arriving in Calais on 22 May, with orders to pick up 2,000 troops, the crew found the quays deserted, and despite enquiries, could not find their intended passengers. A full moon made the ship a sitting target for enemy planes, and so the ship returned to Dover empty.

Another Channel Islands' vessel, the *St Julien* had been requisitioned for government use on 9 September 1939, and after carrying troops from Avonmouth to St Nazaire three days later, moved to Southampton in October where she too was converted into a hospital ship. From 11 to 23 May she was fully occupied in ferrying refugees and casualties from Boulogne to Southampton.

With the fall of Calais on 26 May, the British Expeditionary Force was pushed back to the port of Dunkirk, its tactic being to fight by day, and retreat towards the coast under the cover of darkness, a process which it was hoped would take three days. The seriousness of the situation can be gauged by the comments of the General in charge of the BEF, General Gort, who in a message to England noted

that "I must not conceal from you that a great part of the BEF and its equipment will inevitably be lost even in the best circumstances".[12] Thus the fact that 338,226 troops were evacuated from the port and beaches make the enormity of the achievement all the more important.

The four ships already mentioned, with the addition of the *Roebuck, Sambur* and *Mew*, played an important part in 'Operation Dynamo', and the difficulty of their task cannot be underestimated, since the harbour was constantly under attack from enemy planes and artillery, and the crews also had to contend with wreckage and other sunken vessels as they entered the port itself. Even though the three hospital ships were clearly identified with large red crosses, and were unarmed, this made little or no difference to German forces, who did not discriminate between Allied shipping.

The *St Helier* was the first GWR ship into Dunkirk, arriving there on 23 May, and picking up about 1,500 evacuees, returning to Dover the same night without incident. The next day the *St Andrew* and the *St Julien* arrived off the embattled port at about 4pm. The *St Andrew* managed to pick its way

The SS St Julien, *fitted out as a hospital ship, seen at Penarth Docks.*

Despite all the special trains run, day to day services still continued, all over the network. GWR 2-6-0 No. 6329 is seen here leaving Barmouth in September 1940. (RCTS Collection)

through the smoke now obscuring the harbour, and for the next three hours embarked wounded soldiers. The task was not easy however, since there were no stretcher bearers or medical staff, and thus the master of the ship, Captain H. Bond, called for volunteers from the crew, who bravely responded, dashing to and fro whilst an air raid continued. At 8.05pm the ship sailed for Dover, continuing from there to Newhaven. The *St Julien* had a similar experience, also reaching England safely.

On 25 May, the *St David* managed to reach the harbour, and departed safely, although loaded with wounded, she came under heavy fire from the shore, but managed to reach Newhaven without damage. Both the *St Andrew* and the *St Julien* made fruitless attempts to enter the harbour in the next few days, and it was not until Monday 27 May that the *St Helier*, the *St Andrew* and the *St Julien*, along with two other ships, the *Royal Daffodil* and the *Kyno*, approached Dunkirk on a new longer North Sea route calculated to reduce enemy bombardment. The port was reached about 4.30pm, but the bombardment was intense, with two planes attacking the vessels. The master of the *St Helier* avoided damage by "steering the ship for

the spot where the last one fell".[13] Since the biggest threat to the evacuation was the danger of a ship being sunk at the entrance to the harbour, rendering it unusable, the ships had to wait until the air raid ceased.

The *St Helier* managed to the enter the port during a lull in the raid, but no sooner had it moored, than further planes appeared, and it was forced to leave. Returning to the other ships, she reported that as well as the bombardment, many of the quay walls in the harbour had collapsed, and for the time being the transport officer in the harbour would not let any ships enter. With this news, the Great Western vessels were forced to return to Dover. The next day, it was the turn of the *St David* to enter the fray; lying in the harbour overnight, Great Western crew members were again forced to act as stretcher bearers, helping to load the wounded onto the ship. Matters were not helped by the fact that there were no suitable gangways for passing stretcher cases aboard available, and the ship's engineers therefore constructed improvised gangways to suit.

On 30 May, the *St Helier* once again set sail for Dunkirk, its crew augmented by both naval ratings and 20 soldiers. Fog covered the English Channel, which although protecting the ship from attack by German aircraft, must have been a nerve-racking experience all the same, with the number of craft travelling back and forth. The ship returned safely with over 2,000 troops on board, and having disembarked them, returned without delay to France. Sailing with two French troopships, the *St Helier* distinguished herself when attacked by three planes, and not only did it survive a number of near-misses, it also managed to shoot down one of its attackers. Arriving back in Dover at 7am the following morning, it once again had rescued a further 2,000 troops.

The following day, 31 May 1940, saw all the Great Western vessels in action at Dunkirk; the *St Andrew* arriving in the harbour was instructed to dock wherever she could find room, since by this time, the devastation was tremendous. The scene which faced the master of the ship is difficult to describe in words – wrecked quaysides, sunken ships and other wreckage made it seem that it was impossible to find anywhere to berth, "At ordinary times it would have been considered impossible to berth anywhere in that harbour" he reported.[14] Having finally found a suitable spot, the master could not have been best pleased to learn that further instructions were issued asking him to move elsewhere in the dock. When they arrived at the spot requested by the authorities, it was found that the ambulances had been bombed, and were either empty or full of dead soldiers. Even if they had managed to rescue any survivors, the condition of the quayside would have made matters very difficult. Moving to yet another berth, the crew, like that of the *St David* had to build improvised gangways to allow casualties to be carried on board. A particularly fierce air raid, and the fact that stretchers had to be carried long distances took their toll on the spirit and stamina of the crew and with the falling of the tide, the port transport officer requested that the ship leave immediately, and on her way to signal to the *St David* to enter the harbour. This ship was cruising up and down outside the port, waiting to enter and embark any further wounded.

The trip made by the *St David* was to be ill-fated, since the radio equipment on the *St Andrew* was not working, and thus the message asking her to enter the port was not received. The captain and crew had spent a torrid day off Dunkirk, suffering seven separate air attacks, and also being the victim of a magnetic mine, which when it exploded, lifted the ship out of the water. After attempting to signal by Morse code and megaphone, the master approached the entrance to the harbour, but fierce gunfire, and the fact that no message had been received, led the ship to be steered back to Dover reluctantly, without landing at Dunkirk. The master of the vessel, Captain Mendus, in his report of that day's events wrote that "during the time that the vessel was at sea at Dunkirk, the Navigating and Engine-Room Officers and Ratings, although tired and weary, carried out their duties with great coolness and courage".[15] One can imagine however, that despite all their efforts, the crew must have felt a great sense of disappointment and sadness at having to leave behind BEF troops to what was an uncertain fate.

The *St Julien* also had its crew augmented by naval personnel, and it arrived at 5.58pm, its crew again helping to load casualties under shell fire, although the Captain's log did report that on this occasion mercifully, there were no air raids. This was its last involvement in the Dunkirk operation, since concern for the position of troops in North-West France led to its move to duties evacuating troops from Cherbourg in early June.

The *St Helier*, which had already seen much action, was again in the thick of things on 31 May. The 1,600 French troops she collected on that day were destined to have an eventful passage to England. Leaving the port in the dusk of early evening, she collided with a naval minesweeper, HMS *Sharpshooter* which had passed across her bows. The Great Western ship was not badly damaged, but at the request of the naval captain, the *St Helier* did not withdraw, but steamed along pushing her bow into the damaged section for about 40 minutes, to prevent the minesweeper from sinking. Despite the attention of German planes, a tug eventually came to the rescue of the *Sharpshooter*, after which the *St Helier* continued on. Further excitement ensued, when the vessel was hit by a former pleasure steamer, the *Princess Eleanora*. No serious damage was done to the *St Helier*, although the *Princess Eleanora* was forced to limp home without one of its paddle boxes. The French troops, who by now might have been thinking that they had made the wrong choice of escape vessel, were further shaken when the ship ran over a submerged wreck. Fortunately this was the last episode on an eventful trip, which through great fortune, ended safely.

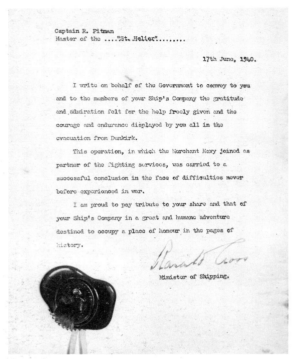

Captain R. Pitman
Master of the ...."St. Helier".......

17th June, 1940.

I write on behalf of the Government to convey to you
and to the members of your Ship's Company the gratitude
and admiration felt for the help freely given and the
courage and endurance displayed by you all in the
evacuation from Dunkirk.

This operation, in which the Merchant Navy joined as
partner of the fighting services, was carried to a
successful conclusion in the face of difficulties never
before experienced in war.

I am proud to pay tribute to your share and that of
your Ship's Company in a great and humane adventure
destined to occupy a place of honour in the pages of
history.

Minister of Shipping.

A notice issued to the captain of the St Helier.

The *St Helier* made two final trips to Dunkirk, the first on 1 June began with the by now usual air attack, and the ship spent an uncomfortable seven hours alongside the quay loading 40 stretcher cases and troops. All the time the ship was moored, the harbour was shelled by German shore batteries and attacked by planes. Despite being slightly injured by a shell, the second mate carried on with his duties, and at 10.15pm the ship left, illuminated by fires burning on the shore, and shelled by coastal batteries until finally out of range. The following day, the naval authorities, considering that the GWR master, Captain Pitman, had done more than enough, offered to put a naval commander and crew to operate the ship. "Not on your life, you won't!" is reported to have been his reply.[16] With the Captain still in charge, the ship left for Dunkirk again with a naval commander and ten ratings on board, in case the ship should be required to pick up troops from the beaches. Once again however, the Captain manoeuvred his way into the devastated harbour, this time rescuing another 2,000 troops, amongst the last members of the BEF to find a safe passage to England.

This last trip by the *St Helier* brought the total

number of people evacuated by the ship to over 11,700; 1,500 refugees and 10,200 troops. The bravery and determination of all the crew was recognised both by the medals awarded to the Captain and Second Officer, who received the Distinguished Service Cross, and the Quartermaster, who gained the Distinguished Service Medal. The efforts were also marked by the Minister of Shipping, who concluded a letter to the Captain, "I am proud to pay tribute to your share and that of your ship's company in a great and humane adventure destined to occupy a place of honour in the pages of history".[17]

Two further Great Western vessels were involved in 'Operation Dynamo'. The first, the *Roebuck*, had been used by the GWR on its cargo service to the Channel Islands, and on 29 May was requisitioned at very short notice. In fact, so short was the notice given, that it could not proceed until the cargo of produce it held was unloaded. It then proceeded to Dover at full speed and two days later was sent to La Panne, some nine miles up the coast from Dunkirk, where thousands of troops were stranded on the beach. Unfortunately a strong breeze made it impossible for craft to get near enough to the shore, and thus it was with some trepidation that the master of the *Roebuck* was ordered into the harbour at Dunkirk itself. Although the jetty to which the ship was moored was in ruins, ramps were improvised by the crew, allowing 47 stretcher cases, 72 other wounded, and another 570 troops to be embarked. Because of the speed of her requisitioning, the *Roebuck* only played a modest part in the Dunkirk operation as she had not been degaussed, and thus was an ideal target for the scores of magnetic mines which were scattered around the entrance to the harbour. Within days she was back at Weymouth, and ready to recommence trips to the Channel Islands.

The final Great Western ship involved was the 117 ton ferry the *Mew*, more usually seen crossing the short distance across the River Dart, between Dartmouth and Kingswear in Devon. With a top speed of only 10 knots, this ship was requisitioned on 30 May, with the authorities presumably hoping that it would join the flotilla of 'Little Ships' that assisted in the evacuation of Dunkirk. Volunteers were asked for, and the ship's crew was quick to respond, having their craft ready to leave for Dover the following morning. Reaching Dover on 1 June, by which time most of the evacuation was complete, the luckless crew were ordered to return

As well as the evacuation of the BEF, the Great Western also had to cope with another evacuation from the South East. Here evacuees are seen at Gowerton on 2 June 1940.

to Kingswear. Although they did not face the hazards of enemy bombing and shelling, the achievement of sailing such a small craft up the Channel, and the willingness of their crew, were as the railway's account of the Dunkirk operation put it, "well up to Great Western standards".[18]

By Sunday 2 June almost all the British elements of the BEF had been evacuated; and we have already seen that the troops embarked by the *St Helier* were some of the last to be evacuated. At 11.30pm, the senior naval officer was able to signal to Vice-Admiral Ramsey at Dover, "BEF Evacuated". For a further two days, another 50,000 French troops were lifted from the beaches and the harbour until in the early hours of the morning of Tuesday 4 June, the last ship left, bringing 'Operation Dynamo' to an end. Later that same morning, the last defenders of the embattled port finally surrendered.

Readers will have been left in no doubt from the description of the Dunkirk evacuation given, that the crews of Great Western ships performed above and beyond the call of duty. Back in England

however, railway employees performed a vital task with no less determination, even though their enemy was not German bombing or shelling, but fatigue. For once the tired and hungry troops had been safely delivered to the Channel ports, it was the railway system which then distributed them to military bases and hospitals all over the country.

As was the case with the naval evacuation itself, little notice was given of the demands that were to be placed on the railways. Speaking in 1943, the Director of Movements at the War Office, Major-General M. G. Holmes noted that "The first warning of the impending evacuation was given by my Directorate to the railways on 21 May, 1940".[19] Most of the heaviest traffic was generated however, between 27 May and 4 June, during which period 569 special trains were run, and over 30,000 troops were transported. As a comparison, in the six days before the 27th, only 55 extra troop trains had been run from ports on the South Coast.

Initially little information was available, with no precise details of the number of troops to be moved, or where they would be landed. More

Few pictures of the actual trains run to evacuate troops have survived; this later picture of an ambulance train taken after D-Day does however illustrate the type of working. GWR 'Grange' class No. 6827 Llanfrechfa Grange *assists LNER B12 4-6-0 No. 8525 at Kennington Junction* en route *to Wheatley for Holton military hospital. (Great Western Trust Collection)*

information was provided on 26 May in the form of a confidential letter to divisional superintendents from F. R. Potter, the Superintendent of the Line at Paddington. "The Company may be called upon at very short notice to cooperate and work with the miltary authorities over a miltary move of a major character" he wrote.[20] However, it was obvious that a large number of men would have to be transported, and thus the Southern Railway, which served most of the ports likely to be used, asked for a pool of 160 train sets, each comprising eleven or twelve coaches to be formed from the stock of the four main line companies. This meant that the Great Western was to provide a total of 480 carriages, making up 40 trains.

It should be remembered that all the railways were already hard pressed with extra war traffic when this request was made; to provide over 400 coaches at short notice was an achievement in itself. The stock from the the other three companies was handed to the Southern at a number of locations; GWR trains at Salisbury, LMS stock via Kensington Addison Road, and LNER rolling stock via Banbury and Reading. Under the supervision of the Railway Executive Committee, the railways operated special Control offices at key locations, to coordinate the movement of trains away from the coast. These were situated at Redhill, Reading, Banbury and Salisbury. At each of these locations the ultimate destination of each train was decided, for in many cases, when trains left the Channel ports, their destination had yet to be agreed by the military authorities. Movement of special trains on to the Great Western system was organised by the Control at Redhill. Almost all of this enormous operation was improvised, since there were no working timetables, and almost all communication was done by telephone.

Although the Southern Railway bore the brunt of the traffic generated by the evacuation from Dunkirk, the Great Western played an important part, handling a large number of trains on from their initial disembarkation points. From a total of 319,116 officers and men moved by the railways during this period, the GWR was responsible for the safe transit of 182,808 men, a good proportion of the total. By far the largest number of trains were run over the three days from Thursday 30 May to Saturday 1 June, and during this period 197 special trains passed through the GWR system. Matters were not helped by two further factors which put additional strain on the staff and equipment of the

railway; firstly additional troop trains, not directly connected with 'Operation Dynamo' were required, returning French troops to Southampton for repatriation, and a large number of supplementary trains were also required to move other military personnel from Weymouth. As a result, in addition to the 293 trains run in connection with the Dunkirk operation, a further 435 special military trains were moved at the same time. If this were not enough the hard-pressed Great Western had to cope with another 31 special trains, this time carrying evacuated adults and children from East Anglia to the Midlands, and Kent to South Wales.

It was not surprising that with such pressure being placed on the network, a number of freight and passenger services had to be cancelled. In some locations, bus services were run, and stations closed to all but essential personnel. Throughout the period of the operation, staff made superhuman efforts to ensure the smooth running of the operation, working long hours, and missing mealtimes and breaks to get the job done. The *GWR Magazine*, adding its own tribute to the staff, noted that "footplate and train men had no regard for their own convenience, and gladly did their parts in taking trains on even though they had already worked long hours".[21] The Secretary of War recognised the magnitude of the operation, concluding that its successful conclusion was "due to the excellent organisation and willing cooperation of all grades of the railways concerned".[22] Expressing his own thanks to the staff in a personal message printed in the July *GWR Magazine*, the Company Chairman, Viscount Horne, argued that the story of the part played by Great Western employees in the Dunkirk evacuation was one which could "be read with the greatest pride by all our staff".[23]

Reporting the tumultuous events of the previous month to the Great Western board on 28 June, Sir James Milne remarked that the operation of the evacuation plan had placed a severe strain on the Company's resources, and on the operating sections of the Traffic and Locomotive Departments.[24] However, following this effort, further long hours of toil were required when the Company was called upon to participate in phase two of the evacuation, which was in effect the movement of members of the British Expeditionary Force from their initial reception stations to their Divisional areas. This task began

Volunteers helping to feed soldiers evacuated from Dunkirk at an unknown location; the rolling stock is Great Western however.

on 6 June, and necessitated the running of a large number of special trains daily.

A week after the end of the Dunkirk operation Great Western ships were once again called into action, this time to rescue British troops trapped at the small port of St Valery 18 miles west of Dieppe. When the *St Helier* now fully seaworthy after its Dunkirk adventures, reached the French coast in the early hours of 12 June, the area around St Valery was deserted and in the absence of any Royal Navy vessel the master, feeling that something was not quite right, returned his ship to Southampton. As things turned out, this decision may have saved the lives of his crew, since when 24 hours later, two further Great Western ships, the *Roebuck* and the *Sambur* approached the port, they received a very hostile welcome indeed.

After her brief visit to Dunkirk, the *Roebuck* had managed one further trip to Guernsey between 6 and 8 June; both she and the *Sambur* brought cargoes of Channel Islands tomatoes to Weymouth

before being once again ordered to stand by for Admiralty service. On Wednesday 12 June they were ordered to sail to a point five miles off St Valery where they were to contact either a British Naval vessel or troops on shore. Reaching the area early on the morning of 13 June, they, like the captain of the *St Helier*, could find no sign of any naval vessel. All that was visible was a train ferry anchored near the shore, and some French fishing vessels, who on being challenged, told the captain of the *Roebuck* to proceed inshore. Taking this instruction at face value, the two ships steamed straight into what turned out to be a trap; about a mile and a half from the port they met with a hail of shells from the German batteries.

It was estimated that some 40 shells hit both ships, the most serious damage being done when the ships turned broadside into the barrage when trying to escape. Helped by fog and smoke from fires onshore, they managed to zigzag their way back to sea. The ships did not escape unscathed however, with two members of the crew of the *Sambur* being killed, and four injured, and on the *Roebuck* three crew were killed and another two seriously wounded.[25] These fatalities were the first involving GWR staff whilst on duty, although the Company magazine had reported the sombre news of the first Great Western employees to be killed in action in April 1940.

Once repaired the *Roebuck* and the *Sambur* did not return to Weymouth, remaining under Admiralty control for the rest of the war. For almost the whole of June, Weymouth, in peacetime a thriving port serving the Channel Islands, was the centre of numerous large scale embarkations and disembarkations associated with events in France. The harbour was crowded with many railway steamers which had been requisitioned and were now far from their normal routes including a number of LMS and LNER vessels, as well as the Belgian Marine mail steamer *Prinses Astrid*.[26]

The additional evacuation of troops of the BEF from Western France created additional work for the Company; for as well as the traffic generated at Weymouth, troops were also landed at Southampton, Plymouth, Falmouth, Liverpool, Milford Haven, Avonmouth and Newport. A total of 254 trains were run for these military personnel between 17 and 21 June, of which the Great Western dealt with 215, the number of troops carried totalling more than 100,000. Some idea of the enormous strain borne by the Great Western during this period can be ascertained by the fact that in the five weeks ending 22 June 1940 the Company had run 1,659 special trains; this staggering number not including a further 671 ammunition and equipment trains, and another 102 special coal trains.[27]

As the military situation in France worsened, so the position of the Channel Islands became more vulnerable and as a result, in the last fortnight of June thousands of refugees, particularly children, were evacuated from the Islands. The Islands were served jointly by the Great Western and the Southern, each handling both the passenger and freight to Guernsey and Jersey respectively. Almost 50 Great Western staff on Guernsey, under the

A very rare photograph of the SS Roebuck *at Penarth for repairs after the St Valery raid on 13 June 1940.*

control of the agent, Mr A. Martin, worked tirelessly in the last few weeks of June, to ensure that as many refugees as possible managed to make the trip to the mainland. With the demilitarisation of the Islands, matters were made much more uncertain, and on 24 June the staff decided to remain at their posts to make sure that "everything is done to maintain a service to and from the Channel islands until such time as circumstances absolutely compel the Company to withdraw it".[28]

The staff had remained at their posts despite an offer of evacuation by the Navy two days earlier, and they managed to organise the sailing of a further twelve boats between 23 and 28 June but as the *Roebuck* and the *Sambur* were unavailable, the Harwich steamer *Sheringham* deputised. German planes were first seen over the Islands on Wednesday 26 June, and on Friday 28th, bombers attacked the harbour doing a great deal of damage, and wounding three Great Western employees. Judging that this might be an opportune moment

to leave, two hours after the first air raid the Agent and 38 of his staff sailed for England, leaving the three injured men in the hospital, and eight unaccounted for. Fortunately most of the families of staff had been evacuated some days earlier, and within two days the Islands were under occupation by the Germans.

Outlining the end of the GWR operation on Guernsey to the board at the end of July 1940 the General Manager, James Milne, also noted that following the evacuation he had to report the loss of three company vehicles, two Commer and one Morris cars, which it was presumed had "fallen into enemy hands".[29] Concluding his account of the last days of the Great Western operation on Guernsey, the writer of an article in the Company magazine hoped that "in due course the Channel Islands will once again be flying the Union Jack".[30] It would be five long years before the Channel Island route was once again run by the GWR.

4-4-0 No. 3205 is seen crossing Barmouth Bridge with a mixed freight in September 1940. (RCTS Collection)

4
Under Siege

By the summer of 1940 Britain was an island fortress, with its government and population fully expecting an invasion at any moment. The country was faced by a vast stretch of hostile coastline behind which the Luftwaffe, which had 2,000 bombers and over 2,500 other dive bombers and fighter aircraft, waited to strike a decisive blow. The victorious German army, which included ten armoured divisions, was only a short distance across the English Channel. Facing them were, apart from about a dozen poorly trained training divisions, the battered remains of the British Expeditionary Force, which only possessed a small number of weapons, having lost almost all its equipment, including virtually every tank it possessed, on the battlefields of Northern France.

Winston Churchill, who had succeeded Neville Chamberlain some months earlier, on 8 May, was still bullishly defiant, proclaiming in his famous 'Finest Hour' speech on 17 June that the Battle of Britain was about to begin, and that Hitler knew that "he will have to break us in these islands or lose the war".[1] The seriousness of the situation had even permeated down to the level of the *GWR Magazine* which, in its July 1940 edition, featured a story about Sir Francis Drake, noting that when "invasion of Britain by a foreign power appears again to be a possibility, it is interesting to look back some 350 years..."[2]

The seriousness of the the situation faced by the country had already been acknowledged, even before events in Northern France and the Channel fully brought home the dangers of invasion. The 'Blitzkrieg' methods used by the Germans during the invasion of the Low Countries had been grasped by the government, particularly the dropping of troops by parachute in advance of the main invasion force. To combat this, and to act as an extra line of defence in covering the 2,000 miles of British coastline which were under threat, The Home Secretary, Anthony Eden, called for volunteers for what he called the Local Defence Volunteers. In a radio broadcast on 14 May 1940, he appealed for men between the ages of 15 and 65. "You will not be paid, but you will receive uniform and you will be armed" he promised.[3]

Within eight weeks of Eden's appeal, more than a million men had answered his call to arms; few had uniforms, and fewer still had weapons, apart from truncheons and a few antique guns borrowed from museums. Soon, these irregulars were renamed by Churchill as The Home Guard. Railwaymen, hard-pressed as they were, still volunteered in their thousands, and over 99,000 came forward in response to this first appeal. This total soon grew to over 120,000, and eventually over 156,000 were enrolled at one time or another. The railways themselves formed Home Guard companies and platoons, and in some cases whole battalions were set up. It was thought that these units could be used to defend railway property particularly, but in most places, Home Guard units formed part of larger groupings protecting towns or particular areas. In Swindon for example, the Works was protected by 'F' Company of the 5th

Battalion, Wiltshire Home Guard, although as the war continued, it eventually had its own battalion, the 13th, to cover GWR property only.

A circular issued by the company some weeks after the official formation of the LDV seems to suggest that the Great Western were themselves hopeful that railway units could be formed to protect their property. Referring to the setting up of the Local Defence Volunteer Corps, the General Manager related to staff that "It had been agreed with the War Office that railwaymen volunteering for service...can be specially earmarked for the duty of guarding vulnerable points of the railway".[4] He went on to note that spare time duty only was involved, and that uniform and arms would be supplied. The company was, he concluded, particularly keen to enrol men with knowledge of firearms.

Railwaymen were of course the best people to protect railway property, already having a good knowledge both of the stations, lines or structures they were guarding and also of railway rules and regulations. The vulnerable points mentioned included bridges, signal boxes, tunnels and dock installations. Work to identify such locations had been going on for some considerable time, and in fact the Great Western had been in contact with the War Office over the subject as early as 1929, when the Army Council set up the Inter-Departmental Committee on the Protection of Railways in time of War. This grouping, chaired by General Anderson, Quartermaster General to the Forces, also included two railway officers, Lieutenant R. Bell, Assistant General Manager of the London & North Eastern Railway, and Lieutenant G. Szlumper, Assistant General Manager of the Southern Railway. Although considering a number of wider issues such as the various routes on which large scale troop movements could be carried out, they were also interested in identifying vulnerable points on the railway system, particularly in the neighbourhood of ports and mobilisation centres such as army camps.

A good deal of highly secret correspondence took place throughout the early part of 1930 with divisional superintendents being asked to prepare lists of strategic points on key routes in their area, including bridges over and under the line which, in the event of war, could not easily be removed, or could be restored within 14 days. Also included were generating stations, pumping stations and

other vital points. Interestingly, these were identified for protection because they had been targeted by striking employees during the General Strike of 1926. A good deal of discussion took place between the Great Western and the War Office as to what constituted important engineering works deserving of protection, and by 1932 a short list of 14 large structures had been initially identified. These included the Severn Tunnel and its pumping stations on both sides of the river, the Royal Albert Bridge at Saltash, Crumlin Viaduct and Chepstow Bridge.[5]

From the tone of the discussion, even at this early stage, it was obvious that only limited protection could be given to railways by the full-time military forces themselves. It was hoped that they would be able to guard large strategic targets like the Saltash bridge, but it was apparent that they would not have the manpower to protect even a small fraction of the thousands of bridges, tunnels and stations on the railway. As a result, it was the Home Guard which stepped into the breach, ending up as the guardian of all strategic points on the line, as the hard-pressed full-time military forces found themselves too short of manpower to even guard the larger sites.

In Swindon, the response to Eden's broadcast on 15 May was immediate with over 500 men attending a meeting at the mess room in London Street, near to the Works entrance, to hear an outline of what was proposed, given by Mr J. Auld, Principal to the Chief Mechanical Engineer. The first five members were enrolled on 30 May 1940, and the patrolling of railway premises started the next day. It was not practical to enrol all those railway employees who wished to join the GWR Local Defence Volunteer Corps without seriously affecting the formation of other local companies. Therefore volunteers were called for to enlist in units near to their homes, thus levelling up the numbers in each battalion. Having mentioned this, it should be noted that the strength of the GWR company at Swindon never fell below 450, even when extra long hours were being worked in the railway works, and the demands of conscription increased.

Another circular on the subject was issued by the General Manager some months later in September 1940, by which time the LDV had been renamed the Home Guard. The circular began, "The Directors are very gratified to learn that a large number of their staff has volunteered for service in the Home Guard, and that a keen interest is being displayed in the general training and parades."[6] The circular went on to acknowledge the problems experienced by Home Guard units in the early months of their existence, with lack of uniforms or equipment. One early report for example, noted that the GWR Battalion at Swindon was initially armed with molotov cocktails![7] To placate the staff further, the General Manager continued "members of the Home Guard will be glad to know that a warmer type of serge uniform will be shortly available for use during the winter".[8] Bearing in mind the atrocious weather endured by railway staff earlier in 1940, this last message must have been a relief to those fearing many a cold night on sentry duty!

The circular ended with an appeal for more volunteers, a plea echoed in an article in the *GWR Magazine* the same month. The writer, Mr G. H. Hemmen, Battalion Commander in the London Division, argued that many more Home Guards were needed, and those who did volunteer would "win the esteem of their colleagues and the silent gratitude of their women-folk".[9] Labouring the point somewhat, he continued, "come along fellows, and do not let it be said that throughout the war you enjoyed the comfort of a cosy bed each night, knowing full well that the next man...was fitting himself to meet an invasion, which if successful, might mean saying good-bye to your job."[10]

An interesting survival is a file of correspondence relating to the enrolment of staff from the Chief Mechanical Engineers Department in 1943. Even though it only accounts for part of the Great Western Railway's staff, it does give a good idea of the level of participation by employees. The GWR were it seems, required by the Railway Executive to supply details of the numbers of the Company's staff enrolled in the Home Guard at the end of each quarter. Thus lists of both numbers and occupations of staff at Swindon and the various other workshops and locomotive sheds were produced. At the locomotive works in Swindon, a total of 1,074 men were enrolled, 405 in the Great Western company and a further 669 in other local units. By far the largest number of Home Guard members came from the ranks of the

semi and unskilled labourers, followed closely by machinists, fitters and turners. Only 20 clerical staff were members of the Home Guard, many were it seems, already enrolled in ARP squads. In locomotive sheds, the spread of occupations was perhaps wider, mainly due to the smaller size of many depots; at Machynlleth for example, of the 40 staff enrolled in the Home Guard, twelve were drivers, 15 were firemen, and the rest included cleaners, clerks, examiners and unskilled staff.

The smallest depot mentioned appears to be St Ives in Cornwall, where one employee, a Mr H. C. Blewitt, whose occupation is given as a carriage cleaner, was noted as being a member of the local Home Guard unit. In total, the Chief Mechanical Engineers Department, which included, the Locomotive Department, the South Wales Docks, the Electrical Department and Swindon Works, had 4,399 of its employees enrolled for Home Guard service. Of this total 2,491 were in railway units, and the remainder, 1,908 in all, were part of local units.[11]

A further precautionary measure introduced against the backdrop of a German invasion was the removal of all but the smallest station signs in June 1940. These instructions, issued by the Railway Executive, also included the removal of bridge signs and street signs directing passengers to stations.[12] Travel in the blackout, already difficult, became rather more problematic as even the most familiar station became almost impossible to recognise in the dark. Reporting the introduction of this measure, the *GWR Magazine* noted that the obliteration of station names was to thwart possible 'parachute invaders' and that to Company employees the identification of a particular station was not likely to cause any difficulty. Nor, it

No. 5042 Winchester Castle *on the 1.55pm ex-Paddington at Tilehurst on 13 July 1941.* (RCTS Collection)

continued would "passengers be in any bewilderment concerning stations they are accustomed to use".[13] Evidence collected by numerous writers and oral historians would seem to contradict this rather high-handed statement, bearing in mind the number of people who remember vividly missing their home station in the gloom. Matters were not helped in the first few months after the removal of signs by staff not shouting out the name of the location on the arrival of each train.

A month later, further instructions were issued to staff directing them to go much further, and obliterate all place names painted on such items as sack trucks, skids, station barrows and ladders. In order that there was no confusion, the circular issued to divisional superintendents clarified that this instruction included any item that could be seen from "a highway, footpath or railway".[14] It also listed items which were exempt from these regulations; these including 'Internal user' wagons used within docks or railway workshops, goods brake vans, passenger branch coach sets or stores vans. An interesting postscript on this particular circular was to the divisional superintendent at Shrewsbury, who was told that "the name on the narrow gauge wagons at Blaenau Ffestiniog need not be obliterated".[15]

As had been the case with blackout measures inside coaching stock, public discontent with the lack of station nameboards eventually led to the issue of a further order by the Minister of Transport authorising railway companies to reinstate station nameboards, providing they could be situated under the station roof or platform canopies and could not be seen from the air or the highway. The *Railway Gazette*, reporting this relaxation of the regulations argued that although the intention of the original order had been to deny possible invaders or aircraft any indication of their location, in practice "the enthusiasm of the obliterators led them to remove all marks of identification and to vie with one another in the creation of anonymity".[16] The *GWR Magazine*, reporting the introduction of these new measures, noted that in the London area, there was no limit on the size of lettering used on station nameboards, whilst in the provinces, the maximum size of lettering was three inches.[17] In the Capital, larger lettering was justified since it was argued that suburban trains only stopped at intermediate stations for short period of time, and

passengers had less time to determine where they were.

Further precautionary measures included plans to evacuate the civilian population in coastal areas in time of real threat of invasion. The official line, as stated by the Minister of Home Security on 20 June 1940 was that "the duty of the public in the event of an invasion is to remain where they are unless instructed to leave".[18] Experience of events in the German campaign in France and the Low Countries showed that attempts to slow the advance were severely hampered by roads being blocked by refugees fleeing from affected areas.

Plans to evacuate the civilian population were formulated, and in late June the *Railway Gazette* hinted darkly that "measures already prepared have now been put into effect, but it is not desirable in the national interest to state what precisely they are".[19] What was proposed was in effect the depopulation of large areas of southern and eastern England, where it was intended to leave only essential workers. As the Great Western had lines which ran in areas which could have been likely invasion sites, some discussion obviously took place regarding the status of staff.

Following a meeting between the Railway Executive and the three railway unions at Euston on the 7th August 1940, the GWR issued a confidential circular to clarify matters. Noting that plans for the compulsory evacuation of a substantial proportion of the population of certain towns were being prepared, it stated that railway staff were seen as an essential service. When the decision to evacuate a town was taken, then a decision would be made as to the level of train service still required; this would determine how many staff were to remain. Wives and children were to be evacuated with the rest of the population, the circular concluded.

Government plans envisaged that once railways had been used to evacuate the civilian population, they would then run the minimum service with the final eventuality being that they would be used for the movement of troops and freight. Instructions issued for the guidance of air raid wardens reinforced this, noting that "Roads and Railways are wanted for essential traffic".[20] Bearing in mind the strategic importance of the railways, a leaflet was issued by the Railway Executive Committee to staff advising them on what to do in the event of an invasion. This document reinforced information given in a leaflet issued to every household called *Beating the Invader*.

Staff were instructed that if they were in areas some way away from fighting, they should carry on as usual, but if fighting should break out in their neighbourhood, they should "carry on as long as possible and only take cover when danger approaches".[21] The leaflet reminded staff that they bore a heavy responsibility in time of invasion, and that it was "imperative that all staff should be at their posts". If invasion came, it concluded, "it will be defeated by calm courage and resolute action and it is confidently expected that all members of staff will play their part."[22]

A further tactic use by the Germans during the invasion of France and the Low Countries was that of disinformation. An official notice distributed to Great Western staff in October 1940 warned that "disorganisation of railway traffic was caused in France by staff being persuaded to stay away from work, or being misled...by false instructions."[23] It was reported that French railway staff had been told by persons working for the Germans that there was no need for them to report for work the next day, as the military would be manning the trains. All notices were to be posted on the official notice boards the circular continued, and any which seemed not to be from the usual source were to be treated as suspect. Employees were also warned about the use of telephones, in the event of an invasion, employees were to be on the alert, and to exercise the greatest care when receiving instructions by telephone. If in doubt, the person who received the message should ring back the

The Emergency Control Room at Paddington. Some of the telephone equipment in evidence seems fairly elderly, even for the 1940s!

This unidentified member of the 'Aberdare' class 2-6-0 was chosen to have the rather undignified job of being used as a target in secret government tests, hence the liberal application of whitewash!

reputed source of the message, to ensure that it was genuine.

In the early stages of the war, it was decided that 'Railway Service' identification badges should be issued to all staff. In the Great War, some railways had done this, but not all, and the Great Western had not issued many such badges. This had lead to problems with staff being attacked by some of the more fanatical women, who stuck white feathers to those who they thought were not doing their bit for the war effort. In the 1939–1945 war, although 'Railway Service' badges were intended to distinguish staff in reserved occupations, this was not their only function. Their other use was to identify staff in times of emergency. The badges issued were of a standard lozenge shape, with the initials of the railway company, and the outline of a locomotive on each. On the Great Western example the engine resembled a member of the 'Castle' class, although the

design was difficult to identify with any precision.

In a notice issued to all staff in July 1940 James Milne, the General Manager reminded employees that "all members of staff are advised to wear their Railway Service Identification badges whilst on duty and when proceeding to or returning from work".[24] Staff were also reminded that they should take great care of these badges, and in the event of one being lost, the individual concerned "must immediately report the loss in writing to his superior officer, giving information as to when and how the loss occurred".[25] This stern warning seems to have gone largely unheeded, since just over a month later C. B. Collett, the Chief Mechanical Engineer at Swindon, wrote to his divisional superintendents suggesting ways that the loss of these badges could be prevented.[26] By January 1941 it was reported that over 1,000 of these badges had been lost, a situation the General Manager argued was "to be deplored",[27] especially

An undated photograph of the GWR Swindon Home Guard on parade in Wood Street.

as the Company was aiming to cut out as much waste as possible.

A further measure on which railway staff had been instructed in the event of an invasion was that of immobilisation. Denying the enemy the use of the railway and its facilities was a vital task, and one which was carried out in great secrecy. Even today there is little information available, but some detail can be gleaned from surviving material. Both the War Office and the railways were faced with difficult choices, since it was easy to quickly and comprehensively destroy bridges, dock gates or other structures, but to make too comprehensive a job of this might prove awkward if an area overrun by the enemy was recaptured in a very short period of time. As a result, the War Office issued orders that no damage should be done to railway bridges which could not be repaired in seven days.[28] In some cases chambers were drilled in the piers of bridges for the insertion of explosive charges, although more time and energy seems to have been devoted towards denying the German army the use of locomotives,

rolling stock and other railway equipment.

Enginemen old enough to have worked in the war period, remember instructions which suggested that staff should remove the coupling rods of locomotives, and if possible dispose of them in nearby rivers or canals, so that they could be retrieved at a future date. How practical such instructions would have been if the situation had demanded it, remained to be seen; apart from the fact that locomotive valve gear was very heavy, the task of immobilising the whole of the Great Western fleet would have taken some considerable time. One surviving circular, issued by Swindon, does give just the smallest hint of the kind of measures that were contemplated. Relating to the immobilisation of cranes, instructions were given as to the various methods of making such equipment unusable. In the case of electric cranes, it recommended the removal of intermediate shafts and pinions; and for steam cranes, connecting rods should be removed. Diesel and electric machines were to have their valve rockers hidden, whilst on the oldest hand cranes, staff next week similar orders were issued for Fishguard Harbour, Port Talbot, Swansea and Newport. On 26 June another batch of orders were placed instructing staff to carry out the immobilisation of electrical equipment at Plymouth, Cardiff, Newport, Barry, Penarth, Kingswear and Fowey, as well as similar work at Cardiff General station.[31]

Few staff seem to have known anything but the sketchiest of details about the immobilisation procedures, with information being passed on a 'need to know' basis. The whole scheme was organised on regional lines, with each major location having one member of staff who was to be advised of "arrangements made for notifying them of a state of extreme urgency".[32] In the case of Swindon Works for example, the 'Responsible Officer' was K. J. Cook, the Locomotive Works Manager.

On a more general basis, arrangements were in place on the Great Western regarding the situation should communications break down in the case of an invasion. In conditions of extreme secrecy in February 1939, the government had set up a system of twelve Regional Commissioners. These officials had sweeping powers to govern if a complete disruption of communications took place between Whitehall and the provinces. In a secret letter to F. W. Hawksworth at Swindon in 1941, the Great Western Superintendent of the Line, Gilbert Matthews, stated that if a Regional Commissioner declared that "communications have broken down...or are seriously impeded"[33] then certain appointed officers would be the "only channel of communication between the commissioner and the railways in that area".[34] It should be noted that this also assumed that communications had broken down between the various divisions of the railway and Paddington. Listed were four members of GWR staff who, had an invasion taken place, would have been in both a very responsible and powerful position. Included were F. G. Pole, Divisional Superintendent at Bristol, who covered the South Western area, H. J. Peacock, Assistant Superintendent of the Line at Cardiff, and W. E. Hart, Divisional Superintendent at Birmingham. Mr A. V. H. Brown, the Divisional Superintendent at Chester covered the North Western area, but at the time the letter was written, no officer had been nominated to cover the Southern area.

Returning to the events of the summer of 1940, Adolf Hitler, in formulating his plans to invade England, at the beginning of August ordered the

A GWR porter, complete with his gas mask, pictured on platform 1 at Paddington station.

were told to remove the operating handle, and the first pinion.[29]

Another measure taken to deny resources to the invader was to prevent them using supplies of oil or petrol; railways stocked large amounts of petrol and more importantly diesel, which could have been of vital importance to advancing motorised divisions. After experiments in the laboratories of the railway workshops, an emulsifying solution was invented, which could be pumped into diesel and petrol tanks, turning the fuel into a thick foam which would block a carburettor or injection pump very quickly.

Although few details of what was actually done to immobilise the Great Western system exist, company records do show that a good deal of work was carried out, especially in the weeks after Dunkirk when the expectation of a German invasion was very high. An example is a series of New Work Orders issued in June 1940 which refer mainly to Great Western dock facilities. On 15 June, an order was placed relating to Plymouth Docks. It instructed staff, "to take account of any charges in connection with immobilisation at the Docks, excluding manning or standby time".[30] The

GWR 0-6-0 pannier tank No. 2785, and 4-6-0 No. 6801 Aylburton Grange *after the Newton Abbot raid in August 1940.   (Great Western Trust Collection)*

The Castle Barr Home Guard Battalion seen here in 1943. By this time Home Guard units were much better equipped, as this picture shows.

Luftwaffe to engage the Royal Air Force, and destroy it. This would leave the way open for his armies, massing in Northern France, to cross the Channel unopposed. Beginning on 2 August, the Battle of Britain raged over the skies of England until 17 September when, having failed to neutralise the RAF, the German invasion plans, codenamed 'Operation Sealion' were postponed until the following summer.

On 20 August 1940, Winston Churchill addressed the House of Commons, praising the Royal Air Force for its struggle against the Luftwaffe. "Never in the field of human conflict was so much owed by so many to so few" he said in a now famous speech; continuing he noted that in contrast to the First World War, this conflict involved "not only soldiers, but the entire population, men women and children..."[35] The Great Western were to appreciate how very true this latter statement was when just

before 6.45pm on that summer evening, three German aircraft attacked the station and locomotive shed at Newton Abbot.

This attack was one of a number of similar incidents involving Luftwaffe planes who were engaged in probing the defences of Southern England. When the raiders had fled the area on that particular evening they left a scene of devastation and carnage. One of the first serious raids on Great Western property cost 14 lives, and left 29 people seriously injured, with another 46 minor casualties. There was little warning of the attack; a 'Yellow' alert had been received at about 6.34pm, but since this did not mean that aircraft were in close proximity, staff and passengers continued about their business waiting for a 'Red' alert to be sounded. There had been no siren or ARP activity when three aircraft appeared, flying at about 200 feet, from the direction of Haldon, a small village to the east of Newton Abbot. It was

Damage to the station at Newton Abbot showing the length of rail which had been blown onto the roof. (Great Western Trust Collection)

thought that there were two bombers and a fighter, since each of the bombers dropped five 250 kilo bombs, and the other aircraft strafed the station and yard with machine gun fire.

Of the bombs dropped, most fell within the precincts of the station and yards; and only one failed to explode, this hitting a rail in the carriage sidings and coming to rest a short distance away from 'King' class locomotive No. 6010 *King Charles I*. As has been already noted, the raid took place at 6.45pm, but the unexploded bomb was not discovered until 7.25pm, after which all work had to be stopped for almost ten hours while bomb disposal experts defused and removed it. The majority of casualties and the most damage was caused by two bombs which fell very close to each other on the down through line and the down relief line. Much of the trackwork in this area was destroyed, and the island platform serving these two tracks was severely damaged. Photographs show the havoc wreaked on the refreshment room, where two staff were badly injured, the waiting room, toilets and bookstall. The roof of the canopy covering the down platform was also wrecked by

both the force of the blast and flying debris.

Further casualties were sustained since a train was actually standing on the down main line at the time the raiders struck, but by good fortune, the 10.32am express from Crewe bound for Plymouth, had left the station only three minutes previously and was at a safe distance from the station. The occupants of the 7pm Newton Abbot to Plymouth stopping service were not so lucky as the first coach, a brake third, No. 4941, was almost completely destroyed. One survivor of all this devastation however, was a small terrier, who had been tied up in the luggage compartment; he was rescued unhurt, although the fate of its owner is unrecorded.

As well as the damage actually caused by the bombs themselves a further hazard, peculiar to attacks on railway targets, was that a number of fairly substantial lengths of rail were blown into the air raining down on the station and immediate area. One 44ft 6in length was blown into the roof, whilst others were propelled out of the station, with one landing in the park opposite, another in a nearby bowling green 200 yards away, and a third

Clearing up operations have started at Newton Abbot to repair the down through and relief roads. The extent of damage to the track and rolling stock can be seen. (Great Western Trust Collection)

in the road outside the station. The nearby wagon repair shop came under attack from another such missile, with a piece of rail being sent skywards with such force that it came down end on. The rail hurtled through the roof covering, through the roof of a wagon standing underneath and after continuing through the floor of the wagon, finally came to rest after smashing the tyre of the van, which caused the wheel to break in two and push the wagon forward about six feet. Amazingly, two men sheltering under this particular wagon, Assistant Foreman Fenning, and wagon repairer Hoyle, escaped unharmed and the Wagon Shop Foreman had an equally lucky escape, being missed narowly by the broken half of the wheel as it shattered.

Less fortunate were two carriage cleaners and a gas fitter from the Chief Mechanical Engineers

Department who were working in and around two rakes of coaching stock stabled in carriage sidings close to the station. They were killed as this stock took the full force of two bombs. As well as this tragic loss of life, severe damage was done to most of the eleven coaches.

Two other bombs fell on the locomotive depot, one hitting the approaches of the coaling stage made a large crater, which rapidly filled with water, pouring from a ruptured water main serving a nearby water crane. The locomotive *King Charles I*, already mentioned, was slightly damaged by the blast, although it sustained more damage from the attentions of the fighter plane which machine-gunned it, leaving the tender particularly badly affected. Worse was to come for the 1901 built pannier tank No. 2785 which took the full force of one of the 250 kilo bombs, suffered a broken frame

'Castle' class 4-6-0 No. 5071 Spitfire, *formerly named* Clifford Castle, *is seen at Swindon with its cab window plated over, and coupled to the unique experimental 8-wheel tender. (National Railway Museum)*

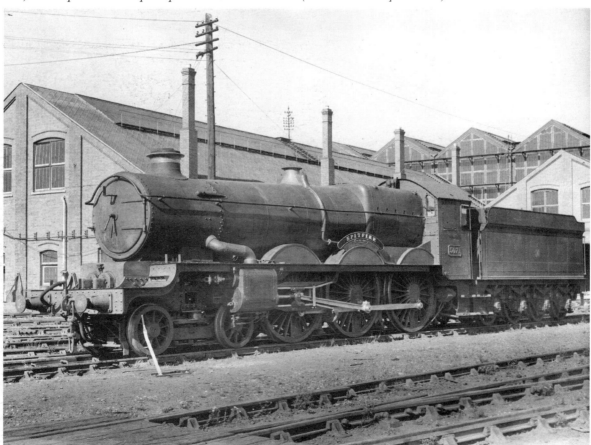

and two broken wheels. The locomotive's pannier tanks were ripped from their mountings, and its coupling rods were bent out of all recognition. It was recorded at the time that the engine was beyond economic repair, and that it was cut up on the spot. It seems however, that this was not the case, and that despite the severity of the damage, the pannier was repaired, since a number of photographers reported seeing it in the years after the war.

In all probability, the wrecked tank engine saved the life of a member of shed staff who was working on locomotive No. 6801 *Aylburton Grange* just yards away shielding the employee from both the blast, and another 44ft length of rail which was propelled over the 'Grange' into fields 150 yards away. Even so, the force of the explosion derailed the engine, and flying debris did cause some minor damage.

A final bomb hit the shed yard next to the No. 1 pit road, near to a group of five locomotives, including No. 6801. A Prairie tank, No. 3180,

was the most directly in line of this bomb blast, along with Churchward 2-6-0s Nos 9311 and 8353. The former was badly affected by shrapnel which left its cab, firebox, rear driving wheel and tender full of holes. The other Mogul and No. 3180 suffered only superficial damage with another pannier tank, No. 1761, escaping unharmed. The final engine in this group, No. 5915 *Trentham Hall*, although protected by a line of ash wagons, still had its chimney blown off and sustained severe damage to its tender. An album compiled by a Great Western employee in the Plymouth Division reveals that the engine required heavy repairs after the raid. No. 3180 was stripped down and sent to Swindon for further attention.[36]

Four other bombs fell outside the precincts of the station and depot; one landing in the front garden of an adjacent house, and another in the nearby Ford Park. These bombs caused no casualties, but the two that hit GWR houses at the back of the wagon shop resulted in a far more

It is hard to believe that, despite the apparently severe damage suffered by this locomotive, it was repaired and put back into service. Note how the coupling rod has been bent and twisted. (Great Western Trust Collection)

serious outcome. Of the six houses, three were completely destroyed, and the other three were badly damaged but amazingly, only one person was killed, the local newspaper reporting in some detail how numerous people were dug out of the rubble. Interestingly however, wartime censorship meant that the account of the raid made little reference to the attack on the station, any damage or injury or loss of life.[37] As a mark of the change in the war, it is also significant that the *GWR Magazine*, which up until this point had reported a great deal of news on the war and its effect on the railway, made no mention of the raid or its casualties.

Of the 14 people killed in the raid, ten were members of the general public, another ten being seriously injured, with four Great Western employees killed and another five badly hurt. With regard to locomotives and rolling stock, five engines required heavy repairs, and ten escaped serious damage, 26 carriages were badly damaged, with another 25 requiring light repairs. Twenty-two wagons also required attention as a result of the raid. The attack was a chilling reminder to the Great Western management, if they needed one, of the vulnerability of railway property against enemy aircraft and gave them an unwelcome preview of the kind of close attention the railway would

receive from the Luftwaffe for the next few years.

As the Battle of Britain raged overhead, moves were being made within the Great Western Railway towards the setting up of a fund to help purchase one or more aircraft to be donated to the RAF. In a circular to the staff at the end of August 1940, Sir James Milne, the General Manager wrote to all senior staff asking for their support in setting up the scheme which became known as the Spitfire Club. A lead was given by the Company's Board of Directors, who personally subscribed £500. All were encouraged to donate, and Milne urged his senior staff to "use your influence to ensure the success of the scheme".[38] Posters and collecting boxes were to be provided at every station, office and depot on the company's network, and it was hoped that if over £5,000 was raised, the approximate cost of each Spitfire, the staff would have the privilege of naming the aircraft. The *GWR Magazine* urged, "Let us give what we can, but all give something – if only a 'lick of paint' towards the Great Western Railway name which the aircraft will be allowed to carry."[39]

A report in the magazine the following month noted that almost £2,000 had been raised, although it was mentioned that the GWR appeal was only one of a number of similar schemes put forward by

Great Western road vehicles were modified as a result of blackout conditions. This photograph of a pickup from Old Oak Common locomotive depot shows clearly the cowled headlights and the white paint applied to the mudguards and running boards.

local communities with the same aim. Despite this, the article concluded, "there is still a great deal of enthusiasm for a 'Great Western Spitfire', and it only needs an average of one shilling from each member of staff to reach this goal".[40] Money was accumulated at a steady pace, until June 1941, when in an editorial in the GWR Magazine it was announced that the fund had been brought to a conclusion. Having raised the £5,000 necessary it was, the magazine noted, "anticipated that an aircraft bearing the Company's familiar monogram will shortly take its place amongst the hundreds of others that are so effectively taking their toll of enemy raiders."[41]

The achievement of this target is all the more impressive when one realises that many staff were also contributing financially to another aspect of the war effort through National Savings schemes.

Instituted in the early part of 1940, groups were set up all over the system to organise the collection of funds. Posters issued during the period urged the public to 'Lend to Defend' and these savings schemes provided an affordable way for many to contribute financially towards the war effort, and to build up savings at the same time. Most savings groups worked through the issuing of 6d stamps, which were fixed to cards. Once these were filled they could be exchanged for National Savings certificates. By the end of 1940 there were over 280 groups already formed, the largest being one set up in the 'AE' Shop at Swindon Works, which boasted over 200 members, whilst at the other end of the scale, there were only eight members of the group at Round Oak. Once the scheme had become accepted by the staff, reports of progress made appeared in every month's GWR Magazine.

5
Under Attack: Part 1

In his New Year message to the staff in January 1941, the General Manager, James Milne wrote that "Last year witnessed the intensification of the struggle which so vitally concerns us all".[1] As well as the fall of France and the events which took place at Dunkirk, he was also referring to the onset of the German bombing campaign which was to continue unabated for much of the year. Staff in the previous year he continued, had been exposed to "long days and nights of unremitting toil, frequently under circumstances of great danger".[2] It is not possible in a book of this kind to record the many thousands of occurrences of bomb damage which effected the Great Western Railway in what became known as the 'Year of the Blitz' between June 1940 and May 1941, but hopefully a survey of some of the incidents will give the reader some idea of the onslaught which the Great Western and the other railways faced in this period.

Although some of the incidents recalled in this chapter were costly in terms of both railwaymen's lives and company property, it will seem fairly evident that the attacks made by the Luftwaffe were largely unsystematic, and that they failed to disable the railway network which, as Evan John noted in his account of the railways work in the Second World War, meant that "Britain as a strategic unit was never put out of action, deprived of the means of defence against invasion nor prevented from turning herself into a military base from which Germany could be counter-attacked...".[3] This was only achieved by the bravery and resourcefulness of railway staff who often worked very long hours in

trying circumstances to ensure that damage was repaired and that trains could run.

It is clear however, that the Great Western, although suffering a great deal from the attention of German bombers, was not as badly affected as some of the other railways, particularly the Southern which, since most of its suburban lines were concentrated in and around the Capital, suffered proportionately more damage than all the other companies. This was particularly so as it had the lowest route mileage of all the Big Four companies. In the years between June 1940 to June 1943, the Great Western had 1,110 incidents caused by enemy action which led to damage or delay. In comparison, during the same period, the Southern was attacked 2,651 times and when these figures are compared with the respective companies' route mileages, the differences are even more marked. The GWR, with a network mileage of 3,652 miles, had an average of 30.4 incidents per 100 miles, whereas the Southern Railway, with a route mileage of 2,135 miles, had an average of 124.5 incidents per 100 miles.[4]

The Railway Executive, who later in the war advised the Royal Air Force on the effect of air attacks on railways, (presumably to assist them in their bombing campaign in Germany), collected a number of useful statistics which give a clearer picture of how the Blitz disrupted railway operations, particularly in the first twelve months. Unfortunately the figures are not broken down by company, but they are still of great relevance to our account of the Great Western's war. In the twelve

Members of the GWR Fire Brigade are seen at Paddington on 7 July 1940. The fire engine is an old parcels lorry. (National Railway Museum)

months from June 1940, there were a total of 6,173 incidents on Britain's railways; of this total, only 214 attacks delayed or affected traffic for more than a week. A total of 1,216 incidents took less than 24 hours to repair whilst 862 only disrupted services for up to six hours.[5]

By far the largest proportion of attacks were the ones which had little or no affect on the track, structures or rolling stock of the railway companies. In that first year, over 30 per cent of incidents, a total of 1,969, fell into this category, and in these cases, it was the disruption in terms of delays to passenger and goods services which were the main casualties. Add to this the number of false alarms and alerts which came to nothing, it becomes all too apparent that attempting to keep the Great Western running during the period must have been a trying and difficult task for management and employees alike. It was no wonder then, that the Company felt compelled to issue additional instructions to staff in October

1940 reinforcing a circular sent some twelve months earlier. In it staff were reminded that "during air raids it is essential that both passenger and freight trains should continue to run as required. Trainmen and signalmen should remain at their posts."[6]

Matters were made even more difficult as we saw in an earlier chapter, by the fact that during alerts, passenger trains were restricted to a speed of only 15 mph. Goods trains should, a Great Western circular instructed, "proceed cautiously at a speed not exceeding 10 mph".[7] As the Blitz increased in intensity, and air raid warnings became for many a nightly experience, the result of these instructions was to slow train movements almost to a standstill virtually causing as much disruption as the bombing itself. Even in the earliest days of the Blitz, the problem was already apparent; the General Manager reporting to the GWR board that "Freight train working has been adversely affected owing to the large number of areas in which public

GREAT WESTERN RAILWAY

Notice to Passengers

Passengers are advised to take shelter during an Air Raid and not to remain on the station platforms, where there may be a serious risk of danger from falling glass and splinters.

J. MILNE,

August, 1940.   General Manager.

air raid warnings were given, and yards and depots in many areas have become congested".[8]

As a result, in November 1940 these instructions were revised, allowing passenger and fitted freight trains to run at 25 mph during daytime air raids, and unfitted goods trains to be run at 15 mph at night and during daytime warnings. In February 1941 the restrictions were relaxed even further when all classes of trains were permitted to run at normal speeds during the daylight hours, and the practice of informing drivers of 'Red' alerts was discontinued. In the blackout however, all trains were still stopped, although they could then proceed at up to 30 mph if conditions permitted.

Some measure of the disruption caused by air raid warnings can be gleaned by the statistic that in 1940 there were a total of 414 'Red' alerts in the London area, an average of well over one a day; a further staggering statistic was that alerts were received on 101 consecutive days from 23 August

to 1 December 1940. Quite apart from the disruption to timetabled passenger, goods and military trains, the effects of such unrelenting pressure on railway staff cannot be underestimated. In Chapter 1, the severe slowing of GWR services was discussed in some detail and matters were not helped further, when in March 1940, perhaps as a precautionary measure, the Chief Mechanical Engineer's office at Swindon issued a notice to all enginemen instructing that, "Until further notice the speed of trains must not exceed 60 miles per hour at any place".[9] By March 1941 the general relaxation of restrictions already mentioned was mirrored by a further letter from F. W. Hawksworth to all divisional superintendents advising them that the maximum speed could be increased to 75 miles per hour.[10]

Air raids occurred regularly from June 1940 onwards, although before this a number of alerts had affected the Great Western. The GWR board heard on 24 May that there had been two 'Yellow' alerts in the early hours of 9 and 10 May, which had not led to any actual raid. On this occasion no public warning was given. German bombers attacked the company's premises at Cardiff Docks, on 20 June, causing some damage; 16 bombs falling in the dock area, two on the East Dock, one hitting the ship SS *Stresso* causing it to list badly. Another seven bombs landed on Great Western property, with a further eight hitting tenants of the company. No casualties were suffered, and damage was judged to be slight, with repairs estimated to be in the region of around £100. The General Manager reported that the Company's air raid precautions had "functioned satisfactorily" although ominously, he further noted that no warning of the air raid had been received by the Company until after the bombs had dropped.[11]

A few days later it was the turn of Bristol to receive the attention of the Luftwaffe. On 25 June 15 bombs fell in the vicinity of Temple Meads station. No casualties were sustained, and damage was restricted since several of the bombs failed to explode but six carriages were severely damaged, and ambulance train No. 28, stabled in the nearby Dr Day's sidings, also required some minor repairs. The next day a bomb was dropped alongside the line at Portbury near Portishead, presumably by a German plane unable to find the larger target of Avonmouth Docks. The attack caused "trifling damage" the General Manager noted in his monthly report to the board. The final incident

A scene of devastation on platform 9 at Bristol Temple Meads station on 24 November 1940.

described in June was another raid on Cardiff Docks; on this occasion it was the Queen Alexandra Dock which was hit, the Company's transformer substation being completely destroyed by a delayed action bomb. No casualties were reported, although once again, it was noted that no public warning was given.

As the months passed, a gradual escalation of the damage and disruption caused by the Blitz can be discerned. In July 137 high explosive bombs, and a number of incendiaries were dropped on company property, principally in the South Wales docks. Damage was reported as being slight in most cases, except in a raid on Swansea on 10 July, when a warehouse on the Mole at the East Dock was hit, killing nine men, including seven GWR employees. A further 21 people were injured in this attack, with another fatality two days later when Newport was raided.

In an earlier chapter the precautions adopted by the Company with regard to air raids were described in some detail. One measure noted was the replacement of the original blue lamps in carriage compartments with white shaded lamps which gave a better light to passengers. By February 1940 almost half of the carriages used by the GWR had been fitted with the new white lighting, and it was reported to the Board that vehicles were being converted at a rate of 250 per week.[12] It was not until the end of September however, that James Milne could report that practically the whole of the Great Western's fleet of almost 6,000 carriages was fitted with replacement lighting.[13]

The new system adopted by all the railways was not without its drawbacks. In May 1940 Swindon wrote to divisional superintendents and stores managers reminding them to keep adequate materials for the repair of the blinds used to maintain the blackout in carriage compartments. A particular problem appears to have been the theft of the stiffening sticks fixed to the bottom of blinds, which were often damaged or in many cases missing. Staff were urged to make regular checks of these blinds, and also to keep stocks of the sticks and the gimp pins that secured them.[14] One further matter was the repositioning of notices reminding passengers to draw blinds

The severity of the Bristol air raid on the night of the 6/7 December 1940 can be seen in the damage to 2-6-0 No. 4358 and its train, which had formed the 7.10pm Bristol to Salisbury.

during the blackout. These were originally displayed in the picture frames which were situated above the seats. With the restriction of lighting within compartments, these were as the Company observed, "practically invisible"[15] and so were moved to the bottom of each window where they could be clearly seen.

Despite all the work done to hide the glare from locomotive fireboxes, there was still some dissatisfaction with the arrangements adopted. Further steps to curb the light emitted from engines were taken in July 1940 when it was decided that the practice of running with the firebox door open and the 'flap' in use let too much light spill out. Swindon therefore announced that for the duration of the war, the characteristic 'flap' was to be removed, firemen being instructed that if they needed to let more air into the firebox, they should open the door slightly.[16] A further modification to all locomotives was the application of gas "detector" paint. As was noted in an earlier chapter, many were convinced that gas would be used by the Germans after its widespread use in the Great War and this detector paint was used in many places, most notably on the tops of Post Office pillar boxes! On Great Western stock, the paint was applied to the cab windows of locomotives, and the drivers' windows on diesel railcars and auto coaches.[17]

The fear of a gas attack persisted, and in the spring of 1941, a further circular was issued by Paddington reminding staff to be on their guard. Perhaps in a move to ensure that people were remembering to carry their gas masks with them at all times, the General Manager argued that it was "necessary in the National interest, as well as your own...that you have available at all times the means of protecting yourself during...an attack".[18] Railways were, he continued, vital to the war effort and, "just as they have continued to operate during the hostile bombing, they will also be required to operate during gas attacks."[19]

Towards the end of August 1940, as the battle for aerial supremacy over the skies of Britain continued, further raids causing damage to GWR property occurred. In a later chapter a number of "hit and run" incidents involving Great Western trains will be described, and although this kind of attack was more characteristic of Luftwaffe attacks in the latter part of the war, it is useful to point out that Great Western trains were targets from almost the earliest months of 1940. With the concentration of naval activity in the Weymouth and Portland area it was almost inevitable that German aircraft would turn their attention on to Great Western and Southern Railway operations in the area. On 11 August the 10.30am Portland to Weymouth train was attacked, with all windows on the right side being reported as being broken by bomb explosions. No mention of any loss of life or serious casualties was made. A more bizarre incident, which illustrated how the war had reached even the most distant corner of the Great Western Railway, occurred on 21 August, when empty stock of the 10.30am Paddington to Penzance express, the "Cornish Riviera Limited", which was stabled in the Ponsandane sidings at Penzance, was damaged by the explosion of a German mine on the nearby beach.

A few days later, on 26 August in a heavy raid on the Birmingham area, the goods empties shed at Bordesley was completely destroyed, with the loss of 75 loaded wagons, 30 horse drawn vehicles, 9 tractors and 21 trailers. Although the cost of replacing all this was high, at over £4,500, no member of staff was injured in the incident. The raid did however demonstrate the bravery and determination of GWR staff. When the warning was sounded at about 9.50pm, an 18-year old engine cleaner, Peter Smout, who was acting fireman on a shunting engine in the Bordesley yards that night, rushed to extinguish a number of incendiary bombs which had landed nearby. On being asked if he could drive a locomotive, he volunteered to take engine No. 7758, which was not his own locomotive, and pulled wagons out of the blazing goods shed. He made three further trips into the shed, by which time the right side of the engine footplate was too hot to touch. One of his workmates, Frederick Blake, a wagon examiner, assisted by acting as shunter, operating point levers with the help of his cap, since the levers had become too hot to touch by this time. Both men were mentioned in an official citation that noted "a good example and acted as an incentive to other members of staff to help save the Company's property."[20] For their courage they were awarded the George Medal.

Some days later, another of the South Wales docks was bombed, the target this time being Swansea. Damage to the hydraulic main and electric power lines was reported, although more damage was done at the nearby High Street station, where the divisional superintendents offices and the goods offices were completely destroyed, with the station roof and permanent way also affected. This time the Company estimated that repairs would cost £24,250; a considerable sum.

Events in the Battle of Britain took a sinister turn for the worse on 7 September, when Herman Goering, the Commander in Chief of the Luftwaffe, changed his tactics, switching the concentration of his attacks from RAF airfields to the cities of Britain. It was from this point that damage to GWR property became far more serious and costly both in financial and human terms. On 7 September itself, the day London faced its first large scale air raid, Great Western facilities in East London were hit in a raid which left 450 people dead, and over 1,600 injured. London's Docklands were set alight by the massive daylight raid; the GWR goods depot at Poplar was destroyed, and further bombs severed access to the Company's facilities at South Lambeth and Smithfield. The General Manager reported to the board on 4 October that goods traffic bound for these depots was diverted to Acton until repairs would allow normal business to recommence.[21] During another raid in the London area on the 19th September, traffic was further disrupted when the 22.10 Paddington to Penzance train was badly damaged, this time by "Friendly Fire" as an anti-aircraft shell, well off target, passed through the roof and floor of one of the coaches bursting on the permanent way beneath it.

The Manager also mentioned that there had been numerous cases where Great Western staff had carried out repairs with "great expedience" even when air raids were still continuing. The Minister of Transport had, he reported, written personally to congratulate the Company on the gallant conduct of its staff who had worked continuously for 17 hours repairing air raid damage near Saltash on 25 September 1940, despite two further air raids which had occurred whilst work was continuing. "This is another incident in Great Western history of which you must be proud" the Minister concluded.[22]

With cities and their people being brought into the war, railways moved firmly into the front line. During the weeks between the GWR board meeting of 4 October 1940 and the next meeting on 25 October, the General Manager reported that there had been 69 serious incidents involving the Great Western. In an attack on Banbury on 3 October, four staff were killed when a porters

mess room suffered a direct hit from high explosive bombs. Two cartage contractors in the vicinity were also killed, and three staff were injured in the attack. In the same incident a freight train was set alight, and two vehicles were burnt out.

London continued to bear the brunt of Luftwaffe attacks, and on the night of 13 October three high explosive bombs fell in the vicinity of the Great Western Hotel at Paddington, one of these hitting the Praed Street (now Paddington) Circle Line underground station. Although not strictly on GWR property, it was Great Western ARP staff who, showing great courage and determination fought their way through the wreckage in the blackout to rescue the injured trapped on the platforms below. All the seriously injured were brought out within half an hour, and treated at the casualty clearing station at Paddington, before being ferried to hospital. The number of casualties in this incident is not known, although it was not a good night for the Capital, with 154 people killed at Stoke Newington when a shelter received a direct hit. South Lambeth Goods Depot, hit in the raid on the 7th September, was further affected on 15 October, when a bomb fell on one of the roadways outside the complex, wrecking 35 wagons, and destroying a number of road vehicles. More importantly, the blast also caused the 35-ton Goliath crane used in the yard to collapse.

With the onset of intense bombing raids on targets in London and the provinces, and the disruption this caused in terms of actual bomb damage, both to everyday life and business, the Prime Minister issued a message urging the continuance of work during air raids. As we have already seen in this chapter, measures were taken to speed up the passage of trains to minimise disruption, especially in areas where, although the alert had been sounded, no raid was in progress. A further measure introduced by the company was the introduction of 'Roof Watching' schemes which involved the use of staff to "give warning of imminent danger when the staff should take shelter, and to give a signal when work should be resumed".[23] These staff enabled work to be carried on far longer than would have been possible if ordinary warnings had been heeded but before this idea was adopted by the Company in late 1940, cooperation with the Royal Observer Corps had already taken place in Cardiff and had, a representative from the Docks Department noted, "resulted in less time being spent by the men in shelters than hitherto".[24]

Where such cooperation was possible it was welcomed by the Company, but in general they preferred to use their own staff. A 24-hour shift was introduced for spotters, with two staff being on duty in rotation at each post. It seems that there was some pressure from the men for increased pay for such duties, but the General Manager was insistent that 'spotters' would only be paid their ordinary rate. Those employed on piecework would be paid an allowance based on their average earnings. It was noted that standard equipment for staff engaged on such duties should be a steel helmet, Civilian Duty respirator, mackintosh and rubber boots. Since spotters were employed to look for enemy aircraft, binoculars were seen as essential items of equipment; unfortunately the only drawback in this scheme was that supplies of these were non-existent. Thus C. B. Collett was forced to write to his staff asking if any of them had binoculars of 6x or 8x magnification which they could loan to the Company for the duration of the war! There was, he noted "little likelihood of the Company being able to purchase their requirements".[25] As we shall see later in this chapter, the Company had to participate further in this kind of system, as in 1941 the Government enacted legislation to compel large undertakings such as railways to set up 'Fire watching schemes' to assist in the prevention of large scale damage in air raids.

One consequence of the Blitz was the temporary withdrawal of Great Western sleeping car services and it was reported in early October that because of damage to the West of England main line, on a number of occasions it had been necessary to divert GWR trains on to Southern Railway metals via Basingstoke and Yeovil. Unfortunately the dimensions of sleeper stock meant that they could not be used on these routes, and as a result, sleepers were withdrawn on 29 August from the 9.50pm Paddington to Penzance service (Sundays only), the midnight sleeper from Paddington to Plymouth, the 1.15am Paddington to Penzance and the 8.45pm Penzance to Paddington. This disruption appears to have been short lived, since on 29 November 1940, the General Manager reported the reinstatement of these services to the board.[26]

Some idea of the intensity of the German bombing campaign can be gained from the fact that from the initial raid on London on 7 September 1940 already mentioned, to 13 November, Londoners experienced only one night on which

In this incident, at the Bath end of No.2 Tunnel at Foxes Wood near Bristol, the carriage was almost completely destroyed when a bomb hit the tunnel mouth and ricocheted into the coach, which was part of the 4.52pm Salisbury to Bristol service. The initial point of impact for the bomb can be clearly seen on the left side of the tunnel.

no bombs were dropped. In fact, it was only on a total of six further nights that less than 50 German planes flew over the Capital.[27] Speaking to the GWR board at the end of November, James Milne reported that there had been 65 incidents in the previous month; as can be imagined, the Company's property in London was badly affected.

On 25 October the second daylight raid in as many days led to severe damage to the relatively new carriage lifting and paint shop at Old Oak Common. A mail coach, No. 836, received a direct hit, and was completely destroyed. More seriously,

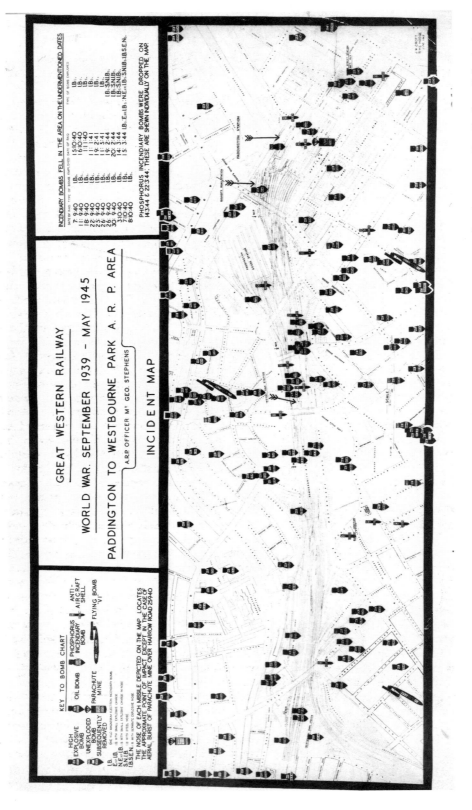

Some idea of the intensity of attacks on the Paddington area can be seen in this incident map compiled by the ARP staff at the station.   (Ian Coulson Collection)

the yardmaster's office, and the seat registration and passenger inspectors' offices were also destroyed. Only two employees were injured, but over £4,000 of damage was estimated to have been done. More loss was reported with further attacks in the Paddington area in early November; 50 cartage vehicles were destroyed when the goods depot was hit on the 12th, and three days later, the efforts of the Company to cut down on waste received a setback when the salvage depot at Park Royal was destroyed by an incendiary bomb.

London was not the only place to be badly affected by German bombing as in October and November, Birmingham also suffered a large number of raids. On 26 October extensive damage was done to the roof of the general offices at Snow Hill station, and the top of the nearby Great Western Hotel was also set on fire. More serious destruction ensued on the night of 19 and 20 November, when the city suffered its 50th air raid of the war. During the intense raid, which lasted from 7pm to 8.30am the following morning, over 1,500 people were killed or badly injured. At Snow Hill, considerable damage was caused to the hotel, divisional superintendent's office, and the district goods manager's office. When a land mine exploded close to Snow Hill, much of the glass in the station roof and concourse was smashed, and the station clock was also badly damaged but the only casualties reported on this occasion were staff who had remained on duty in the ticket office, and were cut by flying glass.[28] Away from the station precincts the running lines at Yardley, Hockley, Acocks Green and Bordesley were put temporarily out of commission. Two days later the up and down lines north of Snow Hill were blown up, and a retaining wall severely damaged. On the same night, 22 November, an empty train was hit at Moor Street station, and the running lines at Hockley were once again blocked.

Another provincial city, Bristol, had suffered a number of 'nuisance raids' in the first 14 months of the war, but on the evening of Sunday 24 November 1940 the first of a series of 30 raids which lasted until 5 July 1941 began just after dark. No one in Bristol could have been prepared for the intensity of the attack as the city was set ablaze by high explosive and incendiary bombs. In the first hour of the raid over 70 fires were reported, mostly in the centre of the city, and as a result, every available appliance of the local fire brigade was brought into action. Bomb damage to water mains caused the supply to fail, and water had to be taken from the docks and the River Avon to augment supplies.[29]

Whilst bombs were raining down on Bristol's mediaeval city centre, its station at Temple Meads was also the subject of three direct hits by German bombers; several platforms and their adjacent tracks were damaged or blocked, and like Birmingham Snow Hill, bomb blasts shattered a good deal of glass in the overall roof. Bombs fell all over the city, well away from the centre, and incidents were reported at Bristol East Depot, Lawrence Hill station and Bedminster. Amazingly, bearing in mind the severity of the air raid, only two employees were killed on this occasion.

It is worth describing briefly, the types of bombs which Great Western ARP squads found themselves dealing with. Three main types were used by the Luftwaffe; the first, containing high explosive were, in the early stages of the war, relatively small, weighing between 50 and 250 kilograms. After May 1941 larger examples of up to 5,000 kilograms began to be used. In the early days of the Blitz, a second weapon was introduced, the large sea mine, which was dropped by parachute. British ARP crews called them 'land mines' and the large 8ft long cylinders were said to float silently to earth like sycamore seeds.[30] If such bombs landed within 400 yards of the railway, they were considered dangerous, and the Admiralty were directly advised whenever one was discovered. Traffic was then not allowed to restart until a member of Admiralty staff had said it was safe to do so. As we have already learned in the description of the raid on Birmingham Snow Hill in November 1940, these bombs were extremely powerful, and could cause extensive damage over a wide area.

The third type of bomb was the thermite incendiary, which although small, was in many ways perhaps the most destructive of the bombs dropped by the Luftwaffe. Weighing only one or two pounds, incendiaries were shaped like hock bottles, and normally about 18 inches long. They were usually dropped in containers which could contain up to 72 incendiaries and if they were not dealt with quickly and thoroughly they could be extremely destructive. Since they were dropped in such quantities, it was difficult to ensure that they had all been dealt with; their size meant that they could be smothered with a sandbag, or doused with water either from a bucket, or from a stirrup pump, which were issued to the general public and Great

Western employees. What was needed, the *GWR Magazine* reported in May 1941 was "a cool head and a quick eye...experience has taught that when approved instructions have been followed the bombs can be effectively dealt with."[31]

The relative ease with which bombs of this kind could be dealt with initially was tempered in December 1940 when it was discovered that the Luftwaffe were placing explosive charges in a proportion of bombs. Writing to staff on Boxing Day 1940, the Superintendent of the Line at Paddington noted that "every 1 kilo incendiary bomb must be regarded as likely to contain an explosive charge".[32] Staff were instructed not to attack the bomb with water or a sandbag until it had been burning for at least two minutes, to ensure that it would not explode; in an attempt perhaps to fool the Germans that the use of explosive charges had not been recognised, staff were also asked to make this information widely known by word of mouth, but that it should "not be published in the press, by poster or on the wireless".[33]

A circular issued by the Great Western illustrates that ARP staff worked under some difficulties. Apart from the obvious physical dangers they faced during raids, in August 1941, perhaps due to the severity of the German bombing campaign, it was reported by the Ministry of Home Security that there was a shortage of jute, which was used to make sandbags. The stores superintendent at Swindon advised staff that apart from exceptional emergency purposes, "no use of sandbags can be regarded as legitimate except for controlling

incendiary bombs".[34] A new 'sand mat' which consisted of half a conventional sand bag, was used specially for this purpose. Another circular was issued by the GWR at the height of the Blitz reminding staff to look after another weapon used against incendiaries, the stirrup pump. Staff were warned not to leave them filled with water in the winter months, since the water had a tendency to freeze, causing the hose to crack.[35]

An example of a serious raid on Great Western property, involving incendiaries will serve both to show how dangerous a weapon this kind of bomb was, and to highlight the kind of bravery and devotion to duty shown by countless Great Western staff throughout the war. On 26 September 1940 the Liverpool area, and in particular the Docks, were the subject of a fierce air attack involving property on both sides of the Mersey. At the beginning of the air raid, it was estimated that about 160 medium sized incendiary bombs were dropped on the Great Western's Morpeth Dock, Birkenhead Goods Depot and sidings. The sidings were the concentration point for all the Company's Liverpool and Birkenhead traffic, but more importantly, they contained a train load of ammunition, a number of wagons loaded with tins of petrol, and a number of other wagons containing 250lb bombs and fuses.

Most of the incendiaries were extinguished by GWR staff, limiting damage to only 17 wagons, but whilst this operation was being carried out, one of the Company's shunters, Norman Tunna, discovered two incendiaries burning in a sheeted open wagon containing 250lb bombs. Showing tremendous coolness, Tunna removed the wagon sheeting, extinguished the bombs, and removed them from the wagon, thus avoiding a serious explosion. Such was the closeness of the call, that the top layer of the 250lb bombs were hot to the touch, and they were promptly removed by the military for examination. Another employee, goods checker Patrick Mahoney, discovered a wagon containing ammunition fuses on fire, and led his gang in extinguishing the flames, then removing the fuses from the van so that they could be dealt with more effectively. Both men were awarded the George Medal for their bravery.

Another view of the anti-glare screens used on Great Western locomotives. The locomotive pictured is No. 4096 Highclere Castle *and shows the top screen that was in daily use after sunset.*

In his last report to the board of 1940, the General Manager gave an account of further raids on Birmingham and Bristol, and he noted that since the last board meeting, there had been incidents of bomb damage at 38 locations. This figure was reduced from previous months since on 15 nights in December weather conditions had compelled the Luftwaffe to abandon attacks on Britain. All the same, there were eleven major attacks, and five serious raids on British cities during the month. On 2 December two platforms at Bristol Temple Meads were damaged by high explosive bombs, and fire also destroyed the ladies waiting room. During this raid a Churchward 28xx 2-8-0 was slightly damaged, and some miles north

of the city pannier tank No. 3632 was derailed on top of a bomb crater between Henbury and Filton West, whilst working a passenger train.

Far worse was to come on 6 December, when in a heavy raid, the 7.10pm Bristol to Salisbury train, which was leaving platform 6, received a direct hit from a bomb, killing the driver of 2-6-0 No. 4358, and badly injuring the fireman. Fifteen passengers in the train were killed, and a further 23 seriously injured. Close by, another rake of carriages was set alight, destroying three coaches, and flying debris hit a third train, causing further injuries to passengers. On top of this, staff had also to deal with a large number of incendiaries, which damaged the overall roof. Five days later,

Every locomotive was fitted with a wooden box containing ARP equipment and this diagram was pasted to the inside of the lid to show how it should be packed.

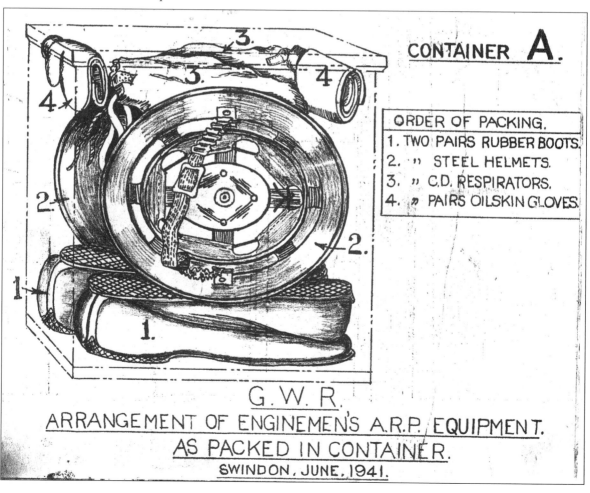

Lawrence Hill station, a mile or so from Temple Meads, suffered severe disruption when the goods shed offices were completely destroyed, and the blast from this bomb also damaged the station buildings.

Birmingham had already suffered at the hands of German bombers, and in December 1940 further attacks caused a good deal of destruction. On 3 December the running lines between Birmingham North and Hockley, and Hall Green and Shirley were blocked, and less than a week later on the 11th, a land mine fell close to Hockley station. When it exploded it caused extensive damage to the station and the nearby divisional offices; the goods offices and bonded stores were also seriously affected, and four employees were injured in the raid. On the same occasion, Handsworth goods offices were demolished by a bomb, and stables on the premises badly damaged. Three employees on Home Guard duties were killed.

In his 20 December report the General Manager also described two attacks in Cheltenham on the same night, 11 December, which illustrate the ease with which German raiders could paralyse the British rail network. The first was the destruction of an overbridge at Dillery Road in Cheltenham, situated between the Gloucester loop and Cheltenham South & Leckhampton. As a result of this attack, the debris from the demolished bridge blocked both running lines, and it took over a week to restore normal services on that stretch of line. The second attack affected the Cheltenham to Honeybourne line at an unnamed location, closing the route for several days.

Although incidents like the ones just described caused a huge amount of disruption, another more problematic source of delay was that of unexploded bombs. It was calculated that almost one in ten of bombs dropped on London was a 'dud', and each of these had to be investigated and disarmed before being removed.[36] A more sinister complication was that the Luftwaffe had fitted some bombs with delayed action fuses, meaning that all 'UXBs' had to be treated with extreme care.

Two examples of incidents early in 1941

Some of the material stored at the Company's South Wales docks could be very hazardous, especially considering the amount of attention paid to the docks by the Luftwaffe. These bombs were stored in 'N' shed, Swansea Docks.

illustrate some of the dislocation and disruption caused by unexploded bombs. The first occurred on the night of 9/10 January when, at just before midnight, a bomb fell on tracks adjacent to a footbridge at West Ealing station. The bomb was only 25ft away from both the up and down main lines and as a result it was felt that some form of screen was essential, thus two rakes of six coal wagons were shunted on either side of the bomb. This meant that the main lines could be opened to all traffic at a reduced speed limit of 5 mph; the task of screening, which in itself must have been a perilous job for staff, was not completed until 4 o'clock in the morning, after which all staff were cleared from the area. The official accident report compiled by GWR staff on the spot records that the bomb exploded at 5.52am causing "very little damage". The force of the explosion however, destroyed three of the wagons, one of which was flung 15ft in the air, demolishing the steps of the footbridge. All in all however, damage was limited, and the main line from the Capital to the West Country was not seriously disrupted.[37]

A further illustration of this ever-present threat to GWR services occurred a month later at Machen in South Wales. One mile above the station the lines were blocked by unexploded bombs on 27 February. Both the New Tredegar lines and the down line between Machen and Caerphilly were blocked, and were only reopened for freight working in the early afternoon of 1 March. The following morning, the lines were once again closed to allow the bombs to be exploded. This was done at 9.20am causing damage to sleepers and seven sets of rails. Single line working was operated between Machen and Caerphilly whilst repairs were instituted, and normal working was not restored until 5.35pm on 3 March. What both these incidents show was that although actual damage from unexploded bombs could be quite small, the disruption caused by their presence could be enormous.

No account of the activities of the Great Western in the tumultuous year of 1940 can be complete without some mention of the most tragic and serious accident to take place on the GWR for some considerable time. The Norton Fitzwarren accident, which occurred in the early hours of 4 November, claimed the lives of 26 people, including one member of Great Western staff, and included 13 naval personnel. A further 56 passengers were seriously hurt, and another 18 escaped with only minor injuries or shock.

Around 900 passengers were on the heavily loaded 9.50pm Paddington to Penzance train which was travelling at about 40 to 45 mph on the down relief line. It passed two successive signals at danger, and ploughed through catch points protecting the down main line, where the two lines converged, about two miles beyond Taunton. The driver of the train for some unaccountable reason thought that he was on the down main line itself, and not the relief line, and thus thought that the signals had been lowered for a following newspaper train. The locomotive, 'King' class 4-6-0 No. 6028 *King George VI* was thrown clear and came to rest, almost 140ft away from the catch points having passed across an open drain. The driver, P. W. Stacey, survived, but his fireman, W. Seabridge died in the accident.

Further casualties were luckily avoided, since the 12.50am Paddington to Penzance newspaper train, which the driver of No. 6028 had thought was in the relief line, was in fact travelling on the down main line at about 55 to 60 mph, and only just overtook the passenger train before the derailment occurred. The closeness of the call was ably demonstrated by the fact that a rivet head from the bogie of No. 6028 was found in the fourth van of the newspaper train, having broken the window of the leading door. Indentations caused by flying ballast from the accident were also found on the side of the fifth vehicle in the newspaper train. Had this train been involved, it seems likely that casualties would have been even higher.

The accident occurred at 3.47am, and GWR trained ambulance staff from Norton Fitzwarren and Taunton were quickly on the scene. Fortunately, a surgeon commander was travelling on the train and was able to do valuable work before other help arrived. Despite their efforts it took over 40 minutes for the first ambulance to arrive, which must have seemed an eternity to those laying injured on that dark November night, especially since rescue work could only be carried out by the light of hand lamps and torches. In his official report, Colonel H. S. Mount, who carried out an investigation into the circumstances of the accident, reported that in the aftermath of the crash there was "evidence to the effect that everyone behaved with complete composure."[38]

The inspector was sympathetic in his summing up, and believed that the issue was "largely psychological"; he noted that the driver's breakdown may have been partly attributed to operating conditions in the blackout, and to more general strain, since his house in Acton had been damaged in the Blitz. Concluding his report, Colonel Mount put the cause of the accident down to an "unaccountable lapse" on the part of Driver W. P. Stacey who, as he noted, was an experienced and capable Old Oak Common man with over 40 years service. Why he mistook the line on which his train was running, we shall never know, but his horror on realising that he was on the wrong track must have remained with him for the rest of his life. The jury of the inquest for the crash victims held at Taunton on 20 November were less sympathetic, finding him guilty of "an error of judgment"[39] although they could not decide on the actual degree of error, and noted that they did not think the error criminal, in view of the weather and other conditions. Neither this sombre conclusion or the accident itself were reported in the company magazine, presumably to protect staff morale, although reports of the accident did appear in other railway journals, most notably the *Railway Gazette.*

The conclusions of the accident Inspector highlight the enormous pressure railway staff were under; like the public at large, they faced the nightly Blitz with fortitude and courage, but they also had the extra responsibility of making sure that the railway network continued to run in both the most efficient and safest way possible. The Norton Fitzwarren accident was perhaps the most dramatic and savage example of the stresses put on Great Western employees, who by and large coped extremely well. Tiredness, coupled with the affects of the blackout, inevitably led to scores of minor accidents and mishaps, not all of which were reported to the General Manager's office at Paddington!

As 1940 drew to a close, there seemed to be no let up for the hard-pressed staff and it was reported that the government had called for continuous production during the Christmas season, and this required delivery to destinations, and thus the railways were a key part of this process. As a result, the Railway Executive requested that passenger services over the Christmas holidays be limited only to the normal daily services, and an appeal was made to the general public not to travel unless it was absolutely necessary. The appeal concluded, "make this a 'stay-where-you-are' Christmas and you will have the satisfaction of knowing that by doing so you are helping indirectly to clear the rails and roads for the munitions and war supplies so essential for victory."[40]

6
Under Attack: Part 2

With the beginning of a new year the Great Western braced itself for a further onslaught from the Luftwaffe. Reporting to the Great Western Railway board at the end of January 1941, Sir James Milne revealed that casualties sustained on Company premises up to the end of December 1940 had totalled 67 killed and 238 injured. Of the fatalities, 27 were passengers, and 24 were staff; the remaining 16 included contractors and municipal ARP staff. Ninety-three members of staff had been seriously injured, and in addition to this, 35 railway staff had been killed and another 86 seriously injured whilst off duty. The General Manager argued that despite the adversities they had faced, the "Company's ARP and fire prevention services have functioned very satisfactorily at all places where heavy raids occurred".[1]

In his January report, the General Manager informed the board of the cost of all the destruction and mayhem described. In the period from the outbreak of war to 31 January 1941, the total cost of enemy action amounted to £423,764. By far the largest proportion of the total was, not surprisingly, damage to railway property, which amounted to £246,309, with the next highest amount, that of repairs and renewals to locomotives and rolling stock, costing the GWR over £67,000. Also noted was that of the houses owned by the Company and rented to its staff, 32 had been destroyed, and another 501 needed repair.

In an editorial in the first *Railway Gazette* of 1941, the editor stated that the New Year was opening with a realisation that, "the war was about to enter a decisive phase".[2] He continued, remarking that a year before, the war had seemed fairly remote to many people, but that during 1940 there could have been few citizens and no industrial undertaking in the country that could claim to have been untouched by it. The "decisive phase" mentioned was to be a sustained attempt by the Luftwaffe to destroy both the military and industrial base of the country and the spirit and resolve of its population; once again the Great Western, like all the other railway companies, was to be at the 'Front Line' of the Home Front.

Over the Christmas and New Year period the appeals for the public to stay at home by the Railway Executive and the Minister of Transport were heeded, but despite traffic being smaller than in previous years, it became apparent as early as 21 December, that if the public were not to be left stranded at stations over Christmas, it would be necessary for the railways to run relief trains or run popular services in duplicate or triplicate. Arrangements were therefore made, and as the Railway Executive reported in a statement issued as a result of adverse press comment, "main line stations were cleared on Christmas Eve, and very few passengers were left behind".[3]

If Company staff had hoped that Christmas and the New Year would bring some respite from the German bombing campaign, they were to be sorely disappointed. During January 1941 there were 69 incidents of enemy bombing, but for this month at least, Great Western property in the Capital

The burnt out remains of the clock tower at Bristol Temple Meads station after the raid on 3 January 1941. Incendiary bombs also destroyed the booking hall, refreshment rooms, telegraph office and waiting rooms.

suffering less damage than that in the provinces. In an intensive air raid on the City of London on the 29th December, the Company's receiving offices at Broad Street and Redcross Street were both destroyed by fire. On 11 January Paddington was attacked, this time by a shower of almost 50 incendiary bombs which fell in and around the area of the station. Fortunately, both staff and members of the travelling public set about extinguishing the resultant fires, and prevented any destruction being done; only 5 minor injuries being reported.

It was Great Western property to the west of the network which received the attentions of the Luftwaffe in early January and on the 2nd, Cardiff station was badly damaged by incendiary bombs. Large numbers of these destructive weapons were dropped on the General station, causing a number of serious fires, the refreshment rooms on platform 6 were destroyed, and three coaches gutted. Extensive damage was done to Stonefield Yard

signal box, and the East Dock engine shed by land mines, whilst several other unexploded land mines caused extremely serious interruptions to the timetable. Bombs also dropped on the docks, causing minor damage to small buildings and the hydraulic mains system; a vessel in the Queens Dock was also hit. Despite the ferocity of the raid, only two fatalities were sustained, one of which was an employee, and a further 19 were injured, eight of whom were GWR staff.

The next day it was the turn of Bristol once again to suffer an intensive raid, something which was to continue until the middle of April. From the evidence of Luftwaffe air photographs discovered in more recent years,[4] it seems likely that as early as September 1940 German Intelligence had specifically identified Temple Meads station and a number of vulnerable railway bridges in the vicinity as key targets. Early on the night of 3 January it was apparent that the station and the nearby City Docks had been earmarked for special attention.

As was the case of Cardiff the night before, the bombers showered the city and especially the area west of Temple Meads, with incendiaries, many of which hit their intended target. Soon the buildings adjoining platforms 9 and 12 were well ablaze, destroying the main booking office and hall, the telegraph office, the refreshment rooms, and left luggage department. When it was thought that all the incendiaries had been traced, one of which had come to rest behind the clock tower facing the station approach ignited, causing further destruction including severe damage to the roof. To this day, the clock tower has never been replaced. Matters were made much worse for fire fighters by the fact that the night was one of the winter's bitterest to date and as they tried to extinguish fires, the water formed great icicles on buildings, and roads and pavements became coated with sheets of ice, making their task even more difficult. A nearby bridge was also wrecked, causing trains to be diverted to the south and worked backwards into the various platforms. Temporary huts for use as booking offices were erected in the station forecourt, until platform 9 and its associated facilities were rebuilt.

Despite all this destruction, the company was able to carry on running trains, albeit with some difficulty. Only one locomotive seems to have been damaged, Company records noting that 4-6-0 'Saint' class No. 2945 *Hillingdon Court* suffered "slight" damage during the raid. No record of any loss of rolling stock seems to have survived. Mention was made in Chapter 5 of the severity of the first serious raid on Bristol on 24 November 1940, when much of the city centre was destroyed. On this occasion, the 12-hour dusk-to-dawn Blitz almost completely obliterated any premises in the city centre which had not been destroyed in previous raids. It was calculated that almost 2,500 houses were damaged, and in total 149 people were killed, and another 133 were seriously injured.

The final raid affecting Great Western property in January was at Swansea, where on the 17th, during a heavy raid, the docks took a severe battering. In Kings Dock two cargo sheds were severely hit, with others escaping with only slight damage. More serious was the loss of two electric dockside cranes, and damage to lines and nearby rolling stock. At the Prince of Wales Dock, two sheds were completely destroyed by fire, and the

whole docks area was immobilised for several days through bombs severing both the hydraulic main and electricity supplies.

One further hazard was one which came not from the Luftwaffe, but from the efforts of the ARP and anti-aircraft staff who were trying to drive off German bombers. This particular problem, which constantly irritated those trying to run a train service was that of the ubiquitous barrage balloon, which seemed to be ever present on almost all skylines. The initial appearance of the balloons seems to have caused some excitement; in an article in the September 1939 issue of the *GWR Magazine*, an unidentified writer waxed lyrical as to their appearance at Paddington. The view from his window was not normally inspiring he noted, and he went so far as to argue that it could often be depressing; but, he continued "Today this depression is gone, for a new wonder has appeared...glistening silver in the sunlight and dark in the shadows, is an anti-aircraft balloon."[5]

Those who had to deal with the problems caused

As a result of the heavy bombing of Bristol, the Great Western carried out an evacuation of children from the area in February 1941. The author's father was evacuated to North Devon on one of these trains, and he can be seen in this picture, third from right, taken at Lawrence Hill station. (Author's Collection)

by balloons probably had a rather less romantic view than the writer of this article. Two examples taken from Great Western Railway incident reports illustrate how, although small, these anti-aircraft measures probably lost the railways as much time as some of the minor air raids they suffered. The first report was sent to the General Manager's office by R. C. Pole, the Divisional Manager at Bristol, and noted that during a severe thunderstorm on the afternoon of 10 March 1941 a barrage balloon caught fire, and the cable fell across the telegraph wires between Ashley Hill and Stapleton Road stations, causing the failure of the block bell equipment. An hour was spent by GWR, staff untangling the cable, and repairing the block system; the report noted that two trains were delayed by around ten minutes, and the branch train to Severn Beach was delayed a matter of a few minutes.[6]

Rather more delay occurred less than a month

later in West Wales, when during a gale, another balloon broke free of its moorings at Neyland, and its trailing cable snapped both telegraph and telephone cables between Boncath and Crymmych Arms. Pilot working had to be instituted at 8.35am between these two stations, since the electric train staff instruments were put out of order. The repairs were not completed until 4pm, causing some considerable disruption, especially since military traffic used this particular line.[7]

The extremely heavy air raids on Bristol led to the evacuation of school children from the city between 18 and 21 February 1941; in mentioning the operation, the *GWR Magazine* paid tribute to the courageous and resolute bearing of Bristolians in general, and to the children of the city.[8] The government plan called for the evacuation of over 7,000 children in ten special trains, taking them to a variety of safer locations in Devon and Cornwall. The author's father was a passenger on one of these

Weymouth, with its proximity to the Naval base at Portland, was the scene of a number of air raids during the war. The destruction seen here was as a result of a raid on 17 January 1941.

trains, departing from either Stapleton Road or Lawrence Hill station, and being evacuated to Bideford and subsequently Westward Ho! in Devon. On the completion of the operation, the Chief Education Officer of the City of Bristol wrote to the GWR expressing his approval at the "admirable arrangements which were made".[9]

There was little let up in the assault on the Great Western network during February; the South Wales ports once again took a hammering, with Swansea being particularly affected over a period of three nights. On the 19th, the High Street station was hit, with damage to the roof, running lines and platform 4 being reported. In the nearby docks, little serious destruction was caused to buildings, but the tug *Carnforth* was hit and sunk. The next evening slight damage to the station refreshment rooms was noted, and the demolition of a retaining wall close to the fish platform. On the night of 21 February, bombs once again fell on the station, causing damage to the ARP control office, the goods office, the district goods manager's office and one of the platforms. The blast injured three Great Western staff, and caused severe disruption by cutting gas, water and electricity supplies for some hours. In the docks another two staff were injured, as bombs set fire to a store and an engineering workshop belonging to the Company. A larger ship, the SS *Tudor*, was hit by a bomb and holed, but not sunk.

Along the coast, Cardiff was also receiving its fair share of bombs in the docks, and on 26 February the Crown Fuel Works, and the Company's stables in the area were both destroyed. Some days later, on 3 March, a high explosive bomb demolished the west abutment of the Rhymney river bridge. This attack caused a great deal of disruption, since the bridge carried a six-track main line; such was the force of the blast, that it distorted the main girders of the bridge, and ripped up trackwork. On the same night, a swing bridge at the Queen Alexandra Dock was hit, and put out of commission; two Great Western employees were killed, and six injured in this incident. Twenty-four hours later, German bombers returned to the Cardiff area, dropping a land mine on the north side of Roath Dock. This caused severe damage to various factories and sidings, and also put the silo of Spillers Ltd out of action, preventing the discharge of bulk cargoes for some time.

Later in March, Bristol received what many locally believed to be the worst air attack of the war. On the night of the 16th and 17th German bombers mounted a raid which lasted from just before 8.30pm to 4.12 the following morning. It was estimated that between 700 and 800 high explosive and several thousand incendiary bombs were dropped on Bristol, causing high casualty figures; 257 killed and 391 injured. Unlike 3 January raid, this time the bombers hit areas just outside the city centre which had suffered so badly in previous Blitzes. As a result, although Temple Meads station was hit, causing serious damage to the refreshment rooms on platform 4, Great Western suburban stations took a heavier pounding than they had done before.

At the first station on the route to the north of the city, Lawrence Hill, which may be remembered, had been hit earlier in 1940; all lines were damaged, and the goods shed destroyed by fire. One station further on, at Stapleton Road, both main lines were hit in several places, and the signal box was put out of action. A banking engine, used to propel trains up the incline to Ashley Hill and beyond, Collett Goods 0-6-0 No. 2253, was hit and the fireman badly injured. On the Severn Beach line at Montpelier, the station buildings, signal box and goods offices all suffered from bomb damage, and the running lines again needed attention.

Much of the information reproduced here has been gleaned from sources such as the General Manager's reports to the Company Board, or Railway Executive logs, none of which were accessible to the general public. There was obviously some frustration amongst both railway travellers and the public at large at the apparent censorship of air raids and their consequences. In late 1940, the *Railway Gazette* had felt it necessary to clarify what it saw as "the apparent inconsistency in the form of official information giving particulars of enemy air raids...especially as affecting transport services".[10] The main purpose of the lack of information was, the article noted, to prevent the Luftwaffe knowing about the success, or failure of its attacks, and government policy was based, it argued, on the "assumption that the enemy knows much less of the result of his raids than he would like to do".[11] Raided towns or districts were mentioned if attacks took place in daylight, or if they were obvious targets the German air crews could not fail to recognise, otherwise the article concluded, the navigation skills of the Luftwaffe could be checked and used in future raids. What was not mentioned was that casualty figures were sometimes not revealed for reasons of morale.

In his monthly round up of air raid damage to Company stations, on 25 April 1941, the General

Great Western Railway 3-ton Fordson flatbed lorry, photographed on 17 October 1940.

Manager had a fairly grim account for board members. Since the last board meeting 75 places had been attacked, and he recounted incidents at Plymouth, Redruth, Birmingham and Paddington, all of which involved severe destruction and loss of life. Our account of air attacks on Great Western property so far has included most of the major stations on the network apart from Plymouth, which although the subject of attack on account of the activities of the Navy in the area, had suffered little reported damage up until March 1941. Two raids on 20 and 21 March, and almost exactly a month later on 21 and 22 April showed that few places could be immune from the attentions of the Luftwaffe.

At North Road station, three platforms were hit, as were the station buildings, refreshment rooms and subway, while a number of coaches were destroyed or wrecked in the raids, and two people, including one member of station staff, were killed. Two locomotives sustained slight damage, 4-6-0 No. 4957 *Postlip Hall* in the first raid, and a 1501 class 0-6-0 pannier tank, No.1900, in the second. The nearby Millbay Station was also attacked, with the station building, refreshment rooms, control office and goods platform all affected. The locomotive shed was completely destroyed by fire,

and a number of goods and passenger vehicles were also destroyed in the raid.

Across the River Tamar in Cornwall, the small town of Redruth was the subject of an air attack on 20 March, the same day that Great Western property in Plymouth was suffering; two persons were killed, including one member of staff, and five injured as the station building was hit.

Birmingham had suffered badly like Bristol from air attack, and bombs had fallen on the lines around the city with monotonous regularity, particularly in December 1940 and January 1941. However, after the heavy raid which had caused destruction in November, no serious damage had been done to Snow Hill until the night of 9/10 April. A feature of this raid was the large number of high explosive bombs dropped and it was estimated that a total of 864 such bombs fell on the city, killing 290 people, and injuring a further 631. GWR traffic was seriously disrupted as a result of the five-hour raid, with trains scheduled to pass through or terminate at Birmingham subjected to severe delays. The diversion of some LMS trains onto GWR metals, further slowed traffic down.

At Snow Hill, one of the high explosive bombs penetrated the station roof above platform 5, and destroyed the ladies waiting room, the bookstall

Damage on platform 5 at Birmingham Snow Hill station on 10 April 1941.

and cloakrooms. The station roof, which had lost most of its glass in the November Blitz, was badly damaged, and a large wooden framed glazed skylight was brought crashing to the ground. Debris blocked the platforms and lines, and the windows of the South signal box were blown in by the blast. Twenty feet of retaining wall was also destroyed.

Another bomb hit one of the station approach roads used by cabs, detonating in the fish dock below, although this caused only minor damage; more serious was the affect of a third bomb which exploded on the steel deck carrying the trackwork to platform 11. It caused further damage in the yard below, smashing glass in the parcel, telegraph and control offices. Derek Harrison, in his history of the station, noted the amusement caused by the scattering of various items of clothing all over the station, including a pair of women's cami-knickers and a pair of RAF issue trousers, which were blown up into the girders close to platform 5![12]

As well as the broken windows suffered by the South signal box, considerable damage was also caused to signal and telegraph wires generally, and these and the block system were not repaired until late on the 10th. Similar damage was done to the signal box at nearby Tyseley, which also had its windows blown out, and as well as the downing of telegraph wires, point rodding was also affected. At Birmingham Moor Street, the goods offices were hit by another high explosive bomb, causing the suspension of goods traffic for 24 hours and the nearby divisional superintendent's office was slightly damaged in the same blast.

Throughout the heavy raids which disrupted most of the major stations and depots on the Great Western network, staff and passengers were forced to take cover in a variety of air raid shelters of differing shapes and sizes. In the December 1940 edition of the *GWR Magazine* some of the arrangements of this nature at Paddington were described in some detail. One innovation was the provision of a creche for mothers and children waiting for trains at night. What had been a store for staff uniforms under platforms 10 and 11 was transformed into a nursery which provided refuge for children from as young as 10 months to 14 years old. The shelves in the old store were converted into bunks, with a small rope barrier being provided to prevent the child from falling out!

A uniformed GWR nurse was on hand to open the room on receipt of a 'Red' air raid warning, and often nursed small children whilst their parents attempted to get a few hours sleep in the nearby subway shelter provided for passengers. The room, which could hold up to 72 children, was busiest on what staff called 'Irish Nights', Mondays, Wednesdays and Fridays, when the Irish boat train left Paddington in the early hours of the morning. For passengers using the subway shelter, there was no danger of them missing their train; a loudspeaker was installed which announced departures, meaning that they could avoid long hours waiting in the cold. Whether they were able to get any sleep with the announcements is another matter!

Staff were also provided with shelter accommodation in the warren of subways and rooms under the station complex. Two hundred bunks were built in a special shelter which catered for staff who were either unable to get home due to working a late turn, or were starting work very early. Those on "Double Home" duties such as dining car or sleeping car staff could also use this shelter, as could those unfortunate enough to have been bombed out by enemy action. Each bunk was provided with a carriage seat, cushion and pillow, staff supplying any other bedding they needed. Accommodation was allocated by a permit system, and appears to have been in great demand; "Many members of staff occupy the same bunk each night" reported the *GWR Magazine*.[13]

A real sense of community and camaraderie appears to have been built up in the Paddington staff air raid shelter, as an article in the February 1941 Company magazine seems to suggest. The writer argued that "a more cheery, warm and comfortable shelter than ours would certainly be hard to find".[14] For those having to spend nights at Paddington regularly the shelter became a second home to many, especially when destruction and mayhem raining from the skies was so close at hand. The writer noted that the shelterers were a mixture of all departments, consisting of both clerical and wages grades, "on common ground as GWR shelterers".[15]

It is likely that the good cheer described by the writer of the article would have been in short supply in the early hours of 17 April, when a land mine exploded in the departure roadway, close to the station master's office at Paddington, causing extensive damage. The Company board room and part of the general offices were demolished and severe damage was also sustained by the waiting

One hazard encountered by footplate crews was the danger of running into bomb craters. GWR 2-8-2T No. 7238 is seen at Hatton on 17 May 1941 having suffered such a fate.

room on platform 1, which unfortunately was kept open at night. A number of passengers were trapped beneath the rubble and debris from the blast, and despite the actions of the rescue services, a number were killed. In total, 18 people were killed, including six members of staff, and a further 97 were injured.

Almost the whole of the side of the station adjacent to platform 1 was affected by the blast and in reporting the incident to the board, the General Manager listed a number of other offices and premises on the station that were damaged or destroyed in the raid. This list included property occupied by Boot's the Chemist, Lyons and Wyman's, as well as Company offices for season tickets, urgent parcels and passenger enquiries. The No. 2 booking office was also wrecked, as was one of the station's buffet's. When the land mine exploded at 2.46am, as ARP and first aid parties went to the scene, other Company staff

immediately began the task of clearance and demolition work. With so many casualties, Paddington Borough Council sent additional rescue parties to assist in the removal of of the injured from the rubble of the waiting room; further help was given by a detachment of Auxiliary Military Pioneer Corps.

Clearing up operations proceeded at high speed, allowing the work of the station to proceed remarkably well, and apart from the cancellation of a few early trains that morning, normal train services were maintained. The maintenance of Great Western punctuality was, the General Manager noted, "the subject of many approving remarks from passengers".[16] Since the booking office had been wrecked in the explosion, the tobacco kiosk, normally found on the 'Lawn' was repaired, since it too had suffered minor damage, and used as a temporary booking office on Thursday, whilst on Friday the main booking office had received enough repairs to allow operations to restart there. Such was the destruction, that for the following four days, No. 1 platform road was taken out of use, and used to stable wagons, into which debris and rubble could be loaded directly.

The attack on Paddington was part of a general increase in Luftwaffe activity during April, which like March, was a month of heavy casualties. On the same night that Paddington was so badly hit, Al Bowlly, one of the top dance band singers of the period was killed, in a raid thought to involve over 680 German aircraft. London continued to suffer heavy attacks; on the night of 20 April it suffered its worst night of raids since the end of December, with over 150,000 incendiaries being dropped, causing a record 1,500 fires.

But it was not just London which suffered in this renewed offensive; Plymouth, which because of the Royal Naval Dockyards at Devonport was a prime target, experienced further sustained bombing in the latter part of April. Much devastation had already been done in the March raids; in all it was estimated that over a thousand civilians died in the raids, and up to 30,000 were made homeless, as 18,000 houses were made uninhabitable. Compared to these dreadful statistics, the losses sustained by the Great Western seem relatively trivial. Once again, the station buildings at Millbay were badly damaged but more serious was the destruction of the goods shed and stables which burnt to the ground, with staff unable to save 32 of the horses trapped inside. In the docks, numerous sheds and warehouses were destroyed by fire, and a salvage ship *Miss Elaine* engaged in recovering the SS *Marie II* which had been used for moving GWR locomotive coal was sunk on the night of 23/24 April; two employees were reported to have been injured in these attacks.

Great Western stations and property in the immediate vicinity of Plymouth also came under attack during these raids, the most notable incident occurring in the early hours of the night of 29/30 April 1941 when the 1.15pm Paddington to Penzance train, hauled by 4-6-0 No. 4911 *Bowden Hall* was halted at Keyham, where it was held due to the fact that an air raid was in progress. Having been halted at the signal box at 10pm, the crew were sheltering under the steps of the box. Some hours later, at 1.45am they had an extremely narrow escape when a bomb exploded inches from the locomotive, causing extensive damage to the engine, the running lines and the signal box.

The signal box at nearby St Budeaux was also destroyed by enemy action, with station buildings and running lines also suffering badly in the same raid; the General Manager reported that considerable interruption to communications had been caused by large bomb craters in the main line east and west of the Royal Albert Bridge at Saltash. As well this hazard, he also noted that a number of unexploded bombs had been found adjacent to the bridge and the nearby Weston Mill Viaduct, justifying the inclusion of the Saltash Bridge in the Company's list of strategic targets.

Mention by the General Manager of delays caused by bomb craters provides the opportunity to deal with this particular hazard in slightly more detail. When looking at records of damage sustained by GWR locomotives during the Second World War, it soon becomes apparent that it was this, not direct attack by German planes, that led to heavy repairs being necessary on a good number of engines. It was a difficult enough task to bring a train safely to its destination in blackout conditions, but the fear of running into a bomb crater in the darkness haunted many drivers and firemen. As Evan John noted, what was particularly grim about this hazard was that unlike cars or lorries, which could be turned aside if a crater loomed ahead, railway locomotives did not have this capacity, and could not be slowed very quickly. Locomotive crews he continued, "had to be prepared not only for death, but for the half a minute or more when death was clearly inevitable".[17] Records show that at least nine locomotives of varying classes were involved in incidents of this kind in 1941, eight of which required heavy repairs to enable them to return to service. Unlike some of the other main line railway companies, there seem however to have been no fatalities amongst Great Western crews, although there were serious injuries.

An example of the problems faced occurred on Monday 28 April, as another 'Hall' class engine, No. 4936 *Kinlet Hall* was slightly damaged when it ran into a crater on the main line at Trerule, between Menheniot and St Germans. The locomotive and the first carriage which were making up the 7.20pm Penzance to Plymouth service ended up on their sides and it was not until 2 May that the stricken locomotive could be removed from the crater. Severe disruption had resulted from the incident, although one of the two running lines had been restored after about 24 hours. Another engine to suffer a similar fate was a 5101 class Prairie tank No. 5181, which ran into a crater between Rock Ferry and Bebington. This locomotive was working the 11.33pm Birkenhead to Shrewsbury passenger service, but unfortunately little else is known about the accident.

In May 1941 the sustained efforts of the Luftwaffe to bomb Britain into submission continued without any sign of a let up. At the beginning of the month, Liverpool suffered seven days of continuous bombing, the first attack coinciding with a cloudless moonlit night and in the week that followed, over 1,400 people were killed, and the centre of the city was reduced to rubble. An ammunition ship, the *Malakand*, loaded with 1,000 tons of shells and bombs, exploded in the docks, the enormous force of the detonation causing extensive damage to the docks, and sank six nearby ships. The Great Western goods warehouse, and several of their other offices in the docks were severely damaged in the blast. Elsewhere in the city, offices and part of another goods warehouse at James Street were destroyed by fire, and at the Company's Lightbody Street Goods Depot, yet another goods warehouse, the offices and a timber stacking yard were destroyed.

Around a week later, London suffered once again, with an enormous 500 bomber raid on 11 May devastating the city. Record casualties of over 1,400 dead were recorded, with a further 1,800 badly injured; such was the ferocity of the raid, that at one time, all the London rail termini were closed by enemy action. Paddington had its fair share of problems, with damage spreading well beyond the environs of the station itself. Just after midnight a high explosive bomb fell on the main lines between East Acton and Wood Lane and a milk train hauled by 4-6-0 No. 5936 *Oakley Hall* ran into the crater produced by the explosion, causing the derailment of the locomotive and six milk tanks. The engine was badly damaged as a result, and normal working on the line was not restored until the morning of the 15th May.

An hour later bombs fell on both Paddington station and the goods depot; damage to the latter being restricted to various lorries and vans which were hit by a high explosive bomb that fell in the yard, with one member of staff being reported as

Although a poor quality photograph this view shows the air raid damage at Totnes on 21 October 1942. (Great Western Trust Collection)

injured in the blast. At the terminus itself, the area around platform 13 suffered a direct hit, demolishing the stairs from the booking office and blocking lines and platforms with debris. Platforms 15 and 16 were also closed as a result, and Hammersmith & City lines were disrupted, and not fully restored until early on 13 May, when trains could again run through to Baker Street. At about the same time, twelve coaches stabled at the West London Carriage Sidings, between Westbourne Park and Acton (Main Line) were burnt out, and the up and down main lines were also closed. Traffic was able to use relief lines, although working was severely limited by broken cabling, which affected signalling and track circuits.

Away from Paddington, South Lambeth Goods Depot, which suffered earlier in the Blitz, was again hit when a bomb fell, blocking the roadway entrance. The Company's Smithfield Goods Depot also sustained damage to its cartage offices and warehouse on the same night. Some indication of the intensity of the attack can be gauged from the fact that between Paddington and Westbourne Park, a distance of less than a mile, there were a further seven serious incidents during that night. In four of these, damage was sustained when retaining walls were hit, spilling debris onto the main, goods, relief or Hammersmith & City electric lines leading from the terminus. Thirty carriages and eleven wagons were damaged in the attack.

Records kept by the Company show that some relief seems to have been given to the hard pressed ARP and fire services in the Paddington area the next night; although further heavy raids were launched on the Capital in the next few days, including one on 13 May which damaged the House of Commons, the focus of destruction suffered by the Great Western once again shifted to the margins of its network. On 12 May minor incidents were reported at such diverse locations as Grangetown in Cardiff, where signal wires were brought down, and glass in the station building was broken when a bomb fell on a nearby embankment. At Wyke Regis Halt, an underbridge and a private siding were damaged, and at Laira, the No. 2 loop line was put out of action for a short time.

The most serious incident occurred at Pembroke Dock when, during a two-hour raid, bombs did extensive damage to the roof and glass of the station buildings, two railway owned houses, and a level crossing. Although Company casualties were not recorded 36 people were known to be killed in the raid. Further east in South Wales, traffic was suspended at Gileston during the night of 12 May, due to the presence of unexploded bombs near the line. Bus services were run from Aberthaw to Llantwit until the bomb was exploded, but normal working was not restored until 12.48 the next day.

Reporting air raid damage to the board on 27 June, Sir James Milne noted that since the previous board meeting in May, bombs had been dropped at twelve locations on the Great Western system, but "no material damage had been caused".[19] Minor incidents at Falmouth, Yealmpton, Tettonhall, Yardley Wood and Great Bridge resulting in little if any disruption or damage to the Company; but the General Manager's report does not mention the more serious derailment of a 7200 2-8-2 tank locomotive at Budbrook, between Warwick and Hatton on Saturday, 17 May. Running lines were blocked when the locomotive, No. 7238, ran into a bomb crater at 2.30am, injuring the driver and the guard. The engine required heavy repairs, and normal working was not restored until 6.30pm the same day.

Another similar incident, again, not reported in the board minutes, occurred between Mountain Ash and Middle Duffryn, when both lines were blocked as the 8.25pm Pontypool to Aberdare goods train was derailed at the site of a bomb crater in the early hours of 30 May 1941. A 4500 class 2-6-2 tank locomotive, No. 4514, needed substantial repairs and both the driver and fireman were injured. The line was not cleared until just after ten in the evening, and normal working resumed half an hour later.

After describing air raid damage in his monthly report to the board, the General Manager sometimes released details of the total cost of enemy action; at the 23 May meeting, he revealed that this amount had risen to £645,795. In the next few months, expenditure to repair enemy action was reduced, especially after 22 June, when Hitler's forces invaded Russia, with a resultant reduction of bombing raids on British targets. One major loss for the Company however, occurred a week or so before this, and involved not a land based Great Western asset, but one of its ships. On 13 June the SS *St Patrick*, whilst crossing the Irish Sea between Rosslare and Fishguard was attacked by a Luftwaffe aircraft and sunk, some 16 miles south west of Strumble Head.

The attack was not the first on the ship; in 1940 it was reported that the *St Patrick* had been bombed and machine gunned on two occasions. During the first, on 17 August, one of the crew, the lookout Seaman Moses Brennan, was badly injured, and later died of his wounds. A passenger was also wounded in the same attack. In the second instance, the ship came across three German bombers attacking a tanker *en route*, and was subsequently attacked itself, with the aircraft dropping five or six bombs but without any casualties being sustained. The October 1940 *GWR Magazine* reported that "no serious damage was caused to the vessel by either of these attacks from the air".[20]

Almost a year later the 45 crew and 44 passengers were not so fortunate. After being at sea for almost two hours, the *St Patrick* received a message that a large convoy nearby was under fierce attack by enemy aircraft. All guns on board were manned, and the ship's speed was increased but less than ten minutes later however, a German aircraft appeared on the port side of the ship, and dropped a bomb or stick of bombs, which hit the *St Patrick* on or near the bridge, just forward of the funnel. Within seconds the ship was well alight, due to the oil fuel tanks being hit; the chief engineer, Cyril Griffiths,

and the second engineer, Francis Purcell, who were housed on the lower deck staggered out of their rooms to find a scene of devastation and confusion.

Showing tremendous bravery and composure, Purcell attempted to get to the engine room; finding one door jammed, he groped his way through the damaged ship to find an alternative way in. Finally entering the engine room, he found it full of escaping steam, but he was able to assist the third engineer, a greaser and a fireman trying to escape. Elsewhere in the ship, stewardess Elizabeth Owen, who was in charge of the third class accommodation, struggled on with her life belt in the darkness, and coaxed seven passengers consisting of six women and a child up on to the deck. She then plunged back into the darkness to rescue five further passengers trapped behind a jammed door.

The whole of the midships of the vessel soon became a blazing furnace, and Purcell, still without regard for his own personal safety, assisted a first class passenger, carrying him with the help of the chief engineer, up on to deck where he was put into the sea before being picked up by a lifeboat. He then found his own life belt and began to swim away from the stricken vessel. Stewardess Owen

A general view of the damage suffered to 'Hall' class No. 4911 Bowden Hall *at Keyham on 30 April 1941. (Great Western Trust Collection)*

The crew of No. 4911 Bowden Hall *were sheltering under the steps of the signal box at the time the bomb hit the locomotive, and had something of a lucky escape. (Great Western Trust Collection)*

assisting a passenger, Miss Dora O'Donahue, who had lost her life belt in the confusion, was forced to plunge into the sea with her as the ship began to sink. Within five minutes of the ship being attacked, it had broken in two and sank, leaving a mass of wreckage and a large slick of black fuel oil which survivors were forced to swim around in until rescued.

Despite the sudden nature of the attack, the chief radio officer, Norman Campbell, had managed to send two distress messages, and these, coupled with the explosion and fire from the ship led two ships, the destroyer HMS *Wolsey* and HMS *Indian Star* to the scene within a short time. In less than an hour the majority of survivors clinging to rafts had been plucked from the sea, but it was almost two hours before Stewardess Owen and Dora O' Donahue were finally picked up by the *Wolsey*.[21] Giving an account of the tragedy, the General Manager reported that the officers and crews of both ships had done everything they could to assist the survivors, even supplying them with their own clothing.

The first survivors did not reach dry land until the afternoon of the 16 June, when HMS *Indian Star* put into Milford Haven with 16 crew and 14 passengers from the GWR vessel. A further 30 survivors, and a RAF Hurricane fighter pilot shot down in the air battle over the area were not landed until midnight. The Shipwrecked Mariners Society at Milford Haven had, Sir James Milne noted, "rendered every possible assistance in securing food, clothing and accommodation for the survivors" and he recommended that the society and the Admiralty should be approached so that any expenses due could be reimbursed.[22]

The ship, built in 1930, was valued at £130,000, and a claim was made to the government for its loss, under the War Damage Provision of the Railway Control Agreement. More important was the loss in terms of human life; 18 crew and eleven passengers, including the vessel's master, Captain James Faraday, the chief officer, Frank Row, the quartermaster, the chief steward and five stewarding staff. Particularly tragic was the loss of the 17-year old James Brennan; it was a double blow for his Wexford family, since his father Moses had been killed on the *St Patrick* in the attack on 17 August 1940. The curtain of censorship which had been drawn across the affairs of the Great Western in its Company journal was temporarily lifted as an account of the loss of the ship was printed in its July 1941 issue. Concluding the report of the incident the unnamed writer noted that "The loss of the Master and other members of the crew, as well as the passengers who lost their lives on this ill-fated voyage, is greatly deplored, as is the sinking of the vessel itself, which had an excellent record of service."[23]

In the aftermath of the disaster, the Fishguard-Rosslare service was maintained by the SS *Great Western*, although it was replaced after a short time by the SS *Hantonia* loaned by the Southern Railway. A more tragic reminder of the attack was the washing up of various pieces of wreckage from the ship along the Welsh coast, including lifeboats and life rafts. The Irish crossing continued to be a hazardous one for GWR crews and even before the *Hantonia* had taken over the Fishguard–Rosslare run, the *Great Western* had been attacked by the Luftwaffe on 3 July whilst approaching Rosslare. Although hit, no serious damage was sustained, and as a consequence of this and other near misses, it was decided that the service should only be operated in the hours of darkness, provided there was no moon. During moonlit periods, Great Western vessels had to brave the route during the daylight hours; air protection was to be provided wherever possible, the General Manager noted in July 1941,[24] although one can imagine that both passengers and crew approached voyages of this type with some trepidation.

One would imagine that news of this and subsequent attacks made passengers think very hard about whether they really wanted to travel or not. The war situation had deteriorated further, with even the supposedly neutral Irish Republic being attacked by Luftwaffe bombers. A serious raid on Dublin at the end of May had killed 28 people and injured nearly 90. Passenger traffic between the two countries declined so much that in December 1941, it was decided to suspend the Fishguard–Rosslare service entirely after the Christmas holiday. The Fishguard–Waterford service was also withdrawn in February 1942, since for security reasons, the departure times of the ship had to be varied from time to time. This meant that no trains could properly connect with the service, and not surprisingly passenger revenue plummeted as a result. The Ministry of War Transport agreed that the crossing could be suspended, providing that a cargo service continued. This was the arrangement that occurred, with the SS *Great Western* being used on what was still a perilous crossing.

Summing up the 'Year of the Blitz', and the hard winter of 1940–41, Lt Colonel Moore-Brabazon, then Minister of Transport, noted that the period was a hard one for both men and machines. Two features of railway working were worth highlighting, he argued, the first being the astonishing powers of recovery shown by railways after attack by the Luftwaffe; the other was the courage and determination shown by railway staff.[25] In the next two years, a determination and courage of a slightly different type was needed, and despite all the adversities, the GWR still managed to win through.

ARP trailer pump competitions were held regularly between different depots, and here the crew from Reading Signal Works go through their paces in September 1943.

7

Is Your Journey Really Necessary?

itler's invasion of Russia in June 1941 eased the almost intolerable pressure brought to bear on the British population by the Luftwaffe during the 'Year of the Blitz'. The start of the campaign, codenamed 'Barbarossa' by the Germans, also marked the beginning of a new phase in the war both for the country as a whole, and for the Great Western more particularly. Until the D-Day invasion in 1944 the war became a long hard struggle, both for the population at large and for the railways, and it became apparent that the end of the war was not remotely in sight. Indeed, up until General Montgomery's victory at El Alamein in November 1942, many were not so sure that the ultimate victory they had been promised by Churchill would ever come.

In describing the next phase of the Great Western's war, the emphasis shifts dramatically away from descriptions of attacks from German bombers, although there were a number of serious raids which will be mentioned, to some explanation of the the railway's role in the 'Long Hard Slog' to victory as it became known.[1] Writing to staff in the winter of 1941, Sir James Milne, the General Manager, noted that "Two years of war have meant for all concerned in the operation of the railways of this country two years of strenuous endeavour".[2] Entering the third winter of the war he continued, meant that even more pressure would be put on the railway, and "we all must make a still greater contribution to the National effort to 'finish the job'".[3] Ending his message to staff, Sir James Milne quoted the Prime Minister who had

argued "We shall not fail or falter. We shall not weaken or starve. Neither the shock of battle nor the long-drawn trials of vigilance and exertion will wear us down."[4] Great Western staff had endured much in the first two years of the war, and were to find the next two no less easy.

In this chapter it is intended to show the hardships suffered by another group during this period, the travelling public. We have already touched on some of the difficulties experienced by them in earlier chapters, in particular the hazards of travelling in the blackout. Few people who lived through the war years remember travelling by train with much affection, since as the conflict continued, so conditions for passengers deteriorated. Train travel was around three times as expensive as it had been in 1938, and as demands on the railway network to carry essential freight traffic increased, it became three times as uncomfortable!

What made conditions particularly bad for passengers was that the Great Western like the other main line railways, was called upon to move increasing amounts of troops, munitions, tanks, equipment and petrol as the war progressed. As an example, it was calculated that in the build up to the North African campaign in 1942, the railways moved 185,000 men, 20,000 vehicles and 220,000 tons of stores. This involved the running of 440 troop trains, 680 special freight trains, and a further 15,000 wagon loads of goods from billets to depots which carried by ordinary goods trains.[5]

A further illustration of the increase in traffic

generated by the war effort can be gleaned by figures reported to the Great Western board at roughly monthly intervals throughout the war; it is difficult to pick out a 'typical' month for the GWR, but some idea of the growth of traffic can be seen from the fact that in the four weeks ending 9 March 1940, the Company ran a total of 399 special trains. This total included 183 carrying troops, and 216 for equipment, petrol and stores. In the corresponding month two years later, these figures had risen to a total of 1,043 special trains including 404 troop trains, and 639 carrying equipment, petrol and stores. By March 1944, in the run up to D-Day, the figures had risen even more dramatically to a monthly total of 2,112 trains; of this number 861 carried personnel, and 1,251 equipment and supplies.[6]

With such demands being made on the Great Western, it was no wonder that the 'ordinary' passenger found travel difficult; there were fewer trains, and those that did run were often late, and extremely overcrowded. As we will see, in addition to the huge increases in traffic for the war effort, there were also increases in a number of other types of passenger, such as civil servants and forces personnel on leave, which put additional demands on the railway. Speaking at the annual general meeting of the GWR in March 1941, the Company Chairman, Charles Hambro, noted that "we are unable to offer our passengers facilities which are in any way comparable with those which they enjoyed before the war".[7] In wartime he argued, "public needs must take second place in railway operation",[8] concluding that if shareholders could be told the demands made daily in connection with the movement of troops and supplies, they would realise that interference with passenger services was "inevitable".

The slogan "Is your journey really necessary?" was introduced as early as 1939, when it was used to discourage evacuated civil servants from travelling back to London from the provinces, but it came to real prominence in 1941, and posters with this message appeared all over the railway network. All manner of variations on the theme appeared, such as "Travel only when you must – Coal & Food & Guns come first – Tracks are filled with war – time traffics" exhorted a Railway Executive poster. Another, headed 'Tanks for Attack' issued jointly by all the Big Four companies, stated that, "we all want to win this war as quickly as possible. This cannot be done without

'Hall' class 4-6-0 No. 4966 Shakenhurst Hall *at Castle Cary in June 1942, with a very young looking fireman on the footplate. (Author's Collection)*

building up vast reserves of tanks, guns and all other equipment of war."[9] Noting that the railways were carrying millions of tons of essential traffic every week, it concluded "This means fewer trains for you, more overcrowding, less peacetime service. Travel only when you must."[10]

Although the government spent a good deal of time and effort in trying to persuade the public not to travel, the public were still determined to do so, despite the difficulties such an operation might entail. Over the 1941 August Bank Holiday the GWR experienced a 23 per cent increase in passenger bookings over the previous year. This total was higher than the prewar holiday period of 1939, and entailed the augmenting of existing services quite dramatically, particularly on Saturday 2 August, and Monday, 4 August. Paddington was extremely busy, and over the weekend, 52,000 passengers departed on 64 long distance trains; the "Cornish Riviera Limited" ran in five separate portions, carrying over 5,000 passengers, and services to the West Country were bolstered by the 10.35am Paddington to Penzance train, which in two portions, also carried over 2,000 people. It was noted in the *GWR Magazine* that much of the additional traffic was generated by relatives visiting evacuees in various reception areas, adding to the total by around 5,000.[11] What was not revealed however, was that 50 per cent of the bookings taken by the Company were for military and government warrant tickets.[12]

It seemed likely that there would be a repetition of these events over the Christmas and New Year period, and in November 1941 the government

The Churchward designed 43xx 2-6-0s were, along with the 'Hall' class, the backbone of Great Western services during the war period. Here, No. 6313 is seen near Gloucester on 25 April 1942. (RCTS Collection)

announced its intention to reduce passenger services on railways during the winter months, and also to withdraw a number of restaurant and sleeping car services on congested routes. These measures were announced in view of a severe shortage of locomotives resulting from the transfer of engines abroad on War Department service, the reduction in maintenance of stock, and the curtailment of new construction. Further details of these particular problems will be given later.

The General Manager believed that as "all our through trains are at present heavily loaded, any further curtailment will undoubtedly cause serious inconvenience to passengers".[13] One significant problem was that trains were often heavily delayed owing to the number of coaches in trains being well in excess of the capabilities of locomotives. With a view to assisting in this instance, the Company planned to withdraw restaurant cars from ten main line weekday trains, and a further two from Sunday services beginning on 8 December 1941. What happened in practice however, was that the restaurant car was replaced by an additional carriage, which although increasing the carrying capacity of the train, did nothing to ease the loads hauled by the hard-

pressed Great Western locomotive fleet.

One measure announced by the Railway Executive Committee was the suspension of travel for military personnel between 24 and 28 December, which it was hoped, would reduce the burden on railway companies. It was not felt possible however to introduce a formal scheme for limiting passenger travel over the Christmas period and in view of the reduction in freight traffic during Christmas week, the Great Western, and the other companies were told to make their own provisions for traffic.

On the 17th December however, the decision of the Railway Executive Committee was reversed by the Minister of Transport, who announced that "in no circumstances shall a greater number of long distance trains be run on any one day during the period 22–27 December than the maximum number run on any ordinary weekday at this time of year."[14] Further to this instruction, the Minister also restricted the splitting of trains into a maximum of three parts. The Railway Executive pointed out to the Minister that these measures could lead to severe congestion at stations, with a consequent risk of crowds getting out of hand and asked for some discretion to run extra trains if necessary, the Minister declined.

Great Western management were most concerned about their ability to run an adequate service on Christmas Eve. The previous year, the Company had run 37 ordinary long distance trains, and a further 20 Relief trains. In the interim period, the ordinary service had been reduced to 32 trains, and under the directive issued by the Ministry, the maximum number of relief trains which could be run was five, this meant that the GWR could only run 37 trains instead of 57. The General Manager argued that there might be a grave risk that up to 5,000 passengers could be left behind at Paddington and intermediate stations which was he concluded, a serious situation.

This episode clearly illustrates the fact that as the war progressed, overall control of the railways moved subtly from the Companies, who at the outset had carried on much as they had in peacetime, to the Government who had the ultimate responsibility for the successful prosecution of the war. The amalgamation of the Ministry of Transport and the Ministry of Shipping, to create the Ministry of War Transport, was an attempt to create an overall body responsible for the coordination of the war effort on rail, road and sea although the respect felt for the Minister was somewhat undermined by the short time that many incumbents of the position actually spent in the job. Lord Leathers, the Minister in charge at Christmas 1941, remained obdurate in his determination to reduce travel over the holiday; Sir James Milne, in reporting the saga to the board noted that the Company Chairman had personally drawn the attention of the Minister to the seriousness of the situation, but he would not give way. A final measure introduced, not previously mentioned, was the withdrawal of all restaurant car services over the Christmas period, something which was to be repeated at all subsequent holiday periods until the end of the war.

Interestingly, the Minister was proved right in the final analysis, since the public appear to have responded to his direct appeal to them to refrain from travelling. Passenger traffic was substantially

lighter than in previous years, and no serious problems were experienced in dealing with traffic. Some idea of the problems facing the railways during the war with increased traffic can be gleaned from the fact that the number of passenger journeys recorded on the Great Western in 1941, excluding the Hammersmith & City and Severn & Wye lines, was 110 million. This figure was an increase of 21½ million from 1938, the last year before the war. The number of first class passengers carried was the highest on record, being ½ million in excess of 1929.[15]

Mention of first class brings details of one proposal put forward to ease the congestion on trains. In the early part of 1941, at the request of the Ministry of Transport, the Railway Executive requested that railways should arrange that where accommodation in third class was fully occupied, and there was space available in first class, then passengers should be allowed to travel without extra charge. The Minister was no doubt

No one was hurt in this incident when 2-6-2T No. 4510 was derailed after bombs had made a crater into which the train ran on 12 January 1941. The location was near Penmere Halt, between Truro and Falmouth. (Great Western Trust Collection)

A number of new halts and stations were built to cater for wartime traffic. This photograph shows North Filton Halt in Bristol, built to serve the nearby aircraft factory.

responding to the annoyance felt by many passengers who had been crammed into compartments or had stood in corridors, whilst empty first class compartments stood only a few carriages away.

Not surprisingly this measure was not universally welcomed by the railways, not known for their egalitarian attitude. Sir James Milne pointed out that first class passengers should have a "reasonable opportunity of travelling in the class of accommodation for which they have paid".[16] Company staff were instructed to use their discretion, and to open first class compartments a few minutes before the departure of the train.

In October 1941 matters progressed further, with the complete withdrawal of first class accommodation on London Suburban trains. As can be imagined, this was not received with much enthusiasm by any of the railway companies, who argued that "operating relief likely to be effected by the withdrawal of first class facilities would not in itself be sufficient to justify such a drastic change".[17] Sensing that there might be powerful political

opinion behind such a suggestion, it was noted that if the government on the grounds of public policy felt that "there should be no discrimination between different classes of passenger", then the proposal for abolition of first class within the London area was acceptable.

So far as the GWR was concerned, with the approval of the measure on 11 September 1941, services affected included all local trains between London and Reading, those between Paddington, High Wycombe, Aylesbury, Princes Risborough and Oxford via Thame. In addition to this, altered coach working meant that first class was also abolished on a few trains between Reading, Savernake, Didcot and Swindon, and also on a number of services between Didcot and Oxford, and Worcester and Oxford. Worried that this innovation might be a precedent, the Railway Companies Association, which represented the interests of the Big Four wrote to the Minister of War Transport, asking for a "reassurance that it is your intention to restore these facilities at the earliest possible date after the cessation of hostilities".[18] Replying, the Minister told the railway companies that "any request for the revocation of the direction would of course receive the most sympathetic consideration".[19] Rather ominously though, the Minister concluded that any decision would have to be taken "in the light of the circumstances then prevailing".[20] This was perhaps not the unequivocal answer the railways were hoping for.

It will be remembered that in describing the large numbers of passengers carried by the Great Western over the 1941 August Bank Holiday it was revealed that 50 per cent of the total were either service personnel, or civil servants on essential business. It was this factor which irritated Great Western management, particularly when they were lectured by the Ministry of Transport and others on the need for a reduction in passenger trains. The *Railway Gazette*, in an editorial published almost a year later, in May 1942, noted that "armchair critics" had levelled criticism against the railways for transporting those "travelling for pleasure" who the magazine described as the "unhappy civilian". Even the most cursory examination of most long distance trains it continued, would reveal that "by far the majority of their occupants are servicemen and servicewomen in uniform, either moving singly or in drafts from one depot or unit to another, or travelling on long or short leave."[21]

In normal conditions, leave for an average serviceman might amount to around 16 travel permits per year, which coupled with the steady growth in the size of the forces, increased the demands for space on most trains. The *Railway Gazette* article concluded that if leave granted by the forces was intended for rest and recuperation, then being crammed into compartments, and having to stand for long periods in corridors was hardly satisfactory for most members of the armed services. The large numbers of servicemen travelling can be judged by the staggering statistic that in July 1942 the number of men or women travelling under warrant was 1,816,000. Over two million warrants were also issued to forces personnel going on leave, and over six million journeys were made at the concessionary rate by members of the services or their families. It was calculated that the average journey made by a member of the armed forces was usually over 150 miles, twice the distance travelled by the average civilian.[22]

In order to reduce some of this pressure on the railways, in October 1941 the War Office announced that all ranks were now to be allowed

ARP cleansing unit coach No. 3478, converted from a 'Dreadnought' coach, seen at Swindon on 22 May 1942.

An example of the tickets issued to service personnel during the Second World war. (Mike Wyatt Collection)

blackout conditions, instructions were issued to fix labels identifying smoking compartments inside as well as outside the carriage. The Chief Mechanical Engineers Department at Swindon issued a circular and a number of charts to each divisional superintendent showing how each coach was to be subdivided.[24] By and large, it seemed that third class stock had more smoking compartments than first class, since presumably it was thought that non-commissioned officers and other ranks smoked more than their commissioned counterparts!

Further attempts were made to reduce service travel after representations from the Railway Executive Committee. In July 1942 it was reported that to minimise journeys of over 50 miles, new arrangements had been agreed with the War Office. These included the issuing of only two leave warrants to each serviceman, the lessening of duty travel to a minimum, and a reduction in concessions offered to the wives and families of service personnel, who could obtain reduced fares in order to travel to meet their spouses. Had these measures not been introduced, the effects on the Great Western and the other railways would have been catastrophic; even with with restrictions, the number of service journeys reported in July 1943 was over 15,500,000, almost double the 1942 figure. A year later in July 1944 there had only been a small decline to fifteen million journeys.[25] A further measure aimed at assisting the railways in coping with the large number of service personnel and government staff travelling was the decision in October 1942 to use the travel warrants issued to the forces as actual tickets. Previous to this decision, these warrants had to be exchanged for railway tickets at booking offices, and this often caused huge queues, to say nothing of the clerical work involved in the administration of the whole system. In 1941 over 30 million warrants were exchanged for tickets, so the saving in time and money was plain to see!

Throughout the period from 1941 to 1944 there was a steady decline in the number of passenger trains run by the Company. At bank holidays, similar restrictions to those at Christmas 1941 were in force; service leave was curtailed, restaurant cars were withdrawn, and warnings were issued to the public not to travel. Some idea of the scale of reductions achieved by the Great Western can be

only one period of 14-day privilege leave instead of two 7-day periods. However, the situation was confused by a further announcement in the House of Commons that members of HM Forces would be granted an additional four free travelling warrants instead of the existing two, a measure which was unlikely to result in a reduction of traffic. The increased use of Great Western trains by service personnel also caused another problem reported to staff by the Chief Mechanical Engineer in February 1941. C. B. Collett reported that attention had been drawn by some passengers to the very soiled condition of antimacassars in some first class compartments. It was suggested that this was "due to the greater use of these compartments owing to troops and other third class passengers being permitted to travel first class when third class is full."[23]

One further result of the increase in service travel, which in today's society seems somewhat strange, and particularly unhealthy, was the announcement that railway companies, the Great Western included, should increase the proportion of smoking compartments to about 85 per cent of their total carriage stock. To assist passengers in grasped when it is noted that the new summer service approved by the Minister of War Transport on the 4th May 1942 showed a 34.5 per cent reduction on the service provided in 1939. Passenger traffic did show reductions at peak periods; the Easter 1942 figures decreased by 35,000 from the previous year, and at Whitsun passenger numbers were recorded as being down by over 20 per cent.[26] In the summer of 1942, the Minister of War Transport relented slightly, and gave permission for relief trains to be run, providing that they did not interfere with the running of essential freight trains. The *Railway Gazette* reported that the Company had shown "commendable commonsense" in including relief trains in their actual timetable, which meant that there would be much less confusion amongst passengers. Before the introduction of this measure, such trains were often not advertised, and could consist of duplicate or triplicate trains run for the benefit of service personnel. Such trains often omitted intermediate stops, and thus there was an element of uncertainty amongst passengers joining such services! The Company also spread the departure of these trains throughout the day in an effort to reduce congestion at Paddington. Those

introduced in the new timetable included the 9.35am to Minehead, 11am to Newquay and Penzance, 12 noon to Kingswear, the 3.30pm to Plymouth, and the 3.55pm to South Wales. All these trains had corresponding return services.[27] Matters were not helped during the summer months, by a serious shortage of coal, and in view of this the Minister decided that passenger train mileage could not exceed that of the previous year.

With the onset of the winter of 1942, the Minister once again intimated that passenger traffic would have to be further curtailed to aid the war effort. As early as May 1942, Lord Leathers argued that although the public and Government Departments had assisted splendidly in cutting our unessential journeys...[28] the stage had been reached where even more drastic steps were required. "Long distance services would have to be reviewed again and carefully pruned" he added. The introduction of some kind of rationing system for railway travel had been discussed, but the Minister agreed with the railways, who saw the scheme as cumbersome to administer, and difficult to enforce. The idea of a 'Train Permit' system had been discussed in early 1942 whereby passengers could not travel without obtaining a permit seven days in

'Castle' class No. 5020 Trematon Castle *at Tilehurst on 13 July 1941. (RCTS Collection)*

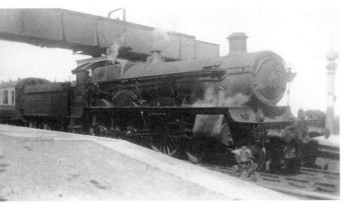

'Saint' class 4-6-0 No. 2949 Stanford Court *at Castle Cary in June 1942. (Author's Collection)*

advance. To add insult to injury, the permits were to cost 2s 6d each. In reporting the scheme to the board, the General Manager noted that however successful it might be, it did not solve the problem of service travel.[29] The Railway Executive was asked to make recommendations on ways of speeding traffic through the winter of 1942/43, and issued a secret report in June 1942.[30] If the Minister was hoping for good news, he was to be sadly disappointed. The 21-page report paints a grim picture of the harsh realities faced by the railways after three years of war. Aside from the continued growth in service travel, a more general increase in traffic as a whole was compounded by shortages of labour, cartage and rolling stock and a backlog in maintenance of permanent way and locomotives. The report also noted that considerable improvements could be made by numerous schemes planned to increase the capacity of lines by doubling, quadrupling or the creation of additional sidings or facilities. Examples of such work will be mentioned in the next chapter.

Conditions for the ordinary traveller continued to worsen as the war continued; in October 1942 all cheap travel facilities were discontinued, the General Manager noting that "all tickets for pleasure travel are to be withdrawn".[31] This included a range of services, including special Sunday trains for anglers, which incredibly had survived up to this point. Parents and relatives of evacuees visiting their children between October and March suffered the reduction of their reduced fare vouchers from six to three.

Another cut was the ruling by the Ministry that after 15 September no special trains or horse boxes were to be run for race meetings. The *GWR Magazine* reported the introduction of the Great Western's new winter timetable in October 1942, noting that certain "necessary" mileage reductions had been introduced on local and branch line services but that the only main line service to suffer was the 3.55pm Paddington to Swansea Saturday train, and the 6.30pm Cheltenham Spa to Paddington train on Sundays. Noting the withdrawal of cheap day tickets, the magazine argued that the object of these stringencies was "to free the lines for additional freight trains for traffic

The severe damage to 0-6-0PT No. 1729 after the Castle Cary raid on 3 September 1942.

GWR 2884 class 2-8-0 No. 3830 at Hereford in September 1941. (RCTS Collection)

directly associated with the prosecution of the war."[32]

For the average traveller, train travel became more and more uncomfortable, as many of the comforts they had enjoyed before the war were withdrawn or discontinued. As early as October 1940, it was reported that supplies of pillows, pillow slips and rugs were running low; the Superintendent of the Line warned divisional superintendents that spare stock kept at Swindon was exhausted, and a special search was to be made for items of this sort, in order that they could be returned to Swindon for laundering and redistribution. The supply of towels in train lavatories was completely discontinued from 1 August 1942, when the company decided that it could bear the constant theft of these items no more. Reporting the end of this facility to the board, the General Manager noted that the Company had lost over 8,000 towels in the last year.

Theft of such items had become a serious problem as rationing was introduced to even the most basic of items. A circular issued to Divisional Superintendents by the Carriage Works Manager at Swindon instructed them to make sure that toilet roll fittings were not damaged or incomplete in rolling stock, since large numbers of toilet rolls were being lost or stolen.[33] Soap too became a valuable commodity, and the supply of this was eventually discontinued in February 1942 to all stock except sleeping cars. The problem of theft was not confined to the GWR, and replying to a question in the House of Commons in December 1941, the Minister of Transport noted that "the loss of towels, soap etc. through pilferage is large".[34]

Despite all the discomforts suffered by railway travellers, it was hunger which caused the greatest inconvenience. Restaurant cars had been withdrawn in the earliest days of the war, but restored within six weeks, however as the war progressed their number steadily diminished. On 18 April 1942 the Railway Executive was informed that the Minister of War Transport had decided that all restaurant and buffet cars should be suspended until further notice. This withdrawal was not total, since it was reported that owing to the difficulties of supplying passengers with adequate refreshment in some station buffets, the Minister had agreed to allow the retention of some restaurant cars on long distance services where there were severe operational difficulties. In the case of the Great Western this meant that the number of restaurant cars operated was reduced from 40 to only 15.

One feature of many prewar expresses run by the Company had been the provision of luncheon baskets for passengers not wishing to use the restaurant car; surprisingly, this facility had survived until the spring of 1941 when it was announced that due to the difficulties the company was experiencing in obtaining food and equipment, the service was to be discontinued. Both this measure and the withdrawal of many restaurant cars put enormous pressure on refreshment rooms at stations.

The huge increases in the number of travellers served in these facilities did nothing to help, as did shortages of food utensils and china. Shortages and theft meant that refreshment rooms were often short of crockery, and it was reported that at one stage, the rooms at Swindon were supplying tea to passengers in jam jars, having run out of cups! By August 1942 the shortage nationally was so pronounced, that posters and notices were issued urging travellers to bring their own cups. Food, which was rationed, was not easy to come by either, and as early as December 1941 the General Manager had reported that the Company was experiencing serious difficulties in obtaining food for its refreshment rooms. The Minister of War Transport was asked to press the Ministry of Food to allocate further supplies, but Sir James Milne noted, with some resignation, he "understood there was little likelihood of this being done".[35]

One measure designed to take some of the pressure off the Company's refreshment rooms was the provision of servicemen's canteens at many

Another view of No. 5071 Spitfire *at Sonning, on an unidentified passenger working. (Author's collection)*

of the larger stations. By December 1941 it was reported in Parliament that there were 119 canteens for members of the armed forces at stations all over the country, including all the London termini. At most of these, cloakroom, washing and lavatory facilities were available, and at a number of the larger stations rest or sleeping accommodation was also provided.[36]

At Paddington, facilities were provided in what had in prewar days been known as the Paddington Passenger Dining Club. Situated at the end of platform 1, this establishment had been converted into a staff canteen, and on the outbreak of war, its facilities were extended to welcome service personnel. Some idea of how busy the place must have been can be gleaned from the fact that it was noted that it served around 1,000 meals per day to service staff, as well as anything from 600 to 1,000 meals per day for Great Western staff. Additional funds from the War Office allowed for its extension, and the addition of rest room facilities similar to those described above. In August 1942 a similar, but smaller canteen was opened at Reading, with seating for over a hundred. Like many of the

canteens, it was manned by volunteers, in this case the WVS; open 24 hours a day, the rooms were presented with a radio by Sir Felix Pole, who had been the Company's General Manager until 1929. The radio, the *GWR Magazine* reported, would be "greatly appreciated by the many men and women of the forces who halt a while to refresh themselves before continuing their various journeys".[37]

For the civilian passenger, who did not have such luxuries, rail travel remained a difficult process. If the problems described already were not enough, they also faced a barrage of war propaganda from a variety of sources. In an editorial in the *GWR Magazine*, the editor noted that the loudspeaker systems which were now common at most stations were being put to a new use, that of spearheading a new campaign against "Careless talk". Many travellers the magazine article noted, "still speak unguardedly of matters which greatly interest the enemy...concerning things the enemy would like to know, silence is golden".[38] Notices warning of the danger of idle or careless talk were also placed in every railway compartment, restaurant and sleeping cars and station waiting rooms. In August 1941 F. W. Hawksworth instructed his divisional superintendents to renew what the Company called 'Anti-gossip' notices, which had originally been introduced in December 1939.[39]

Railway stations were also ideal sites to display posters passing on important information relating to the war and many readers will be familiar with some of the more famous posters issued not only by the railways themselves, but by the Government, which became part of the folklore of the war period. In June 1940 the Railway Executive agreed to put 50,000 free 'Double Royal' poster advertising spaces at the disposal of the Ministry of Information for use for publicity purposes. Things did not always run smoothly however, and in his report to the GWR board on 29 October 1943, the General Manager related a dispute which had taken place between the REC and the Ministry of Health. The latter had wished the railways to display a poster warning of the dangers of venereal disease, which in wartime conditions could be quite serious. It seems however, that the railways were not happy about having such material on display at their stations. The General Manager reported that the REC regretted that "The Ministry of Health should have selected a poster for display to which the railways objected".[40] Once again, the increasing influence of the government over the operation of the railways is apparent, since the General Manager concluded that despite their objections, the railway companies had agreed to display the poster "in view of the direction of the Minister of War Transport".[41]

In a booklet published in 1943, the government's principle for the operation of railways during wartime could not have been more clearly stated when it noted that "the needs of the war must come first".[42] Arguing that absolute priority was given to service movements, it then identified a second group of travellers who took priority before the poor "ordinary" traveller. These were workers travelling to and from the many factories engaged on war work. This traffic was considerable; in 1942 for example, a total of 400 million passenger journeys were made by those issued with workmen's tickets, an increase in 75 million from the previous year.

The refreshment stall set up at Birmingham Snow Hill for service personnel, which was run by volunteers from the Church Army.

As well as the adoption of war work by existing factories, like the Great Western's Swindon Works, scores of new factories sprang up all over the country engaged in government work. It was calculated that nationally around 7,000 additional trains were required to move workers to and from these factories; often special services were run for workers, and in some cases, lines were reserved specifically for them. A good example of this was the suspension of passenger services between Wrexham and Ellesmere in order to improve the working of traffic in connection with the construction and opening of an Ordnance Supply Factory at Marchwiel. From 10 June 1940, two small stations, Highrow Halt and Trench Halt were closed for the duration, and a Crosville bus service was run for any passengers who usually used trains on the line. The only trains then to be run on the route, were workmens trains.

A report of a derailment of a workmens train in South Wales illustrates the kinds of pressure GWR staff were placed under with the extra demands placed on them by services of this kind. On 3 December 1941 an 8-coach 'Workpeoples' train was derailed at Margam Moors in South Wales. The 1.30pm Neath to Tremains service was hauled by 2-6-2 tank No. 3101, which left the track at about 70 mph and tipped itself and all but three of its carriages on their sides. Fortunately, injuries were relatively slight and there were no fatalities which, considering that the locomotive left the rails at such a high speed, was almost miraculous. The official report compiled after the incident concluded that the accident had occurred since the

locomotive with its small driving wheels originally built for suburban trains, was completely unsuitable for the almost main line duties it was performing. The report recommended discontinuing the use of this class of engine "on services so markedly different from those for which it was intended".[43] The shedmaster had probably had little choice about which engine he could roster on the service due to wartime stringencies, but the incident does show the problems faced during the period by the locomotive department.

We started this chapter by remarking on the reduction in bombing raids on Britain after the German invasion of Russia in June 1941. In concluding it would be useful to look briefly at the more important incidents in the year after this significant development in the war. In his first report after the beginning of 'Operation Barbarossa' the General Manager noted that bombs had been dropped at twelve locations, but "no material damage had been caused".[44] In July the trend continued, with the exception of an attack on Penarth Docks on the 1st, which caused substantial damage to buildings, and left two dredgers, the *Graball* and the *Peeress* in need of repair. During the summer of 1941 the Great Western network had a welcome break from the attentions of German bombers, and summing up the air raid damage for the previous three months, at a board meeting held in October, the General Manager described it as "only trifling".[45]

In October itself, there were reports of three incidents, the most serious occurring at Rogerstone on the South Wales main line. On the 7th a land mine caused great destruction, its blast damaging both the North and South signal boxes, wrecking track circuiting and injuring the signalmen. More serious was the death of a shunter, and the eight other railway staff injured in the attack, which also affected nearby homes. On the same day bombs damaged the Bulleymore underbridge near Shepton Mallet, causing extensive damage to the embankment and trackwork. Later in the month, on the 24th, the focus shifted further west, with a raid on Hayle in Cornwall which damaged both the up and down main lines. A few weeks later a Cornish station was once again targeted, with the goods yard at St Austell suffering minor damage in a raid on 13 November.

An interesting feature of reports of such damage

A GWR guard giving the 'Right Away' at Paddington in July 1940.

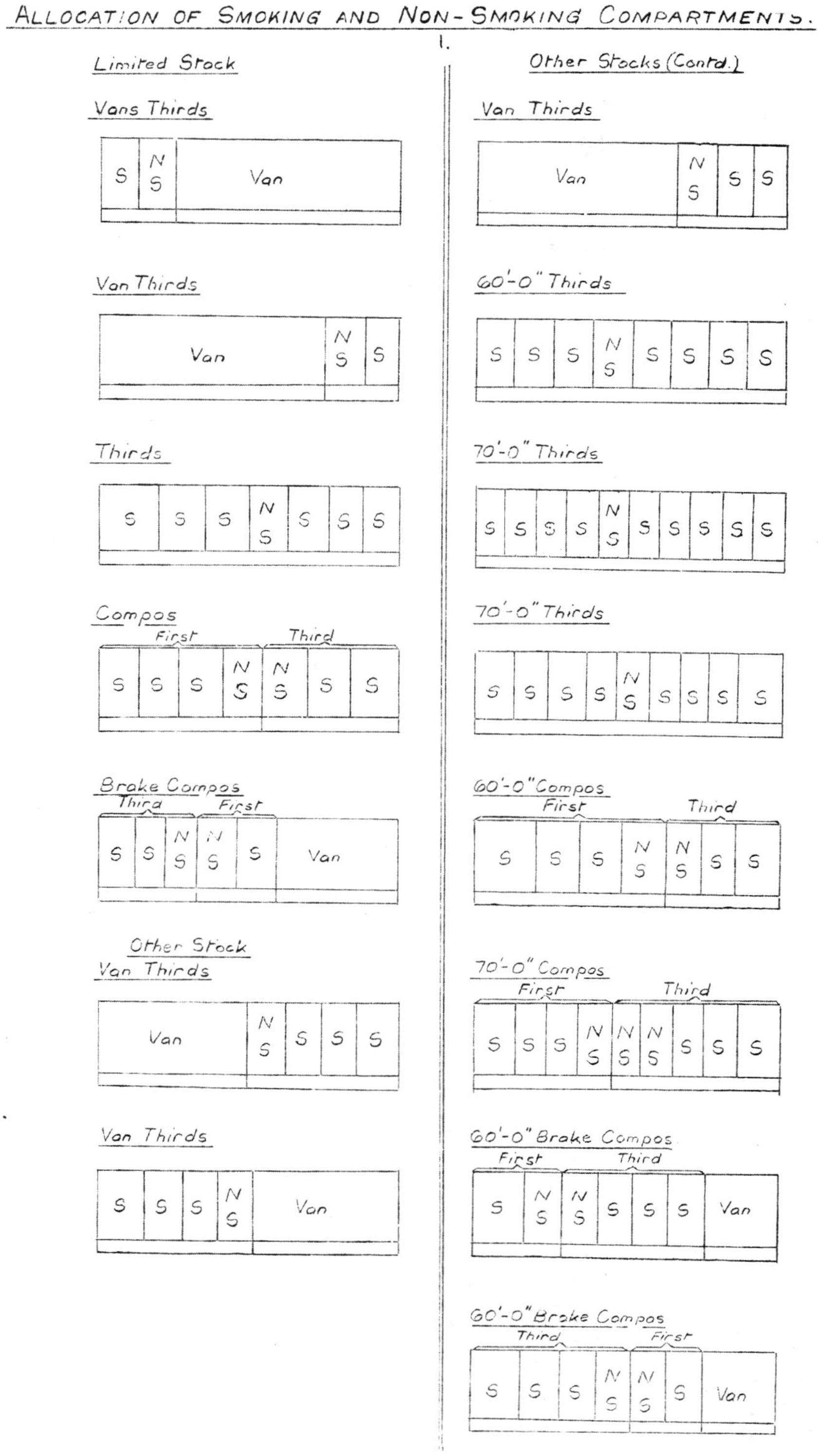

ALLOCATION OF SMOKING AND NON-SMOKING COMPARTMENTS.

I.

Limited Stock

Vans Thirds

| S | N S | Van |

Van Thirds

| Van | N S | S |

Thirds

| S | S | S | N S | S | S | S |

Compos

First / Third

| S | S | S | N S | N S | S | S |

Brake Compos

Third / First

| S | S | N S | N S | S | Van |

Other Stock
Van Thirds

| Van | N S | S | S | S |

Van Thirds

| S | S | S | N S | Van |

Other Stocks (Contd.)

Van Thirds

| Van | N S | S | S |

60'-0" Thirds

| S | S | S | N S | S | S | S | S |

70'-0" Thirds

| S | S | S | S | N S | S | S | S | S |

70'-0" Thirds

| S | S | S | S | N S | S | S | S | S |

60'-0" Compos

First / Third

| S | S | S | N S | N S | S | S |

70'-0" Compos

First / Third

| S | S | S | N S | N S | N S | S | S | S |

60'-0" Brake Compos

First / Third

| S | N S | N S | S | S | S | Van |

60'-0" Brake Compos

Third / First

| S | S | S | N S | N S | S | Van |

A diagram prepared at Swindon Works showing the increased allocation of smoking accommodation in carriages.

The Great Western was called on to move many unusual and sometimes 'out of gauge' loads during the war. This photograph shows a naval gun at Old Oak Common on 10 April 1942.

by the Luftwaffe does not seem to have included many attacks by lone aircraft which characterised the period after the end of the German intensive bombing campaign. The historian Angus Calder noted that although air raids had become a much less important part of peoples' lives, the new tactic adopted by the German Air Force were "Tip and Run" attacks by fighter bombers flying fast and low across the south and east of the country, paying

particular attention to coastal areas.[46] Examples of such 'lone wolf' attacks abound; on 27 July 1942 4-6-0 'Saint' class locomotive No. 2947 *Madresfield Court* was machine-gunned by a German bomber at Westbury whilst working the 4.30am Swindon to Weymouth parcels train. This was the second time the engine had been attacked; in March it had also been machine-gunned this time between Westbury and Weymouth; fortunately on both occasions,

United States Sherman tanks loaded on 'Warwell' wagons ready for dispatch. (D. J. Hyde Collection)

"Tickets Please!" – women ticket collectors at Paddington on 28 May 1942. Army and RAF personnel are prominent in the picture, perhaps for propaganda reasons.

there were no casualties, and damage to the engine was only slight. On the same day, a GWR 2884 class 2-8-0, No. 3828, was also machine-gunned, this time between Lavington and Patney & Chirton; records unfortunately not showing if it was the same aircraft which caused the damage, bearing in mind the close proximity of both attacks.

Perhaps the most serious attack of this kind, which again was not mentioned in the General Manager's report to the board, was a serious attack on the station and goods yard at Castle Cary in Somerset on 3 September 1942. A lone Junkers Ju88 aircraft bombed and machine gunned the area, causing extensive damage. An 0-6-0 pannier tank No.1729, which was working the Yeovil to Durston goods train was hit, killing the driver, and another bomb which hit the signal box, also killed the signalman. The goods clerk was seriously injured, and three permanent way staff were also hurt. The somewhat elderly locomotive, built in 1891 was deemed to be beyond repair, and was cut up a month later. The goods shed, signal box and yard were badly affected, and two milk vans stabled in the sidings were derailed, one suffering considerable damage.[47]

In the early part of 1942 there was little damage to report, and on 20 February Sir James Milne noted that no bombs had been dropped in the period since the previous board meeting, the first occasion this had happened for some considerable time. In April only two places were attacked; the first location was Rodwell near Weymouth, where 100ft of parapet wall, station buildings, the signal box and telegraph wires were all damaged on 2 April. The second incident was another attack similar to those just described, when on 16 April two Luftwaffe aircraft machine-gunned the 7.40am Newton Abbot to Taunton train on the sea wall near Dawlish Warren. The locomotive, 'Star' class 4-6-0 No. 4034 *Queen Adelaide* was slightly damaged and its fireman was wounded.

If the GWR board had thought that the General Manager's reports of bomb damage were a thing of the past, then they were to be sadly disappointed. At the meeting held on 29 May 1942 they heard a harrowing account of destruction and loss of life, which harked back to the darkest days of the 1940–1941 Blitz. In late April and early May, the

Luftwaffe launched what became known as the 'Baedeker Blitz', an offensive against British towns and cities that had no strategic importance, but were chosen because of the beauty of their mediaeval or regency architecture. The raids were so named because it was thought that the Germans had chosen their targets by consulting the famous Baedeker travel guidebooks and were in retaliation for an RAF attack on the historic German city of Lubeck, half of which was destroyed in an incendiary raid in late March.

None of the cities attacked by the Germans were well defended, and their ARP services were not up to the standards of those in larger cities more used to the Blitz. Two cities on the GWR network, Bath and Exeter, were attacked during this series of raids, both suffering very badly in the process. Bath was attacked for two successive nights on 25 and 26 April, with over 600 people being killed in the air raid. It was reported that Bath Spa station suffered considerably with 60ft of platform wall being demolished, and the goods shed, stables and

SAFETY FIRST

BEFORE ALIGHTING BE SURE YOUR COACH IS AT THE PLATFORM

Notices like these were vital to prevent passengers falling from trains, after mistakenly thinking they were at station platforms. (Author's Collection)

weighbridge office being badly damaged. More serious was the fact that the line between Bath and Twerton Tunnel was hit in nine places, destroying over 100ft of a 30ft high retaining wall leaving the up main line totally unsupported for a similar distance, and the down line undermined.

Repairs were difficult and slow; the Chief Civil Engineer carried out the work, along with Sir Robert McAlpine Ltd and by 28 April single line working had been restored by slewing the down line inwards as far as possible which allowed piles to be driven into the 100ft gap beneath the up line. A temporary arrangement was constructed to allow both lines to work pending the completion of repairs. Thus by 15 May, traffic was finally running on both lines.

The first raid on Exeter had occurred two days before the Bath Blitz on 24 April, when about 25 bombers carried out a low level attack, but the raid on 3 May was far more destructive, and the 90 bombers succeeded in destroying much of the mediaeval city centre and hit many buildings, including the cathedral. St David's station, the locomotive shed, the goods shed and various signal boxes were all hit, and the running lines were hit by debris; most tragic was the fact that an air raid shelter situated in the station yard received a direct hit, and the eight men sheltering in it were all killed. At the end of May a totally unrelated attack took place on Severn Tunnel Junction, an extremely important location on the Great Western network; fortunately damage was light, with the running lines needing repair, and the loop lines

obstructed by crippled rolling stock.

With the conclusion of the 'Baedeker Blitz', throughout the rest of 1942 Luftwaffe attacks affecting the GWR network reverted to the more random and scattered pattern described earlier. A raid on Weston-super-Mare on the night of the 28th and 29th June caused considerable damage, with the goods shed, goods agent's office, and weighbridge all being destroyed, and the down platform and waiting room needing considerable repair. Additionally, three coaches were destroyed, and a further six needed attention. In July Swindon Works was attacked, details of which are contained in Chapter 9; elsewhere the Birmingham area suffered once again, with the goods shed at Small Heath being burnt out in a raid on 30 July. Two company staff were killed in the attack, and a considerable number of wagons were also destroyed. More staff casualties were reported on 6 August, when Truro station was machine-gunned, killing one member of staff, and injuring others.

Only three further raids of any significance occurred on the Great Western before the end of 1942; the most serious was a raid on Totnes on 21 October, which demolished much of the station building, including the station master's office. One passenger and an unidentified member of staff were killed in the blast, which also left a further two passengers injured. The second incident occurred at Menheniot when blast from bombs in the vicinity did a good deal of damage to the station buildings, and the final and perhaps most interesting report was of a number of bombs which fell on the main line at Teignmouth on 3 November. It was noted that four Focke-Wulf Fw190 fighters attacked the Teignmouth area, and also machine-gunned 4-6-0 No. 5900 *Hinderton Hall* before two were shot down by Typhoon fighters, scrambled by 257 Squadron.

GWR railcar No. 29 at Ledbury station in September 1941. (RCTS Collection)

8
Salvage and Staff

With the fall of France in the summer of 1940 Britain became an island at bay, and as the grip of German 'U' boats drew tighter in the western approaches, so the supply of raw materials and manufactured products to help sustain the country dwindled. Not surprisingly the government was quick to set up schemes to cut down on waste, and to salvage scrap material for recycling. One of the earliest of these schemes was the infamous 'Saucepans for Spitfires' campaign launched by Lord Beaverbrook in July 1940. Although the aluminium donated by all sections of the population was in truth not of a high enough grade to really be useful in fighter production, it did show that the public could be mobilised to save and recycle vital raw materials for the war effort.

Up and down the country Salvage Shops were opened, and small dumps and depots appeared at strategic locations. As usual, the Great Western was not slow to join what was a national scheme and in August 1940 a small leaflet was issued to all staff inviting them to "Join the GWR Salvage Corps". Inside the leaflet was a personal message from Sir James Milne, who urged staff to join and "help the County to win the war".[1] He argued that staff should look at every piece of material from a new angle; "Is it wanted now, or ever? If it isn't then it is due for the salvage dump".[2] "Do not delay" he concluded, for "salvage feeds the guns that fight the Huns."

An article in the December 1940 issue of the Company magazine rather belatedly reported the distribution of this leaflet, and noted further developments in the battle to save scrap material. Special measures had been taken to ensure that scrap from the engineering departments had been specially dealt with, the writer commented, but apart from this, it was necessary for Great Western staff to be particularly vigilant in identifying items which could be reused. Even items which had previously "been regarded as rubbish and of no commercial value, have assumed a new significance in the war economy".[3] Particular members of staff, known as 'Salvage Leaders' were appointed to drum up enthusiasm for the salvage campaign, and dumping grounds were provided at larger stations, docks, depots and offices. Scrap was separated into four different categories: iron, steel, brass and other metals, sacking and rags, tins and miscellaneous materials such as light bulbs, rubber and paper, as well as a few which did not easily fall into any of the categories noted above!

To service these salvage dumps, four special wagons were introduced, converted from iron 'Mink' wagons. Each was fitted with four separate bins to cope with the various categories, and the wagons were rostered to make regular visits on a roughly monthly basis to all the principal stations. In the austere atmosphere of the war years it would have been hard to miss these vehicles, since they were painted bright blue, with large letters which read 'Salvage: Save for Victory'. It seems that initially the scheme was tried experimentally in the Bristol and Cardiff areas, as the March 1941 *GWR Magazine* noted that the operation of the Salvage vans had now been extended to the whole network.

A view of one of the converted iron 'Mink' wagons used for the salvage campaign.

Once the scrap had been unloaded at one of the specially set up depots it could be sorted and then distributed to a number of different sources. In the case of iron and steel scrap metal, some was sent to an unidentified ironworks which, in 1942, was dealing with 500 tons per week. It was noted that 100 tons of good quality metal was enough to make seven medium sized tanks, or 100,000 rifle barrels. It seems that a good proportion of the iron and steel rescued found its way back to the rolling mills at Swindon Works, where it was recycled into side stanchions used on wagons, and other parts of Great Western vehicles. Cast iron salvaged was returned to the Iron Foundry, where it could be recast into such items as axleboxes, vacuum cylinder pistons and the like. With new metal hard to come by, this operation was indeed useful to the Great Western.

Even before the salvage campaign began, in October 1939, staff were being urged to look for ways of saving steel and iron scrap. The Chief Mechanical Engineer wrote to all divisional

superintendents and docks engineers, reminding them of the "importance of augmenting national supplies".[4] Arrangements for the reclamation of ferrous material were to be made he added, which, as well as being in the national interest, were also useful from the point of 'economy of working'.

Interestingly the latter point, which confirmed the fact that the railway also stood to gain financially from the whole business of reclamation and recycling was further emphasised in January 1940 when it was reported that the War Office had requested 30,950 tons of scrap steel rails for use by the British Expeditionary Force. Of this total, 26,000 tons were required by March, with the balance to be shipped by August. Of this amount, the Great Western was to supply 3,640 tons at £5 5s per ton.[5] No record has been found of exactly how much rail was actually supplied, since the fall of France curtailed the full completion of the contract. At the same time, the British railways were also asked to supply approximately 72,000 sleepers to the RAF and the War Office; once again, the GWR

Scrap metal being salvaged at an unidentified location, although the address painted on the side of the van suggests it may be Hockley, Birmingham.

had to supply a proportion of the total, in this case its balance being 10,000 sleepers.

It is to be assumed that having to supply the BEF with a great deal of scrap steel, could not have assisted the Company in its quest to conserve iron and steel; indeed only a few weeks after the fall of France, C. B. Collett was once again writing to his staff asking them make sure that they had looked carefully for any surplus material. The Chief Mechanical Engineer argued that there was no doubt that "in many places there are odd things which seem hardly worth collecting but, under present circumstances even these should be gathered up".[6] Just over a year later, as the grip of the German blockade of Britain grew tighter, one can sense an air of desperation in the circular issued by Collett's successor, F. W. Hawksworth in August

1941. He wrote that the Company was "most urgently in need of further large supplies of scrap cast iron chairs to keep the foundry going at Swindon".[7]

Perhaps the most famous of salvage campaigns was the compulsory one involving the removal of ornamental and decorative railings from around parks, gardens and public buildings. This process began in 1940 and continued throughout the war years. Although the Great Western played its part, losing a good few miles of fencing around many of its stations and depots, it is obvious that the large lengths of fencing that still remained was something of an issue to some, particularly those in government. A letter from the Great Western Chief Engineer, then based at Aldermaston, reveals that the railway was under a great deal of pressure to

remove any further unnecessary iron railings around company property. The Chief Engineer requested an urgent survey of railings around all Great Western stations and depots noting that these should all be considered redundant unless they were essential for the following: "Defence of the Realm, Public Safety, Preventing the straying of livestock, Protection of Public Utilities". The latter category included gas, water, electricity and sewage, and also transport, vehicles, stores and secret war industries.[8]

Non-ferrous metals such as aluminium, phosphor bronze, copper and brass were also salvaged, since they were of great use to the munitions and aircraft industry; one way that raw materials of this sort were conserved was by the substitution of such metals in construction. Aluminium for example, was used extensively in the construction of carriages, being utilised for numerous fittings, in roof guttering, beading and tread plates. In austere times such as those faced by the GWR alternative materials were used, and, the *GWR Magazine* reported, "every bit of salvaged aluminium goes to the aircraft factories with a

minimum of delay".[9] Such was the demand for non-ferrous material that even the caps of light bulbs were saved. Staff were instructed to keep these, and to send them back to the general stores at Swindon for salvage.[10]

One further, more personal effort that each Great Western employee could make towards the salvage campaign was by saving his razor blades. In the February 1942 issue of the *GWR Magazine* staff were urged to save such items, which the magazine noted "find a ready market at about 1s 6d per gross".[11] The proceeds of this venture were donated to the GWR Staff Association Comforts Fund for Great Western men in the forces. By donating their used blades, the article concluded, readers would be both conserving steel supplies for the nation, and helping their colleagues in the forces. By May, it was reported that over 40,000 blades had been handed in, and after being disposed of as steel scrap, had raised the princely sum of £12.

Another of the materials used in great quantities by the railways was of course timber, and after Dunkirk, this too became scarcer, since much of the wood used in the construction of railway vehicles had come from abroad. Even before the fall of France, Managers had been warned of the serious shortage of timber, and "the urgent necessity...for the strictest economy in the use of all classes of this material, particularly softwoods".[12]

One of the committees set up by the Railway Executive dealing specifically with stores, issued a minute in April 1940 which suggested ways in which stocks of timber could be conserved. This was circulated by the Company to all stations and depots the same month. Five measures were mentioned, most of which initially did not seriously affect the working of the railway. The first was that hotel furniture should not be replaced or renewed unless absolutely necessary; secondly, the erection of advertising hoardings should be discontinued. The third measure involved the issuing of stricter instructions to the users of chocks and packing timber; they were urged to take care in the use of such wood, and to make sure that it was returned to its originating depot. On a related subject, the fourth measure was that users of packing cases should be reminded to return them promptly for reuse. The final proposal was rather more drastic; it was that wooden buildings should be examined to see if they could be dismantled and the timber recovered.

Another national body, the Railway Clearing House, also issued guidelines to the railway companies, this time on the sort of timber to be used in wagon construction. Anticipating the end of plentiful supplies of foreign timber, the specification was for 'home grown timber' and comprised the use of home grown oak for underframes, spruce, larch, Scots fir or poplar for wagon bodies and Scots fir, silver fir, spruce, ash, poplar, larch or beech for flooring battens.[13]

As the war continued, and shortages worsened, the Great Western was forced to improvise and recycle materials to keep the railway running; one example of this was the reuse of coal picks. These were used by firemen to break up large lumps of coal in tenders, and had heavy use, which often resulted in the breaking of handles. Staff were requested to return them to Swindon where they could be turned on a lathe down to hammer handles if suitable. This task was in all probability done by apprentices in the Carriage Works, but was a clever reuse of a valuable material.

In a previous chapter the withdrawal of towels in GWR carriages was noted, and this was symptomatic of a general shortage of cotton and other similar material for such items as dusters, towels and cloths. One way in which the life of such items in use by the Company could be prolonged was by the introduction of longer delays between washes. All linen was returned to the Company's laundry at Swindon on a weekly basis, but in 1941 it was decided that to try to reduce the wear and tear on towels they would be sent to Swindon at monthly intervals instead. A four-week cycle was introduced, with Paddington being dealt with the first week, Aldermaston the second, Swindon Works the third, and docks and other establishments being dealt with on the fourth week.[14]

Matters were so serious that oily and greasy rags, used extensively in the Locomotive Department, the Road Motor Department and Swindon Works, became extremely difficult to obtain. As a result, in 1942 an appeal was made to staff asking them to

Another Porter Gone: the front cover of a leaflet exhorting the travelling public to send lighter parcels and loads to make life easier for women staff.

return as many as possible of these items to Swindon where they could be cleaned in the Oil Works.[15] Presumably an extra saving was that oil recovered from the rags could also be reused.

All manner of materials became hard to come by, some with extremely severe consequences to the running of the railway; ropes were an essential part of the operation of the Goods Department being used to secure loads in both wagons and road vehicles. Soon after the outbreak of war the Chief Goods Manager wrote to staff warning them of the "extreme shortage of ropes which is resulting in delay in the dispatch of wagons and consequently leading to congestion".[16] Superintendents were asked to keep stocks to a minimum, and to send any spares back to the Goods Department at Paddington. By 1942 matters had worsened, and even twine and string was in short supply; the grandly named Hemp Controller, part of the Ministry of Supply, noted that he had endeavoured to keep legitimate users supplied since the beginning of the war, but that with the situation in the Far East, economy in

HEAVY PARCELS BY PASSENGER TRAIN CAUSE DELAY

SMALLER PARCELS —QUICKER DELIVERY

BRITISH RAILWAYS
RY1990/406

the use of sisal and hemp had to be exercised.

Despite the shortages of textiles, it was reported that large quantities were still salvaged in the Company's campaign; most of it was classified as rags by the Ministry of Supply, but it was still deemed useful for recycling as blankets, rugs and cleaning cloths. Rope was also recycled, particularly the old Manila type which the *GWR Magazine* reported, could amount to up to 100 tons a year in some cases.[17]

Perhaps one of the most lucrative and well publicised items salvaged was paper. In 1942 it was noted that over 900 tons per year was sold to contractors and that a single ton of waste paper could be converted into 9,000 shell fuse components, 47,000 boxes for .303 ammunition, or 3,000 boxes for aero cannon shells. Such was the enthusiasm with which the salvage campaign was charged, the amount of paper collected for pulping in the first two years of the war was 2,400 tons, well above the total noted earlier. With the enormous size of the Great western network, the amount of paperwork generated was enormous; thus staff were asked to make a detailed examination of all

the files and records at their particular station or depot. The *GWR Magazine* reported that they were glad to know that staff were "busily engaged in turning out from their cupboards and stores, books, records and correspondence that are no longer required."[18]

The zeal with which this drive to salvage paper was carried out can be judged by the fact that in the first three months of 1942, 437 tons of paper were collected, an increase of 100 per cent from the previous year. Staff were urged to salvage "all accumulations of old books, catalogues, magazines and spare copies of documents not likely to be required".[19] Later the same year the Audit Department at Paddington sorted and salvaged over 10 tons of old books, forms and other paperwork. Bearing in mind the enthusiasm with which this task seems to have been undertaken, it is interesting to wonder how much important historical material was destroyed in the process. Unfortunately we shall probably never know, but when historical information on aspects of the Company cannot today be found in the various record offices scattered around the country, it may be that it was destroyed during the war period.

The salvage drive described at Paddington also led to the reclamation of 1,100 reams of paper which had been used on one side only; many letters of the period were often written on the back of other correspondence, and one dilemma for the researcher is to decide which side of the piece of paper is most interesting! Economy in the use of stationery generally was encouraged very early on, in October 1939, when staff were instructed to use single-line spacing in letters and it was impressed "to all concerned the necessity for saving stationery in every direction".[20] The efforts to reduce the consumption of paper did work; in 1944 the General Manager told the GWR board that consumption of new paper had been reduced from 1,783 tons in 1939, to 570 tons in 1943, even though traffic had increased by 50 per cent since the outbreak of war.[21]

As the war dragged on, another important resource which became scarcer was fuel, in all its various forms. In early 1942, a fuel crisis, exacerbated by yet another severe winter, and poor productivity in the coal industry, meant that the government contemplated the rationing of coal, gas and electricity. Both the public and industry were urged to save energy, on both a voluntary basis, and thorough statutory means such as the Waste of Fuel

Order of 1942 which prohibited the "wasteful and uneconomical consumption of fuel of all kinds".[22]

Through all the remaining winters of the war, staff were urged to save energy; the government made it clear that output of coal and other fuel was insufficient to meet the normal demands of both the domestic market and the growing demands of an industry gearing itself up for the campaign to open a new front in Europe. The General Manager, in a message to staff in October 1942, outlined a scheme to restrict the use of coal in stations, staff rooms and signal boxes, with the maximum quantity available being an amount which was 75 per cent of the previous year's total. He wrote that he was "confident that the whole-hearted cooperation of the staff will be forthcoming in this and any other restrictive measures which it may be necessary to impose at the present critical stage of the war."[23]

Company employees were asked not to light fires in mild weather, and fortunately, the following two winters were not as harsh as those which had preceded them, and so economies could be made. In the winter of 1943 there was a renewed drive for fuel economy and on 29 September, a special meeting of all the main line railways, the unions and representatives of the ministries involved was held to discuss further measures which could be adopted. Much discussion ensued about the movement and supply of coal, and some aspects of this will be discussed in more detail in Chapter 10; what did emerge however, was that in the final analysis, fuel economy rested with "the man on the spot. This was true on the locomotive footplate, in the hotel and workshop, and in the porters' room on the station."[24] All Great Western employees were called upon to "exercise every care to prevent wastage or misuse of coal, gas or electricity".[25]

One problem encountered as a result of these campaigns was that the Company found that the

Female carpenters at work at the Road Motor Depot at Slough. (National Railway Museum)

LIGHTING

The question of the visibility of railway signals, engine head-lamps, etc., from the air has been a matter of experiment over a long period with the Royal Air Force.

The present signal lights of all descriptions have been approved by H.M. Government and are essential for the efficient continuance of British Railways' vital Services. Railway signal-light beams are bright only in the immediate path of the beam, and lose their brilliance rapidly when viewed from other angles.

Master switches control the whole of the lights at large passenger stations and large goods yards so that the lighting, approved by the Government, can be extinguished immediately the warning is given.

In spite of wartime handicaps

BRITISH RAILWAYS

still provide generous Public Services

blackout measures adopted in the early part of the war did not assist in fuel economy; windows had been boarded or bricked up, and roof lights had been painted over. Instructions were therefore issued to allow for the replacement of this permanent blackout with removable blinds, which would allow daylight to be used during the day, thus saving energy. In Swindon Works, this proved to be quite an expensive process, with many acres of workshop rooflight having to be tackled.

One final item on the subject of fuel economy related to the Locomotive Department is however worth repeating at this point. In November 1942 F. W. Hawksworth wrote to divisional super-intendents on the subject of "Economy in the use of paraffin". He complained that at many depots, locomotives were left with headlamps burning after they had arrived on shed and were waiting to be coaled; all lamps should be taken off the engine, and handed in at the shed he instructed, with one lamp being moved from locomotive to locomotive as they passed under the coal stage to save fuel.[26]

By 1942 however, the Locomotive Department was facing more serious problems than running

out of paraffin; staff shortages were making it extremely difficult to run the railway at all. Indeed, the shortage of labour was not confined to the running side of the Great Western's operation, all departments needed additional staff. "It is now impossible to obtain adult male labour" wrote the author of a secret report on preparations for the 1942/43 winter service in June 1942.[27] It was estimated that around 11,000 additional staff would be required by the railways as a whole to cope with the demand forecast by the Railway Executive.

The deterioration in the supply of labour had come about as a direct result of the war; the fall of France, and the mauling which British forces had received led in August 1940 to a request from the Army for 357,000 recruits in March 1941, and from then on, a further 100,000 per month. By July 1941 matters had worsened still further, and it was estimated that two million men and women were required for the armed forces and the munitions industry in the next twelve months.[28] To find this enormous number of people, the basis of the Reserved Occupation system was drastically changed. When war broke out, a schedule of such occupations was issued, followed by a handbook which was received by every household in the country which listed all the various important jobs valuable to the war effort. This was designed to try to prevent a repeat of the situation in the First World War, when industry had been decimated by the enlistment of its most skilled labour into the forces when war first broke out. Just such a situation had occurred on the Great Western in 1914, and management were no doubt relieved when such measures were introduced in 1939.

On the outbreak of war, the National Service (Armed Forces) Act was passed, making all men between the ages of 18 and 41 liable for conscription, but the actual process of call up was extremely slow, with those aged 40 not registered until the summer of 1941. Those whose occupation appeared on the Reserved schedule were exempt from military service if their age exceeded the stated age. The introduction of these measures raised the issue of restricting the conscription of railway staff completely, but the government was unwilling to do this, instead including railwaymen in the Schedule of Reserved Occupations. For most staff the age of reservation was 25, although in the case of permanent way staff, goods checkers, porters and ticket collectors it was 30, presumably on the grounds that their work did not entail quite such skill or experience, and thus replacements could be found if employees were conscripted.

Following discussions with the authorities, it was announced some months after the outbreak of war that certain grades of staff who were conscripted, would only be called up for service in Transportation Units; not surprisingly, staff included in this arrangement included drivers, firemen, engine cleaners, platelayers, shunters and lengthmen.[29] In May 1940 a revised Schedule of Reserved Occupations noted further railway occupations from which men would be enlisted only into Royal Engineers Transportation Units. In 1941 however, the demand for manpower led to the complete overhaul of the Reserved Occupation system, and the scrapping of the Block Reservation system. Instead, workers in particular factories or establishments would be reserved, and in some cases at a lower age than in unessential industries. The deferment of conscription was therefore judged on an individual basis. A revised schedule was also issued, and the age of reservation of each occupation was raised by a year each month after January 1st 1942. Reporting the new arrangements, the *GWR Magazine* noted that any staff "de-reserved as a result of the raising of the age limits would be notified by the Ministry of Labour, and they should let their departmental officer know immediately".[30] Before looking at the ways in which the Company attempted to combat the increasingly difficult staff situation they faced, it would be useful to mention briefly measures taken by the railway to protect the prospects of staff called up for military duty during the war. An announcement was made that staff serving with the forces would be treated as if they were "absent from duty with leave", and that on their return they would be offered their old post or one of a similar grade, providing they were fit to do the job. Arrangements were made to allow staff to keep up contributions to superannuation or pension funds, and if their service wages were less than that earned whilst working for the Company, then the GWR

The suspension of compulsory retirement meant that experienced drivers continued to work during the war years. This 1943 view of Driver Luscombe of Wolverhampton shows him, complete with waxed moustache, on the footplate of No. 5081 Lockheed Hudson.

would make good the difference. These payments were known as Service Emoluments; an example of this system can be seen by the case of a painter's apprentice from Swindon Works who was enlisted in the Royal Artillery in September 1939. His service pay was 14s per week, but this was boosted by a further contribution of 8s from the Great Western. By 1944 his service pay had risen to 45s per week, and the Company contribution another 9s.[31]

Returning to the theme of staff shortages, a number of different measures were introduced to try to combat the problem. The number of staff called up grew steadily; in November 1939 it was reported that 3,310 staff were "Serving with the Colours", with a further 120 engaged in other National Services. Within these totals, the largest number, over 1,200, had been drawn from the Chief Mechanical Engineer's Department; only one member of staff had joined up from the General Manager's Department. By January 1941 this figure had risen to over 8,200, and thirteen

months later the *GWR Magazine* reported that this total was now 11,620.[32] The number of Great Western staff to serve in the armed forces was to eventually exceed 15,000, with over 400 employees killed in action.

A number of relatively minor measures were introduced by the Company to try to ease the problems of staff shortages; one of the most obvious was the abolition of automatic retirement for drivers when they reached the age of 60. Although shortages had occurred in all grades, it was the loss of experienced staff such as drivers which the Great Western felt most keenly, and thus in January 1940 it was announced that enginemen reaching the age of 60 during that year would remain in service until they were 61 or until the cessation of hostilities. Those staff not wishing to carry on could retire by applying in writing to their divisional superintendent, but the tone of the circular issued by the Company certainly made it

clear that unless drivers were in poor health, then they were expected to carry on for the war effort. The suspension of retirement seems to have become the norm within the Company, and in December 1940 C. B. Collett reported that in view of the demands likely to be made on staff by the conscription of men into the forces, "it has been decided that all retirements shall be postponed unless there are strong reasons why the staff concerned should not be retained in the service".[33]

Some of the most acute shortages of staff were suffered by locomotive depots, and correspondence of the period is full of references to problems suffered at sheds from the lack of both skilled and unskilled labour. To help replace conscripted drivers and firemen, the Company increased the speed with which engine cleaners, the lowest grade of locomotive staff, were promoted to Firemen. This naturally led to the promotion of firemen of the right qualifications

An obviously posed publicity picture of women at work at Reading in April 1944. (National Railway Museum)

and experience into driving positions. Some concern was expressed in Company circles that this quicker promotion of staff might lead to a drop in safety standards, and in May 1941 a circular was issued by F. W. Hawksworth, reminding divisional superintendents that, "engine cleaners, regardless of age should not, in any circumstances be utilised for temporary firing duties until they have been in the service for three months as an engine cleaner".[34]

With more rapid promotion of firemen, the demand for engine cleaners became more acute, and staff were urged to process applications for such positions with the greatest possible speed. Hawksworth wrote to his divisional staff in August 1942 informing them that "the necessity to obtain as many lads as possible...will be apparent", and that "the matter is viewed in a very serious light by the authorities."[35] The use of young staff in such demanding jobs was not always a straightforward procedure. In late 1942, whilst working a night shift, an engine cleaner who was under 16, suffered a serious injury in an accident, and Hawksworth noted that apart from any safety regulations which might have been broken, "it is very undesirable that young persons under the age of 16 should be employed during the night shift".[36]

Ultimately however, it was only the employment of women which would really make any impression on the severe shortages faced by the Great Western and the other railway Companies. However, as usual, it seems that the Company, and its staff, not always renowned for their progressive attitude, were slow to embrace the opportunities presented by the availability of female staff. In March 1941 C. B. Collett had written that "the present and prospective situations in the matter of man power are such that it is essential, from a railway point of view, as well as in the National Interest, to employ women and girls to the utmost possible extent, not only in Railway Offices and Workshops, but also in the Railway Operating Grades."[37] Staff were asked to make their comments known to him as soon as possible, and to suggest suitable posts which could be occupied by women. It was also noted that women should be given jobs such as telephone operators, and other attendant jobs in locomotive sheds, allowing boys

As the war progressed, women were employed all over the Great Western system in a wide variety of jobs. This view shows one of the many female staff employed in Swindon Works, operating a steam hammer in April 1944.

to be transferred to tasks such as engine cleaning.

Confirmation that the Chief Mechanical Engineers Department was slow in employing female staff can be gained from the fact that in his report to the GWR board on 21 March 1941, the General Manager stated that up to that date 2,052 women had been employed, with the vast majority, over 1,300, employed as porters. The rest were used in other occupations within the Traffic Department such as van guards, ticket collectors and carriage cleaners. An article in the *GWR Magazine* for the same month was headlined "Women Porters 'Go to It' on the G.W.R.", and reported that like most boys who, it argued, had an ambition to join the railway when they grew up, "this urge, coupled with a desire to perform work of national importance in the country's hour of need, now seems to have permeated the fair sex".[38] "We have every confidence" the article continued, "that they will not let the company down during the momentous times ahead."[39]

Sir James Milne added that, "to assist the women porters, in handling traffic, an appeal is to be made

to government departments, traders and the public to restrict the weight of packages including luggage."[40] An undated leaflet, issued as a response to this appeal, gives a good example of the often somewhat patronising attitude prevailing towards female staff. "Women cannot be expected to lift such heavy loads as men" it argued, noting that "railwaymen liberated for the Fighting Forces are being replaced by women."[41] An article in the *GWR Magazine* went further, arguing that the plea for lighter parcels was a 'gallant' one based on respect for the 'weaker' sex, who had come to the railway for the 'duration'.[42] In March 1942 the Minister of War Transport ruled that passenger luggage was to be restricted to 100 lb, introducing an element of compulsion into the plea to help women porters.

As the year wore on the number of female staff employed steadily increased, in August 1941 the *Railway Gazette* reported that the Great Western now had more than 8,000 female staff on their books; this figure did of course include around 4,000 clerks and typists who had been employed by the Company for many years, as well as refreshment room and Hotel staff.[43] A revealing quote in the *GWR Magazine* noted that every month brought "an increasing number of women into temporary service of the Great Western Railway, and these employees are certainly revealing notable versatility and adaptability."[44] The sight of women on GWR stations both large and not so large became commonplace, although some obviously still found their presence somewhat alien, as the *GWR Magazine* reported the sight of a women porter almost bowling over a curate with a mailbag, and another nonchalantly signalling a train away by whistling through her fingers with "professional aplomb".[45]

At the end of 1941, as part of a package of measures which included the ending of the old system of reserved occupations already described, a further more revolutionary scheme was introduced, the conscription of women. From 2 December, women between the ages of 20 and 30 were to be called up, either for service in the armed forces, or in important war industries, of which the railways were considered part. There was some considerable press opposition to the introduction of such a programme, but the government had little choice, their exhortations for volunteers having had only minimal effects.

By the summer of 1942, although as we have seen, large numbers of women had been employed

in the Traffic Department, the Locomotive Department was still suffering from severe shortages of staff, due in part to resistance from some staff to the utilisation of women in sheds and depots. A letter from the staff office at Aldermaston highlights concern felt by Great Western management to the rather slow progress made by the Chief Mechanical Engineers Department. Writing to F. W. Hawksworth, Mr H. Adams Clarke noted that "a stage has now been reached when we must give further and close consideration to the increased employment of women and part time staff in locomotive running sheds".[46] Figures were quoted for the number of women employed in place of men showing that the LMS had 1,317 female staff compared with only 87 on the Great Western.

It seems that management were suspicious that shed foremen were the cause of the problem, and were unwilling to approach the local offices of the Ministry of Labour in order to obtain suitable labour. It was also suggested that women should be employed as engine cleaners, freeing up male staff for other duties.

Two circulars issued on the same date, 17 July 1942 illustrate that there was still stubborn resistance from shed staff to the use of women in their empire. The first instructed staff that, "it has been decided to proceed with the recruitment of female engine cleaners."[47] It was noted however, that the recruitment of such women should "in no way interfere with the recruitment of male engine cleaners...as and when lads are available". A second, further letter written by Hawksworth that day touched on the apparent lack of progress being made; it compared the staff employed in sheds by the Great Western to those of the LMS and the LNER who had made much further progress. The figures are listed below for comparison:

Job	GWR	LMS	LNER
Caller-up	2	86	17
Engine cleaner	–	332	224
Shed labourer	36	894	88
Messenger	–	11	2
Sand dryer	–	6	–
Telephone attendant	7	54	14
Tube cleaner	–	45	5
Total:	45	1,428	350

Clearly, these figures were something of an embarrassment, and Hawksworth noted that in comparison with the other companies, "we fall far

A further view of women workers at Reading, on this occasion they were part of a permanent way gang. (National Railway Museum)

short in our efforts".[48]

Less than a month later it seems that the situation had not improved, and Hawksworth was once again urging his divisional superintendents to ensure that every means possible should be used to fill vacancies for shed staff, and that, "females should be employed wherever possible". He continued, "I think perhaps the poor results obtained up to now may be due to the fact that some foremen are prejudiced against the employment of female labour, but this prejudice must be broken down".[49]

Eventually the number of women employed did increase, improving the situation in locomotive sheds, with other additional labour being obtained by the recruitment of many more part time staff, Italian prisoners of war and workers from Ireland, who were used at various locations.

Another area where female staff were used extensively was in the cleaning of rolling stock,

particularly carriages. The reduction of male staff in such positions and their movement to other duties had led to a deterioration in the standard of Great Western stock, and consequently complaints to the Company. As a result, in the spring of 1942 it was decided that cleaning gangs of female labour were to be recruited to improve the general condition of the Company's stock. The circular announcing this measure noted that, "it is thought and recommended that it is advisable to employ three women to every two men previously employed".[50] By the end of 1942 the situation had improved considerably, and it was recorded that 976 carriage cleaners were now employed by the Company.

One problem which became most apparent when large numbers of female staff were recruited was, that since the Company had been staffed largely by men for most of its history, there were no toilet or rest room facilities for female staff.

One effect of the war was to prolong the life of locomotives which were ready for scrapping. No. 3568, seen here at Oxford in 1941, had been built as early as April 1894, but was not withdrawn until November 1945. (RCTS Collection)

Throughout the system, new facilities had therefore to be provided; one example being at Cardiff Canton shed where, in 1943, rest and messroom facilities were built. Company records list in detail the furniture needed to fit out these rooms; in the rest room two chairs, a table and a couch were supplied, along with linoleum for the floor. In the messroom, 20 lockers, a 12ft-table and benches, 30 coat pegs and a tea urn were also supplied. All this new equipment cost £105, and similar expenses were incurred all over the system.[51]

A Women's Welfare Supervisor, a Miss Brennan, was appointed by the GWR, and any proposals for improvements or new facilities were first submitted to her before being sanctioned at a higher level. Miss Brennan appears to have been something of a champion for the women in her care as, despite a gradual grudging respect from many male staff, women employed by the Great Western still had to battle against entrenched attitudes. In 1943 Miss Brennan reported to the Great Western Staff Committee that, "there was a mistaken belief that...heavily built women were necessarily best suited for manual work. This was not the case and should be borne in mind by all those concerned".[52]

Space precludes a more detailed description of the role of women on the Great Western in the Second World War, but hopefully the information imparted so far is enough to show what a critical part they played in easing the shortages suffered by the railway. Numerous female staff were employed in Swindon Works, and some of the work done by them will be briefly mentioned in the next chapter. By the middle of 1943 over 16,000 women were working for the Great Western in a huge variety of jobs; a photograph taken at Paddington shows staff employed in such diverse occupations as porter, painter, coilwinder, machinist, carriage oiler, trolley driver, lift attendant and policewoman. Nationally, over 124,000 women were employed in railway service, and their contribution cannot be too highly valued; and as numerous writers have noted, many not only did their allotted job well, but also maintained a home and looked after their children.

In the course of this chapter we have dealt with how the Great Western Railway tried to cope with two major shortages, that of materials and staff; both these factors contributing towards the final problem to be dealt with in this section, that of lack of motive power. As early as the spring of 1940 the Chief Mechanical Engineer's Department were warning that the largest number of locomotives should be kept in good order, and that those awaiting repair or under repair should be out of service for the shortest possible time. By the summer of 1941 management were aware that the position regarding locomotives was worsening; lack of staff to enable, often very simple repairs to be undertaken at depots, were causing large numbers of locomotives to be out of service for long periods of time. The huge increase in munitions work at Swindon had also hit both the usual repairs done at the factory, and the new construction programme. Engines were also being worked much harder than they had done in peace time, with heavier trains and longer journeys run. This meant that when they were due for repair, the work done was often more substantial than it would have been in normal conditions.

Hawksworth wrote to his superintendents in August 1941 urging them to do everything possible to reduce the number of engines out of service, "in view of the fact that the coming winter will tax all our resources for engine power".[53] Matters had not improved by November, and because of the large number of freight trains being run, he recommended that 2-8-0 and 2-8-0 tank locomotives be tackled as a priority, at the expense of other types of engines.

The situation was seen as being so serious that special meetings of all the locomotive super-intendents were convened at Bristol and Swindon on 29 and 30 December 1941, and these continued until the end of the war. At the first meeting, it was noted that the availability figure for locomotives was 80 per cent, and this was not, in the General Manager's opinion, sufficiently high.[54] Through-out the war, the figures varied, although not by large amounts; on 24 January 1942 for example, the committee were told that out of a total stock of 3,878 locomotives, 644 were not available for traffic because they were either awaiting or under repair in Swindon, Wolverhampton or Caerphilly Works, awaiting attention in locomotive depots, or 'stopped' awaiting repairs. This total equalled 16.61 per cent of the total number of locomotives in stock. For comparison, only the LNER had a worse record on this particular day, with 17.87 per cent of its stock out of action, with the Southern figure being 14.07 per cent and the LMS the lowest at 11.13 per cent.

Poor coal was also blamed for many of the failures suffered in traffic, as was the slackening of the rigorous prewar maintenance regime for GWR locomotives. In happier times, locomotive boilers were regularly washed out, and tubes cleaned out as a matter of course; with regular staff conscripted or deployed elsewhere, the old systems broke down, and locomotives did not receive the high level of maintenance they had previously done. In 1944 the committee were receiving reports of boilers being overdue for washing by 20 or 30 days; delays of these kinds led to boilers being in far worse condition than they needed to have been when they finally were repaired, and also caused locomotive failures or poor running.

Tools and spare parts for locomotives were also in short supply, but matters were improved when the Chief Goods Manager gave the Chief Mechanical Engineer's Department the use of the Green Arrow Registered Transit parcels service to allow parts to be moved between running sheds, factories and depots. This concession was granted only because Hawksworth had given a "personal understanding to the Goods Manager and the Superintendent of the Line that the use of the facility will be strictly limited".[55] Writing in June 1942, the author of the secret Railway Executive Committee report already mentioned, which detailed the railway's preparations for the coming winter's traffic noted that despite the railway companies giving continuous attention to the time spent by locomotives under repair, the position had not improved dramatically since the early months of the war. The demands which were to be placed on the Great Western and all the main line companies in the run up to D-Day and beyond would mean, that despite the introduction of female labour and other improvements, the motive power position would still prove difficult for some considerable time to come.

9
Swindon Works at War

When war broke out in 1939 it is probably true to say that the Company's Locomotive, Carriage and Wagon Works at Swindon were in excellent shape. Covering an area of 323 acres, the GWR at Swindon had some of the most up-to-date equipment and machine tools, and a well trained workforce, more than capable of handling most jobs given to them. In the years following the outbreak of hostilities, the resources and staff of the factory would be pushed to their limits, and by the end of the war, much work would be needed to restore the works to its prewar glory.

Swindon Works had played an important role in producing munitions and other equipment during the First World War, with demands being made by the War Office, the Ministry of Munitions, the Admiralty and Woolwich Arsenal amongst others. During those years the factory turned out shells at a rate of around 2,500 per week, built 6in naval guns and mountings, carriage limbers, water carts and a host of other items. The Carriage Works also built a number of ambulance trains for use both at home and overseas.

The pressure of this work, coupled with the existing work planned by the Company put great pressure on both the workforce, badly weakened by enlistment in the forces, and the equipment and facilities of the workshops. It is perhaps for this reason that C. B. Collett, Chief Mechanical Engineer in 1939, when another world war began was said not to be particularly enthusiastic about involving the works in government work once

more. Collett had been Locomotive Works Manager between 1913 and 1920, and had therefore been able to see at first hand the disruption and problems caused during the Great War.

More than one writer has remarked on the Chief Mechanical Engineer's reluctance, and it seems that he did object strongly to munitions work affecting the day-to-day maintenance of the Company's locomotives and rolling stock.[1] K. J. Cook, in his reminiscences of the period,[2] noted that Collett was fond of recalling a statement by Walter Runciman, the President of the Board of Trade during the First World War, who argued that "if the railway service is impeded...owing to the railway rolling stock getting out of condition in consequence of the railway workshops being engaged in the manufacture of munitions of war, I must hold the Railway Executive Committee responsible."[3] Bearing in mind the sacrifices made by the railways in the service of the government, this statement could hardly have been encouraging to them, and it is clear that Collett felt sure the GWR would be put into the same no-win situation once again.

Clearly however, the gravity of the war meant that Collett could not resist the call to assist in the war effort indefinitely, and the works soon found itself a a key part of munitions production once more. One further pressure on Collett came from a perhaps less obvious source, the workforce. The conversion of casualty evacuation trains and ambulance trains already described in earlier

What the company called the 'Brake, Infectious and Boiler Car', converted for Ambulance Train use by the United States Army, at Swindon in 1943.

chapters had been done without recourse to the use of overtime; most other factories in the area were working as much overtime as possible on war work, and the Works Committee pressed Collett for the extra money that war work would bring to employees.

What this situation does highlight strongly was that Swindon Works did have some excess manufacturing capacity, which could be taken up with work for the government. Before the end of 1939, the works was involved in a number of government projects, although it was only during the period 1941 to 1943 that war work really reached its peak. Before describing some of the projects undertaken, we will first look at the impact that the threat of air attack had on the vast site, and how the Company's air raid precautions coped with this.

Swindon Works covered an enormous area, on a site divided by both the main Bristol to London main line, and the branch to Gloucester and Cheltenham. With almost 12,000 people on the payroll, air raid precautions were a huge undertaking. The works hooter, two large steam whistles situated on the roof of the hydraulic power house, whose mournful tones had summoned men to work for over 70 years, were pressed into service to warn of impending air raids. Bearing in mind that the hooters could be heard up to 25 miles away with a following wind, they also provided warning for the whole town, although the more conventional sirens were installed as well. As a result the hooters were not used to mark the beginning and end of shifts in the factory as they had done, which must have been a strange experience for Swindonians who had set their watches and regulated their lives by the hooter for years!

A large number of air raid shelters had to be provided for the staff, because of the scale of the works, and these were situated all around the site. Details of some of these measures have been taken from New Works Orders issued by the Company. These were used to instruct staff to undertake work, once permission to spend money had been made by the Locomotive Committee or the GWR board. These orders give estimates and actual costs, as well as a description of the work done, and provide a fascinating insight into the workings of the CME's Department, not only for the work they did, but for the work they carried out for other departments of the Company.

Instructions for the provision of shelters had been issued as early as May 1939, when the Locomotive Works Manager was instructed to "provide shelter accommodation for staff at the Locomotive Works, general offices and running shed".[4] This work was estimated to cost £1,876; shelters provided for the Carriage and Wagon Works were to cost far more, the estimate being £23,000. This large sum may well have been due to the fact that in the Locomotive Works, many of the subways used by the staff to move from one part of the works to another could be utilised as shelters. One of the shelters for the large A Erecting Shop was the subway which connected the workshop with one of the works entrances in nearby Dean Street.

As well as providing shelter accommodation, further measures were required. A good number of the individual workshops had considerable acreages of glass roof panelling, which in peacetime had made them light and airy. The great A Shop, completed just after the Great War, covered an area

of over half a million square feet, and its roof therefore contained huge amounts of glass. All these roof lights presented the Company with a formidable blackout problem, and thus it was therefore necessary to blacken the roofs of all workshops and stores in the Locomotive, Carriage and Wagon Works, the stock shed and the running shed to make sure that the works could not be seen from the air at night. Windows were painted with thick black paint, plunging the workshops into a seemingly never-ending night shift. Thus most work was done by the light of either electric or gas light, which no doubt added to the difficulties faced by the workforce at Swindon during the war years. One benefit for the workforce of this situation however, was that it speeded up the replacement of old gas lighting by electricity, the most immediate sign of this being the fitting of individual electric light fittings to machine tools in the factory.

The cost of this task was not cheap; blackening the roofs of the buildings was estimated to cost over £7,000.[5] Further examination of works records does however reveal that the painting of roof windows was not completely successful, and two

Work in progress on 25-ton tanks in the AE Shop at Swindon Works in 1941.

The machining of part of the structure for the 'Hyper velocity' gun mounting is taking place in this 1942 photograph.

New Works Orders record that some of the paint was removed in the spring of 1940 and replaced by canvas blinds which could be removed during the day. Not surprisingly the canvas was supplied by stocks held by Mr E. T. J. Evans, the Carriage Works Manager at Swindon. Only a few workshops seem to have been treated in this fashion, with the machine and erecting shops being noted in the New Works Order.[6]

Further similar expense was incurred with the provision of curtaining and screening for the many ordinary windows in the works, general stores and general offices, as well as work done on the wiring of buildings to allow internal lighting to be dimmed. This task cost a further £2,525.[7] Records also note that the telephone exchange, clearly an important strategic part of the Swindon operation, was also provided with structural alterations for its protection.[8]

In earlier chapters the great fear of attack by poison gas was mentioned; at Swindon, with around 12,000 people employed, the affects of such an attack would have been extremely serious. Thus, in July 1940 the Company authorised the provision of decontamination centres at a number of locations around the works; these including the A Shop, the general offices, the London Street messrooms, 24 Shop, the gas works, the fire station and the saw mill. Fortunately these facilities were never used, but the £135 expenditure was a necessary precaution.[9] One final air raid precaution not mentioned was the painting of white lines in various locations around the works, much in the same way white paint was used on stations to mark platform edges, doorways and the like; the same process took place in the works, although on a much larger scale! Over 400 staff became part of the Company's ARP scheme at Swindon, with the factory being divided into ten separate areas; 40 were used in each zone, 20 each for the day and night shifts. With the introduction of firewatching, a much larger problem was created, and over 600 men were required each night to watch the huge works site and warn against incendiary attack; fortunately no bombs of this type landed in the Swindon area.

Swindon Works did have its own fire station, situated in Bristol Street, close to the Carriage

Works, where presumably the greatest risk of fire existed. At the outbreak of war the most modern fire appliance owned by the Company at Swindon was a Dennis fire engine built in 1912. This elderly vehicle is thought to have been the first motor fire engine in Wiltshire, and apart from the replacement of the original wooden wheels with a set of steel wheels a year after purchase, the vehicle remained largely as built until it was withdrawn in the late 1940s. The fire engine did attend the fire caused by an air attack on the works in 1942 when one of the gas holders at the Company's gas works in Iffley Road was hit, and it is thought that this was its last major incident.

In 1942 the vehicle became a reserve when the Great Western replaced it with another Dennis, fitted with a semi-limousine body capable of seating up to seven firemen. Like its predecessor, it was not fitted with ladders, but was essentially a

One of the anti-aircraft sites at Swindon Works. This particular post was situated on the roof of the nearby Compton Sons & Webb factory.

mobile pump, capable of pumping around 600 gallons of water per minute. The body of the new fire engine was specially cut down, allowing it to run through some of the larger subways under the running lines. When delivered it was finished in wartime battleship grey livery although after the war it was repainted in a more familiar red livery.

Reporting the acquisition of the new vehicle, the *GWR Magazine* noted that "telephones, fire-fighting installations, static water and considerable mobile equipment are at the disposal of the Swindon Works Fire Brigade".[10] The brigade itself consisted of a chief officer, a second officer and 36 firemen, with twelve available for immediate call, and the remaining 24 being brought on duty when circumstances dictated.

The Company magazine article concluded by reporting that the changed circumstances of wartime had meant that the fire engines and other equipment were dispersed at various locations rather than concentrated at the works fire station, and that ARP fire squads were available in various parts of the works should an outbreak of fire be detected. A new ambulance was purchased by the Company in 1939 which was used in conjunction with fire brigade vehicles. The vehicle was a 4-cylinder 15cwt Fordson van which was converted into an ambulance by the Express Motor & Body Works Ltd of London. The vehicle was ordered by the Road Transport Department on behalf of the Locomotive Works Manager at Swindon on 5 October 1939, and cost £294 10s.

In 1942 a problem arose when the Auxiliary Fire Service requested that for uniformity, all hydrants and water valve covers should be painted yellow to aid identification in an emergency. This caused difficulties, since at Swindon, yellow paint was used to mark gas hydrants and valves, quite a different substance altogether! A GWR circular noted that in future, gas hydrants should be painted white to avoid any confusion.[11]

Bearing in mind the fairly elaborate precautions described, it comes as something of a mystery to discover that relatively speaking, Swindon escaped very lightly from the attentions of the Luftwaffe. During the course of the war Swindon was attacked a number of times, but in each case the raid was undertaken by small numbers of bombers or lone aircraft. Considering the immense size of the railway works, its strategic importance and the close proximity of other war factories and airfields, it seems amazing that it was not singled out for attack by German planes; in fact most of the attacks caused more damage to property outside the works perimeter when bombs fell wide of their target. In an article published on VE Day, the *Swindon Evening Advertiser* reported that in the Swindon ARP area, which also included some outlying villages such as Wroughton, there had been a total of 158 alerts and 104 bombs actually dropped. Casualties for the war period were 48 killed and 105 injured, 38 seriously; more than 50 houses were destroyed in air raids, and a further 1,852 suffered some form of damage.[12]

Considering the German forces extensive use of the rail network during their conquest of France and the Low Countries, perhaps Swindon was left alone by the Luftwaffe for future use when the Germans invaded England. We shall probably never know the reasons for Swindon's reprieve from bomb damage, but for the Company, it was a huge relief, since had the works been badly damaged, the railway would have been severely affected.

The first real test for ARP services within the town was on the night of Sunday 20 October 1940, when bombs fell on houses in Roseberry Street, near the Carriage and Wagon Works further bombs fell in nearby streets, but there was no damage to Great Western property. Extensive damage was caused, and ten people were killed in this attack, and in a further raid on the night of the 19/20 December 1940 when more casualties occurred. Once again the bombers missed the most of the works, bombs dropping in sidings and causing some damage to rolling stock. Beyond the

The shell production line in 24 Shop, Swindon Works with a predominantly female workforce.

Coaches provided for the firewatching parties at Swindon Works. In the foreground some of the 'cut and cover' air raid shelters can also be seen.

boundaries of the works five houses were completely destroyed and a number of others badly damaged. Many lucky escapes were reported in the local paper, amongst them a number of evacuees brought to the town by the Great Western to escape the Blitz.

Eighteen months later the most serious attack on Swindon Works took place; at 6.40am on 27 July 1942, another lone Heinkel He111 bomber attacked the northern part of the works, dropping five bombs, and causing extensive damage to the roofs and windows of the running shed and 24 Shop, which was being used by Short Brothers for munitions work. The oil gas main was damaged, and one of the gas holders in the gas works was machine-gunned by the plane, which set light to the gas. Local folklore has it that when the gas holder was hit, flames shot from the bullet holes burning furiously; gas works staff were said to have plugged the holes with clay until proper repairs could be carried out and the holes patched. It should be noted at this point that there were a number of anti-aircraft gun posts situated around the works, one being mounted on the roof of the Carriage Works offices, and another on the roof of one of the station buildings at Swindon Junction. Those around at the time of the raids reported that these positions were not terribly effective, partly because of the small calibre of the guns mounted on them, and also because staff were said to have

not reached their positions until the plane was nowhere to be seen! In his usual air raid damage report to the Great Western board, the General Manager noted that two Company employees had been injured in the raid, but the author has not been able to discover how serious the casualties were.[13] One minor casualty was an eyewitness to the raid who 44 years later remembered being knocked off his bicycle in the nearby Rodbourne Road, by a bomb blast, sustaining injured ribs.[14]

There were two further raids in 1942 which had worse consequences than those previously endured by the Swindon population. The highest number of casualties suffered in any one raid occurred at 11pm on 17 August 1942 when a lone German bomber swooped low over the town and dropped bombs which hit houses in Ferndale Road and Kembrey Street, again close to the Works, which suggests that the bombs may have fallen wide of their target. In this raid 24 people lost their lives and 35 were injured. The final attack of the war occurred on the 29 August, when the town suffered its only experience of stratosphere bombing, when a single bomb was dropped from a height of about 38,000 feet killing eight and damaging over 300 houses. Once again the railway works was not hit in the raid.

The general secrecy about many aspects of the railway's workings was remarked on in the introduction to this book, and nowhere was this

A general view at Swindon, taken from the roof of the A Shop in March 1941. The camouflaged Newburn carriage shed can be seen in the background.

secrecy more apparent than in the work undertaken by Swindon for the war effort. There is only limited information and correspondence available, and descriptions of some of the jobs undertaken can only be gleaned from New Work Orders issued by the Company, and a number of photographs which were taken for future reference by the works photographer. These pictures, and their negatives were always kept locked away from view, and even after the war, access to them was limited.

Alan Peck, in his comprehensive history of Swindon Works (OPC), noted that most of the munitions work was done between 1941 and 1943; the entry of the United States into the war, and the resultant influx of American equipment eased the pressure on the munitions industry in Britain. Looking at the surviving Swindon records, the New Works Order books which were full of orders for all manner of munitions and military equipment in 1942 and 1943, change character markedly in 1944. From this date their content becomes predominantly concerned with modernisation and upgrading of Company facilities such as the installation of electric lighting and the provision of additional facilities for the increased traffic using the railway; this category including the installation of extra sidings, water columns, and staff messrooms, especially those for female staff.

It is not proposed here to describe in detail every job undertaken by the works in this period; that task would fill a book in its itself, and hopefully the following will instead give the reader some idea of the broad range of tasks carried out by the factory. A good proportion of the work done was concerned with the production of bombs and shells; by 1941 demands were being made for both mortar and aircraft bombs and the order books are full of references to these, with over 60,000 being produced in total. Swindon, always known for its ability to turn its hand to any task allotted to it, undertook the design of various sizes of bombs, including over 2,000 of the heavy 4,000lb type.

Such was the urgency of the task, that the first dozen bombs of this type were constructed within a few days of discussions taking place between Swindon staff and ministry officials; a further 88 were supplied, and subsequently used on a raid on Essen. It was said that to maintain the veil of secrecy over their production, the 2,000lb bombs were always referred to as a 'Goebbel' and its heavier counterpart was called a 'Goering'.[15] An example of a typical job was an order for 2,000 500lb bombs placed by the Ministry of Aircraft Production in May 1942; these were presumably done in batches, since records show that the job was not completed until June the following year.[16]

A much quicker turnaround was required for an order for the machining of 30 1,000lb bombs, which was completed in around six weeks in the spring of 1942. The skills and precision techniques available in the numerous machine shops in the works were in great demand by munitions manufacturers; often material was required very quickly, and an example of this occurred on 5 March 1942 when an order for 448 copper bands for 9.2in howitzer shells was placed by the Dundee firm of Urquhart, Libdsay & Robertson Orchar Ltd. Records show that the rings were ready within two weeks.[17] Whilst this order was being worked on, another was received, this time placed by the Royal Arsenal at Woolwich, who needed 2,400 annealed copper rings for shells.[18] Presumably some discussion had already taken place about the order, since the original letter from the military authorities had been written in January. Even so, the order was executed extremely quickly, and the rings were finished by 13 April 1942, just over a month after the order was placed.

In the months that followed the Battle of Britain, the works also provided components for aircraft; over 171,000 parts for Hurricane fighters were produced, and it was also reported that the Carriage Finishers Shop did build some timber assemblies for this particular fighter. In a good example of the secrecy prevalent at the time, a later order placed in 1943 refers to work done for the Hawker Aircraft Company, but gives no detail as to its nature. In general however, the workshops were more concerned with the production of component parts rather than the assembly of larger pieces of equipment; an example of this occurred in February 1942 with an order for "Sundry work for Fairey Aviation of Hayes".[19] One of the bigger orders discovered however, was one for the supply of 30,000 suspension lugs for 500lb bombs carried out for the Ministry of Aircraft Production, which lasted for well over a year.[20]

The Works also had a hand in the production of guns of various sizes and types; the largest by far dealt with was the redesign of the mountings for a 13.5in 'hyper velocity' gun which was to be situated on the Kent coastline for firing at German positions on the French Coast. Swindon draughtsmen made alterations to the arrangement of the gun and its mountings, although the actual

The crew of HMS Australia *are seen on a visit to Swindon Works in July 1945, lining 'King' class 4-6-0 No. 6021 King Richard II. F. W. Hawksworth, the Chief Mechanical Engineer, can be seen in the middle of the group.*

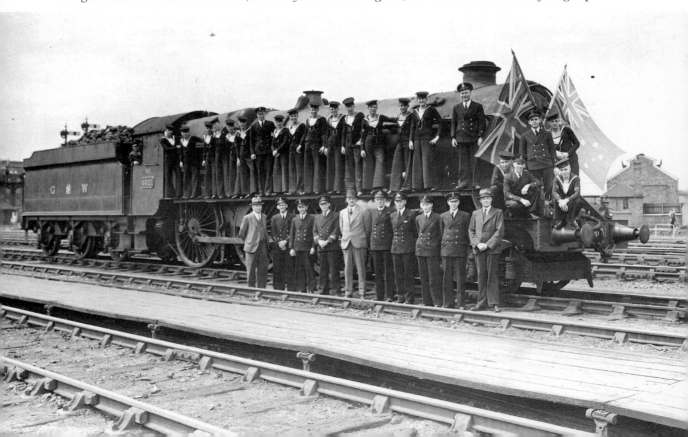

assembly and installation of the equipment was done by a specialist firm. Less powerful, but no less important was the construction of literally thousands of parts for Hotchkiss, Oerlikon and 'Pom Pom' guns; an example of this work was an order for 7,000 covers for 40mm Bofors anti-aircraft guns placed in December 1941 which was not completed until February 1944.[21] Another similar task was the manufacture of 4,000 steel springs for 3.7in anti-aircraft gun mountings placed in February 1942; this too was a long-term job, not being completed until the following March.[22]

One of the first tasks to be completed by Swindon for the military authorities was the machining of 12,500 turret bearings for armoured cars, and throughout the period the works made many thousands of component parts, such as clutches, final drives and other similar items. On 13 February 1942 an order was placed for 500 base junctions for the traversing gear of Cruiser tanks.[23] This task was undertaken for the Tolworth firm of Powered Mountings Ltd and was finally completed in September the same year. An example of the variety of different organisations asking Swindon for assistance can be gained from the case of a request in early 1942 by a Major J. H. Fox of the 5th Canadian Armoured Division, for the manufacture of 'special tank tools'; unfortunately yet again, no detail of what was produced has survived.

Thus far much of the discussion has centred around work done by the Locomotive Works; the Carriage Works played an important role too, and its reputation for work of the highest quality led to it undertaking projects requiring great skill and precision. One good example of this was the construction of a full size replica "Besa" machine gun, used by the military authorities in ongoing tank design; another model constructed was that of a midget submarine; this was intended for training in loading and unloading from parent ships, but its production ultimately led to the building of 50 superstructures for these craft. Constructed in mahogany, they carried two personnel, and were mounted on what were essentially torpedoes. Craft of this type were used in the successful attack on the German battleship *Tirpitz* in September 1943.

Two other fairly unusual tasks carried out by the Carriage Works for the war effort illustrate the need for the works to adapt to all requests from outside sources. The first was a request to kiln dry an unspecified quantity of timber for the Bristol firm of May & Hassell in December 1943,[24] and the other was on order from the Somerset shoe manufacturer C. & J. Clark of Street, for 250 pairs of wooden soles for shoes in November the same year. The size 6 soles were delivered as requested and the order was recorded as being completed on 16 December.[25]

As early as August 1941 preparations for the opening of the Second Front in Europe began to gather momentum, and the Carriage Works did further important work for the Admiralty, in the form of the construction of powered landing craft for the coming invasion. Swindon also assisted in the production of Bailey bridges and supplied 25,157 timber components and 13,700 packing timbers.[26]

Much work was done by the workshops in manufacturing items for use on the Home Front including parts for searchlights, radar equipment, and the production of 21,685 sets of 'quick release' gear for barrage balloons. The latter item must have been a somewhat ironic task for the Swindon authorities, since within the same New Work Order books used for this job are contained many requests for repairs of GWR equipment damaged by barrage balloons!

The secrecy mentioned earlier in the chapter was apparent by the use of canvas screening around 'sensitive' locations; staff were also discouraged from wandering around the factory, and many temporary staff employed in munitions work were totally unaware of the magnitude of the factory, since they were only allowed to walk from the works entrance to their actual place of work. To the north of the works, part of 24 Shop, one of the more modern workshops was handed over to Short Bros for the production of Spitfire aircraft, and functioned as a separate entity, even to the extent of being protected by a different Home Guard Unit than the rest of the works complex. The new carriage shed on the site of the Chief Mechanical Engineer's residence Newburn House was also handed over to the authorities for use as a store in 1939; within months of its completion, its new paintwork was covered with camouflage. Extensive alterations were made to the building, costing £18,000 these were paid for by the Ministry of Supply, who were also to pay for its reconversion after the war.[27]

This brief sample of some of the work done by the Great Western at Swindon for the war effort will hopefully have given the reader some impression of the strain put on both management,

One of the landing craft built for the admiralty, seen outside 13 Shop, Swindon Works on 22 January 1943.

men and machines during the period. Inevitably these stresses took their toll in a number of ways not least on the staff itself. The shortages described in the previous chapter were mirrored at Swindon, with the gradual increase in conscription reducing the numbers of skilled workmen available. A further problem was that under the concept of Direction of Labour the government could send skilled staff to other locations to run the many new factories and munitions facilities being set up. Writing to the Great Western at the end of 1942, the Regional Controller of the Ministry of Supply in Bristol noted that what he called a "comb out" of staff had enabled British forces to "smite the enemy so effectively".[28] The substitution of skilled men he added, would " inevitably cause inconvenience and throw a heavier burden on those already, no doubt in many cases, overloaded".[29] As early as the autumn of 1940 it was reported that nearly 900 staff had already been loaned to outside firms; new staff, often female, had to be be trained, and as was mentioned in the last chapter, facilities and amenities had to be provided for their use too.

Conditions for those staff not conscripted can hardly be described as ideal; long hours were worked, and many men worked day and night shifts in weekly rotation. That most famous of Swindon institutions, the Trip Holiday for employees and their families was cancelled in 1940; even if they could have travelled, the men would probably have found beaches at their favourite locations, such as Weymouth and Weston-super-Mare, covered in tank traps and barbed wire! The war situation was so serious in 1940 that a GWR circular noted that the government had decided that "the usual Bank Holiday on Boxing Day, December 26th will be cancelled this year".[30]

Perhaps as a result of the more difficult working conditions, and the stresses of wartime, Swindon management made a quite significant concession to staff in September 1940; this was to allow staff to smoke in the workshops. This concession was however limited to overtime hours only, and was not permitted in workshops where woodwork or inflammable material was used. In March 1941 however, the ban on smoking generally was completely withdrawn, on the proviso that staff were to "avoid annoyance to non-smokers and...they do not in any way add to the risk of fire."[31] Despite this relaxation of the rules, the Company attempted to maintain discipline within the factory; a circular issued in 1942 recorded that "office messengers are frequently being used for carrying out private commissions in the town for members of staff to the detriment of their proper duties".[32]

Another more long standing concession was the supply of coal to Great Western staff; despite the many shortages suffered by the population during the war period, staff were still able to maintain this privilege. Coal was bought by the Company in bulk, and sold to its staff at a discount rate; in view of the difficulties experienced in obtaining it, staff were urged in May 1941 "to build up stocks during the period June to September inclusive".[33] In the same month, a list compiled by the staff office at Swindon illustrates just how many staff did make use of this facility; within the Chief Mechanical Engineer's Department 16,652 staff received coal from the company. This total included 1,500 retired workmen, and 700 widows of company servants.[34] An additional perk was the supply of scrap or refuse timber which again despite shortages, continued throughout the war period, albeit at a reduced rate on occasions.

The effects of the war and the concentration of workshop activity on munitions production had serious effects on the maintenance of Great Western locomotives and the building of new stock. At a special meeting of superintendents held at Swindon in July 1943, Hawksworth referred to meetings he had attended at the Ministry of War Transport, where it had been emphasised that new building, and the maintenance of repairs were of the highest importance. He went on to note that the availability of GWR locomotives had actually declined in the previous year the total awaiting repair increasing from 260 to 373. This poor result had meant that the construction of new locomotives had been reduced as a consequence, from 120 to 67 locomotives. He had called the meeting he noted, to put before them "the importance of keeping as many engines as possible turning their wheels."[35] At the end of 1944 an analysis of locomotive failures was done, and some of the main results are listed below:

Class	1941 No. of Engines	Failures	1944 No. of Engines	Failures
49xx	231	81	270	196
43xx	242	119	242	111
30xx	50	25	50	66
26xx	32	24	31	37

Figures based on three months ending 6/12/41 and 25/11/44.

A picture taken at the opening of the new canteen in the Carriage and Wagon Works at Swindon on 16 September 1943.

Looking at the causes of locomotive failure, by far the highest proportion of problems were related to boiler, firebox and smokebox defects which in most cases accounted for over 50 per cent of the faults reported. Many of these problems were caused by shortages of staff, and poor maintenance at sheds. Basic tasks such as the cleaning of boiler tubes, and the regular washing out of boilers were not done properly; a circular issued in August 1943 revealed that some locomotives were over seven weeks overdue for boiler washing, and the number of overdue locomotives each week had significantly risen from the previous year.[36] New systems were introduced to try to improve matters, and by 1944 it was reported that boilers were getting more attention, but Mr Hawksworth thought there was still plenty of room for improvement.[37]

What these problems meant to Swindon was that many locomotives came into the works for repairs needing much more work than they would have done in normal peacetime conditions. The introduction of a new organisation the Locomotive Shopping Control in 1943 was intended to improve matters by identifying engines which needed repair, allowing the work programme to be forecast and planned, rather than having locomotives idle waiting to be taken into the works when space and time was available. Lists were compiled, noting locomotives needing repair, and these were then circulated to each depot in due course.

New construction did continue during the war years, and although what follows is an outline of some of the main developments at Swindon during the 1939–1945 period, it is not proposed however, to devote a large amount of space to a subject already covered in some detail by other distinguished railway historians. Between the two World Wars, C. B. Collett, the Chief Mechanical Engineer at Swindon continued the process of development of Great Western locomotives begun by his predecessor Churchward in the early years of the 20th century. With the outbreak of hostilities, construction therefore initially continued on a 'business as usual' basis with further examples of 'Castle' and 'Hall' class 4-6-0 designs, and various heavy freight locomotives including the 2800 class 2-8-0, and the 4200 class 2-8-0 tank locomotives. It was intended to build 60 of the former locomotives for overseas service, but after the fall of France this order was cancelled.

In 1940 in response to events happening in the

skies over Britain, the Company decided to rename a number of 'Castle' class locomotives after various British aircraft, some of which had played an important role in the Battle of Britain. Fittingly the first to be renamed was No. 5071 *Clifford Castle* which became *Spitfire*; it was thought at the time that the action of renaming the locomotive would also boost the collection of funds for Spitfire aircraft, a scheme mentioned in an earlier chapter. The other names chosen included *Hurricane, Blenheim, Hampden, Wellington, Gladiator, Fairey Battle, Beaufort, Lysander, Defiant, Lockheed Hudson* and *Swordfish*. Some of the aircraft listed were, even by 1940, fairly elderly and not quite in the same category as the Spitfire or Hurricane! The *GWR Magazine* however, proudly announced the decision arguing that the development would have the enthusiastic approval of our patrons and the staff.[38] A major milestone occurred in 1941 however, with the retirement of C. B. Collett, after 19 years in charge at Swindon; reporting the end of the 'Collett influence' the *Railway Gazette* remarked that his "quiet and helpful manner overcame many difficulties and gained for him the confidence and respect of the men in the department over which he presided".[39] His replacement was F. W. Hawksworth, Swindon born and bred, who already had over 40 years service on the Great Western, having joined the company in 1898. Few observers were expecting any radical departure from Great Western tradition, and in any case, the stringencies of the war gave Hawksworth little opportunity to introduce too many new developments; however, having waited a good many years for the chance, Hawksworth was keen to introduce some of his own ideas.

It was not until March 1944 that the public saw the first of his designs, the 'Modified Hall' class, which included a new frame design, and new cylinder and superheater fittings. The first engine, No. 6959, was followed by a further 70 locomotives, the last not being completed until 1950. Both the modified type and the original Collett design of 'Hall' class locomotives built after June 1941 ran unnamed until after the end of hostilities. The public had to wait until after VE Day to see Hawksworth's first completely new design for an express passenger locomotive; in August 1945 the first of the 'County' class, No. 1000 *County of Middlesex* was built at Swindon. Although superficially bearing many of the characteristics of previous Swindon designs, the

'Counties' had a number of new features, including a one-piece frame design, similar to that used in the 'Modified Hall' class, and a new design of boiler with a higher working pressure of 280lb sq inch.

The works also turned out locomotives for the War Department as well as producing its own engines and as the war progressed locomotives were required for use overseas, especially for routes such as those linking Russia and Iran. In October 1941 the General Manager reported that the 'Controller for Railways' had informed the Railway Executive Committee that the cabinet had decided that 150 locomotives belonging to the British Railways must be released "as a matter of urgency" for use overseas.[40] This request could hardly have come at a worse time for any of the Big Four railways, and as we have seen at Swindon, the increase in munitions work had led to a consequent reduction in the construction of new locomotives, while freight traffic in the coming months and years was likely to dramatically increase not decrease.

Swindon's contribution towards the solution of

the problem posed by the government was to construct 80 LMS 8F class Stanier 2-8-0 freight locomotives; orders for the engines were placed in 1942, and production was limited by the availability of raw materials. As a result, 27 were built at Swindon in 1943, a further 36 in 1944, and the final 17 in the final year of the war. It was perhaps rather ironic that Swindon was building locomotives originating from one of their closest rivals, but apt that they were to the design of a former Swindon man, William Stanier.

The conversion of elderly Dean Goods locomotives is probably better known. At the outbreak of the war, a good number of the class had already been withdrawn, and nine which had recently been taken out of service, were hurriedly reinstated. On 5 October 1939 the Chief Mechanical Engineer reported to the GWR Locomotive Committee that the reconditioning of 100 Dean Goods locomotives was to take place for the War Department for service overseas. To ease the pressure on the works, he further reported, 20 were to be dealt with by the Southern Railway.[41] In the event only 15 were prepared at Eastleigh, while

A wooden mock-up of a Besa 95mm machine gun, which shows something of the craftsmanship practised in the Carriage & Wagon Works at Swindon.

One of the Dean Goods locomotives converted for War Department use, somewhere in France. This particular engine, formerly GWR No. 2533, was renumbered 101 by the War Department. (Steamchest Collection)

Swindon dealt with the rest. Conversion involved the removal of Automatic Train Control apparatus and the fitting of Westinghouse braking; all were turned out in War Department black livery, and a number were fitted with pannier tanks and condensing equipment. With the invasion of France, 79 Dean Goods locomotives fell into German hands; reporting the loss of these in July 1940, the General Manager also noted that 39 wagons and two containers had also been lost. With this development the engines, which had been loaned to the government, were formally written off, and compensation paid by the government for their loss. Not all the locomotives were destroyed in the retreat from Dunkirk, and some continued to work on French Railways during the occupation. A further eight engines were requested by the War Department in December 1940, and the subsequent travels of the surviving engines led them to far flung parts of the globe such as China, Tunisia and Italy.[42]

To compensate for the loss of these locomotives, the Great Western borrowed various 0-6-0 tender engines from the LMS and the LNER; in 1939 26 ex-Midland Railway 2F class locomotives were loaned by the LMS, with a further 17 being borrowed in 1940. The LNER supplied 24 J25 class locomotives in 1939, adding another 16 the following year while 30 O4 class 2-8-0s were also sent to the Great Western in the same year.[43] Further Great Western 2251 class Collett designed goods locomotives were also built at Swindon in 1940 to bridge the gap.

One further method by which Swindon attempted to cope with the shortage of locomotives during the war period was by the reinstatement of withdrawn engines, and the retention of old designs which were due for scrapping. Statistics noting the number of engines withdrawn during the period clearly identify how the GWR 'made do' with aging locomotives. In 1939 114 were withdrawn, and the following year the total was 112; this figure was deceiving however, since it included the 'Dean Goods' locomotives just referred to. The following year, 1941, when the effects of the war were really being felt, only two locomotives were withdrawn, one of these being No. 4911 *Bowden Hall*, which had been badly damaged in the Keyham incident described in Chapter 6. Figures for locomotives withdrawn in 1942, 1943 and 1944 were five, four, and 19 respectively and it was not until 1945 that withdrawals restarted in earnest with 91 being recorded.[44]

What this process meant was that numerous elderly locomotives such as 'Bulldog' 4-4-0s and 'Aberdare' 2-6-0's, many of which had over 40 years service, continued to run, giving sterling service in the cause of the war effort. In both 1939 and 1940 withdrawn locomotives were reinstated and placed on 'government account' and loaned back to the GWR for the course of the war. One example of this group was 'Bulldog' class locomotive No. 3378 *River Tawe*, built in 1903, the engine was withdrawn in February 1939, and the nameplates removed. The engine was returned to stock on 26 October 1939 and ran for the rest of the war until being finally withdrawn in December 1945. The locomotive had accumulated an additional 123,261 miles of service before scrapping, having run a total of 1,192,738 miles.[45]

Before leaving discussion on Swindon locomotive matters during the Second World War period, it ought to be finally mentioned that the austerity and drabness caused by the shortages of materials described earlier in the book also manifested itself in the livery adopted by the Company for its locomotives in 1942. In April of that year, paint was in such short supply that F. W. Hawksworth was forced to write to all his divisional superintendents informing them that in view of the difficulties being encountered, "all engines and tenders, with the exception of 'Kings' and 'Castles' will be painted black when they require painting after building or repairs. No engines will be lined after they have been painted."[46]

Matters were no easier for staff in the Carriage and Wagon Works; a similar circular was issued less than a month later, instructing that, due to a shortage of constituents for the mixing of cream paint, and also to increase the output of the coach painting section, it had been decided that for the war period coaches should be painted all-brown instead of brown and cream. The circular actually listed the new method of painting to be adopted

The Swindon Works Home Guard Battalion march past the Iron Foundry in the Works on 17 November 1940.

which entailed the following: "Coach Sides: 1 coat of grey on all cream panels, 1 coat of brown on sides complete, 2 coats of varnish on sides complete. Ends: 1 coat black, 1 coat varnish."[47]

The only exception to this ruling was to be what Hawksworth termed 'special coaches' which included "Cornish Riviera" stock, Super Saloons, and diesel railcars. Mention of the latter merits noting that the Second World War saw the construction of the first diesel railcars to be built by the Company rather than purchased from outside contractors. Railcars Nos 19 to 38 differed from those previously operated by the Company in that they did not have the aerodynamically streamlined bodywork of the first 18 vehicles, the GWR opting instead for a more angular and workmanlike design.

Fitted with two AEC engines, the railcars had a lower top speed than the streamlined batches, being limited to 40mph, with the exception of Nos 19 and 20 which were built to run to a 60mph maximum, and the last four cars which were designed as two-car units capable of 70mph. The Swindon Works drawing office description of the interior of the railcars noted that "the saloons are pleasingly decorated in coloured rexine effect with polished mahogany mouldings".[48] It was also noted that owing to blackout regulations, "additional curtains have had to be fitted to the vestibule, windows darkened, and blinds added in the luggage compartment".[49] The first railcar completed was No. 20, which appeared in June 1940, and the last, No. 38, finally emerged from the works in February 1942. It should also be mentioned that two of the earlier type of railcars, Nos 6 and 19, were loaned to the LNER in 1944, being used in the Newcastle area, although their trip north lasted less than a year.

Enormous problems were experienced in the wagon repair section of the works, which was under great pressure even from the earliest days of the war; demands from the government and the railways themselves for the rapid turnaround of rolling stock, compounded by shortages of labour and materials made life very difficult. The Chief Goods Manager at Paddington wrote to C. B. Collett on 3 December 1940 regarding the problems of wagon stock facing the Company, and although unfortunately his original letter has not survived, the reply given by Collett does give a good idea of the difficulties faced. He wrote that he fully appreciated the situation and said that he was

doing all he could to help.[50] The problem was, he noted, the movement of vehicles to Swindon and other repair workshops. He continued, "there are plenty of wagons marked off for repairs but we are unable to get them expeditiously to the shops, neither are we able to clear the shops of those that are repaired."[51]

The Chief Mechanical Engineer reported that there were 200 wagons waiting to be taken away, and that similar problems were being experienced at collieries, where there were plenty of loaded wagons ready to be collected, but not enough motive power to move them. As a temporary measure, divisional superintendents were instructed to ask staff to work overtime on Saturdays and Sundays to try to alleviate the situation. The pooling of wagon stock described in Chapter 1 had also not helped, since not all the private owner wagons now part of the 'Common User' fleet had been particularly well maintained in the past, and some considerable effort was expended in some cases in keeping the maximum number of vehicles in use. As a result, a large amount of paperwork was generated by the Railway Executive Committee and the railway companies about the level of repairs to be done on private owner wagons, since the railways were obviously reluctant to spend large amounts of money on rolling stock they did not own.

As the war progressed, and demands for rolling stock increased, a priority system was introduced for the repair of crippled wagons. In September 1942 a circular was issued which listed in detail which wagons should be tackled first. At the top of the list were brake vans, which were in very short supply, next came specially constructed wagons and bogie bolster wagons used for the transportation of tanks and other military equipment, then covered vans, and finally open wagons last.[52] Shortages of paint, also affected wagon stock and in 1942 it was decided that all covered vans should be painted in bauxite residue livery. The circular continued, "open goods wagons will in future not be painted, with the exception of left hand quarter boards".[53] This panel was used for lettering and numbering, which itself was smaller than in prewar days, again to conserve zinc white paint, which was in extremely short supply. The shortages suffered even at this early stage in the war were to continue for some time yet, and it would be many years before Swindon Works fully recovered from its wartime exertions.

10
Prelude to D-Day

On the afternoon of 22 February 1944, General Sir Bernard Montgomery met in secret a group of railwaymen of all grades and from all companies, to ask for their support for their part in the operation which was to open up the Second Front in Europe. He said, "I am confident that I can rely upon you continuing to give your utmost cooperation in providing the necessary transport for the forces..."[1] This cooperation he continued, would lead to complete victory. The extensive preparation and planning for D-Day will be touched on later in this chapter, but it is important to note that the speech delivered by Montgomery on that February afternoon was not only a prelude of things to come, but also an affirmation of the valuable work done by the railways up to that point.

Preparations for the opening of the Second Front had started many months before Montomery's speech, and the Great Western, like the other main line railways, had played a crucial role in the movement of military personnel and equipment, to the detriment of the ordinary travelling public as we have seen. As D-Day approached however, the demands placed on the Company would be greater than they could imagine.

Without doubt the dock facilities owned by the Great Western, particularly those in South Wales, played a crucial role in the war effort, not only as a place where raw materials, military equipment, food, troops and other items were unloaded, but also as sites for the departure of the invasion forces in June 1944. In a promotional handbook issued in 1938, the Company boasted their docks had been the "greatest sustaining factor in the power of South Wales to resist the adverse blows of the general world depression in trade".[2] The total value of trade dealt with at the docks in the previous year had been over 24 million tons, a considerable amount, but one which was to be exceeded in the very near future. The optimism shown in the Company's official publications was not reflected by the trade figures reported the following year; the uncertainties caused by the international situation had led to decreases in both coal exports and exports of other British industries such as steel and tinplate. This meant heavy losses being suffered by the Company compared with the previous year.

Although the docks owned by the GWR were well equipped and maintained, the factor which changed their destiny during the war years was the switch from east to west coast ports caused by the German invasion of Europe. This move had been foreshadowed by a more general campaign which the Great Western participated in during the years running up to the war. Anticipating that London and the South East might be a target area in any war, the Company advertised what they called the "Call of the West", a poster issued in 1939 urging industrialists to resite their factories in the West. "It may be vital to your business in the future" the poster warned.[3] The campaign was fairly successful, with 91 businesses relocating to GWR territory in South Wales and the West Country; unfortunately, moving west did not guarantee safety from bombing raids, as the inhabitants of

United States troops disembarking form the SS Santa Rosa at Swansea Docks wait for a train to their new base.

Bristol, Exeter, Plymouth and Cardiff among others could testify.

The Atlantic blockade however, meant that the Great Western's docks in South Wales became the nearest and best equipped port of call for ships which had made the hazardous crossing from America. The number of ships using Great Western facilities and the tonnages of cargoes loaded and unloaded was often recorded in the General Manager's board reports, and these give a clear indication of the way in which traffic handled increased as the war progressed. At the end of January 1940 it was noted that since September 1939, 194 ships had been loaded for the government, consisting of over 213,664 tons of stores, petrol and ammunition. This figure included 10,000 vehicles and over 13,000 troops. All this activity had been due to the movement of the British Expeditionary Force to France. Only 19 vessels had been diverted from East Coast ports since the outbreak of hostilities; the low number of ships being diverted did not increase until the fall of France in June.[4]

In the early part of the war little traffic is noted as being unloaded, and this was still the case even in October 1940, when the General Manager's report records that only 414 vessels had been loaded with cargoes totalling 487,555 tons, between July and the end of September. The tightening of the Atlantic blockade was becoming apparent though, with 45 ships carrying over 244,000 tons of imports being diverted from East Coast ports. This situation changed dramatically as the war progressed and large amounts of Lend-Lease goods from the United States began to arrive. By August 1942 American supplies began to arrive in great quantity; in October 1942 for example, 29 ships had berthed at South Wales docks, with over 57,000 tons of traffic being unloaded.[5]

Much of the material unloaded was vital equipment for the prosecution of the war; aircraft, tanks and other items of equipment were the norm, and as preparations for D-Day began, armoured cars, locomotives, landing craft and other supplies arrived in ever larger quantities. The pounding taken by the British fleet in the Battle of the Atlantic led to the use of mass produced Liberty ships being supplied by the United States. These vessels maintained the lifeline between Britain and America. Collie Knox, in his wartime account of the Great Western described the arrival of such ships at Cardiff Docks, writing that, "their cargoes gave me a thrill of pride when I reflected on all that these brave ships and their crews had dared before they could arrive at their destination".[6]

Although well equipped, the docks required a good deal of new craneage, to make sure that the facilities were kept free from congestion and in April 1941 it was reported that the Prime Minister considered it essential that the tonnage of imported traffic dealt with at the South Wales docks should be materially increased forthwith.[7] Over 50 new electric cranes had been installed in the previous year, and ten more 6-ton electric cranes were supplied to Swansea in 1942, with Barry receiving a further four of the same type. Swindon Works, which was responsible for the repair and maintenance of dock facilities, had helped in the construction of these cranes, and also assisted in the provision of all manner of other equipment and facilities such as improvements to lighting, staff accommodation and extra sidings.

The situation had not improved even by December 1943, when the General Manager reported that "freight traffic is extremely high, particularly at the Company's Docks, where large numbers of heavy cased vehicles are being landed".[8] The lack of high capacity cranes to lift cases from quays had caused difficulties he noted, and staff sickness had also slowed down the task of unloading. The Great Western did have a floating 100-ton crane, but this was not enough on its own, and the government approved the construction of seven 50-ton floating derrick cranes designed by the Chief Docks Manager, Mr W. J. Thomas. Further 30-ton floating cranes were also loaned to the Docks at Cardiff, Newport and Swansea by the United States forces, doing sterling work before being moved across the Channel after the Allied invasion.

As well as dealing with the loading and unloading of cargoes of all shapes, sizes and weights, Great Western docks also carried out repairs to ships which had suffered at the hands of German 'U' boats or mines *en route* from the United States. Such was the volume of work that in March 1942 the Chief Mechanical Engineer's Department at Swindon was asked to "provide improved electric lighting at dry docks to enable repair work to be carried out during the hours of

Three very different 2-8-0 locomotives about to leave Oxford North Junction for Yarnton Yard, to work cross country freight trains: LMS 8F No. 8427, GWR 2800 class No. 2805 and USA S160 class No. 2270. (Great Western Trust Collection)

The SS Santa Rosa, an example of one of the ships which braved the Atlantic, bringing troops and supplies to Britain, is seen arriving at Cardiff Docks in 1943.

darkness".[9] This order referred to facilities at Barry, Cardiff and Newport Docks. On occasions however, the company also had to carry out repairs to damage caused by the 'guests' they were entertaining in their facilities and on 24 July 1942 the American ship the SS *Henry R. Mallory* struck the west inner gate of the South lock at Newport Docks, knocking the gate from its pivot, and completely paralysing the port by blocking the whole lock complex. The boat was finally moved into the dock the next day, but the renewal of the gates was not completed until the beginning of September, causing a great deal of inconvenience.

Considerable new facilities also grew up around the South Wales docks, many built for the government or the War Department. One of the largest cold stores in Britain was constructed at the Queen Alexandra Dock in Cardiff and costing over £300,000, the store was the repository for cargoes of meat and butter discharged from ships from Australia and New Zealand. Having inspected the inside of this great warehouse, Collie Knox, writing

in 1944 when rationing was still all too familiar a part of British life, wryly noted that "ton after ton of food comes in...ton after ton goes out...and our Food Minister in his wisdom doles it out to us in driblets".[10] At Barry and Port Talbot, facilities for the discharging of oil and other petroleum products were also constructed.

The strategic importance of the docks had meant that they suffered a great deal from the attention of the Luftwaffe; some of the damage done in the early part of the war has already been described, and as preparations for the invasion of Europe built up, so air attacks continued. On 16 February 1943 over 300 wagons and large amounts of trackwork were destroyed in a raid on the Kings Dock at Swansea;[11] in May a serious attack on Cardiff caused slight damage in the Docks, although the General station seems to have suffered more, with the refreshment rooms and staff hostel being badly affected. During the raid the 9.25pm Paddington to South Wales train was machine-gunned, with two soldiers being injured, one fatally.

The labour shortages suffered by the railway in general were mirrored in the Docks Department; the need to unload vessels quickly was all important, and matters were not helped by shortages or the traditionally poor labour relations in the docks. Matters were improved however by the introduction of what later became known as the National Dock Labour Scheme, which abolished the old casual labour system, and replaced it with arrangements whereby dockers were registered as a permanent labour force, and received a guaranteed minimum wage, in return for agreeing to work where and when they were needed. Port Labour Inspectors could then direct labour to where it was required, and meant that congestion in ports was not a major problem after 1941.

Under these arrangements some dockers were redeployed from East Coast ports to locations such as South Wales and Bristol, relieving some of the shortages; even with these extra staff, Company officials had to resort to assistance from the British Army, and the United States Army who supplied large numbers of troops to unload Lend-Lease cargoes. Troops undertook a variety of work including quayside and stevedore work, crane driving, and cargo checking duties.[12] Knox remarked that American troops working at Cardiff Docks in 1943 made a heartening sight, with "their mouths working steadily the beloved products of Mr Wrigley's Gum...they looked reliant and tough".[13] Large numbers of women were also employed in the docks, and in 1943, Cardiff alone employed over 100, carrying out a wide variety of

Paddington station was the scene of a number of serious air raids, this incident taking place on 22 March 1944 when a bomb hit platforms 6 and 7. (National Railway Museum)

An Ambulance Train at Kennington Junction near Oxford in 1944; LNER B12 class 4-6-0 No. 8557 is being piloted by GWR 2-6-0 No. 5303. (Great Western Trust Collection)

tasks, including crane driving, loading, checking and labelling.

The hive of activity which the docks must have presented in the war period is hard to imagine; however, their primary aim was to unload cargoes as quickly as possible to enable them to be moved to depots, factories and stores well away from the coast where it could be safely housed away from the attentions of German bombers. Thus the Great Western played yet another key role: the movement of goods from ports, which was only one part of its enormous freight operation during the war period. In 1944 the BBC broadcast a now famous radio programme entitled *Junction X*, which painted a portrait of a day in the life of railway junction during the build up to D-Day; the programme showed the enormous pressures railwaymen were under, and highlighted that although the safe arrival of a convoy in the docks was a victory, "The railways have to pay the price of that victory".[14]

One traffic traditionally handled in great amounts by the Great Western in South Wales was coal. All the docks had been built for, and set up to handle large quantities of coal which was exported

all over the world. Coal exports had begun to decline before the outbreak of war, but the fall of France in 1940, had a catastrophic effect on the coal business in South Wales. In 1941 it was reported that exports had declined by 13.5 million tons since June 1940, and faced with this loss of trade the colliery companies made strenuous efforts to increase sales in the domestic market. Due to increased freight traffic generated by the war however, the Great Western was not prepared to accept additional coal traffic to inland destinations; the General Manager reporting the matter to the board in January 1941 and declared that despite criticism from coal owners, the Company did not feel that they could accept any more coal traffic than in the previous year.

Eventually a compromise was reached whereby the Company and the South Wales Coal Executive Board met on a weekly basis to agree a weekly total of coal to be moved, based on a list of areas where demand for coal was highest; the two parties also agreed a list of collieries from which the coal was to be exported in that particular week. The Company also made a number of special arrangements to increase the number of trains which could be handled; a number of passenger trains were suspended including the 3.55pm Paddington–Swansea service, and the 5.30pm Swansea–Paddington train. Two trains in each direction between Cardiff and Bristol, and Cardiff and Gloucester were also discontinued. The Severn Tunnel, which was normally closed on Sundays for maintenance, was kept open from March 1941.

By April 1941 these arrangements were allowing the movement of 120,000 tons of coal per week, an increase of 20 per cent on 1939. The General Manager reported that the government was pressing for this total to be increased to 150,000 tons, involving the running of a further eight trains per week. Matters were improved further in 1942 with the upgrading of signalling in the Severn Tunnel which had the effect of creating two block sections within the tunnel itself instead of one. Until the installation of new equipment, the 4-mile tunnel had been considered as one section only, allowing one train through in either direction at any one time. The addition of the extra section which included intermediate signalling inside the tunnel, meant that freight timings could be tightened up, reducing the bottleneck[15]

From time to time, the GWR was also asked to move large quantities of coal for other purposes, and on 16 January 1941, it arranged at very short notice to transport over 2,520 tons of coal from South Wales to Birkenhead at the request of the Navy. The diversion of much coal traffic from sea to rail because of the dangers to shipping placed extra demands on the railways, as did shortages of coal faced by various public utility companies such as electricity and gas companies. In the four weeks ending 21 February 1941, the Great Western ran 80 special coal trains of this type; it should be added that in the same period it also ran 297 troop trains and 228 munitions and equipment trains,[16] as well as its advertised passenger services and other freight trains, a situation which clearly illustrates the pressures faced by the Company in the war period.

A constant problem throughout the war period was a shortage of freight stock; the Company's circulars and reports are full of appeals to staff to make sure rolling stock was unloaded quickly and released back to collieries and depots as fast as possible. Writing to staff in August 1943, F. W. Hawksworth stated that freight train traffic was increasing, and considerable numbers of special trains were being run on behalf of the government.

He wrote, "Traffic Department staff are having to face up to the fact that there is every indication that in the coming months traffic will become heavier."[17] Even as early as 1940 the GWR was having considerable difficulties in meeting orders for vans and meat vans, and Swindon was urged to expedite repairs as quickly as possible. One solution to the shortage of vans was to convert the Company's stock of banana vans into ordinary box vans; in November 1942 orders were given to remove the flexible steam heating pipes from this stock, which also allowed these items to be used on other vehicles.[18] By this point in the war, bananas were almost impossible to obtain anyway, and the regular trains from Bristol's Avonmouth Docks were a thing of the past.

New wagon stock was ordered to attempt to combat some of the deficiencies, but shortages of materials and labour meant that new construction was not a speedy process. An example of this can be seen with an order for 1,500 open wagons, approved by the Locomotive Committee on 14 March 1940. Although a very basic design, the order was not completed until 13 January 1945.[19] A few months later another order was passed to the Carriage Works Manager Mr E. T. J. Evans, this time for 100 brake vans. These particular vehicles always seem to have been in short supply during the war era, and once again, there were regular calls to goods yards and depots to make sure that all such vehicles were released as quickly as possible. The order for 100 vans was finally finished in November 1943.[20] A further measure taken to increase the availability of brake vans was to abandon the system of allocation of vehicles which had been used for some years, in favour of the 'Common User' scheme adopted for most other freight vehicles. The only exception to this was the marking of vehicles running on special lines, such as those used on trips to the Smithfield depot in London.[21]

Two further measures to improve the wagon stock position were firstly to implement a scheme of uprating all open goods wagons built to the 1923 Railway Executive Committee standard, from 12 to 13 tons capacity; this covered all the requisitioned wagon stock, so this enormous task was done by a large number of depots including Wormwood Scrubbs, Newton Abbot, Pontypool Road, Bristol Barton Hill and Neath, as well as Swindon.[22] This increase in capacity made a substantial difference in the amount carried by the railway for a minimal

One of the 'Warwell' wagons loaned to the GWR for the carrying of tanks and other heavy military equipment. Photographed at Swindon in October 1943.

cost. The other measure carried out was a slight relaxation in the standards adopted by inspectors in withdrawing stock with defects. In January 1941 it was noted that concern had been expressed that vehicles were being taken out of service for repairs which did not interfere with their safe running.

A GWR circular of the era stated that "in other words, during the present emergency, more risks can be taken than in normal times".[23] Staff were instructed to allow more latitude in their examination of stock, and not to "mark off" a wagon unless it was strictly necessary. This lessening of standards must have come as something of a shock to older GWR staff, and the circular gently reminded superintendents that "the instructions to examiners will have to be given in as tactful a manner as possible".[24] Related to this measure, as a wartime measure, the instructions relating to the examination of freight trains were also altered in 1941; instead of having to stop for examination every 50 miles, as was the case before the war, trains were only required to be inspected every 85 miles.

By far the biggest increase in traffic for the Great

Western and for all the railways during the war period was in the movement of personnel, equipment and munitions; the large numbers of trains run, and the special equipment sometimes needed put a great strain on the Company's resources. Writing to staff in 1940, the district superintendent at Bristol reminded them that the "success of arrangements under active service conditions depends on the full cooperation of the railways..."[25] The confidential circular then listed the various regular government stores and ammunition trains which ran through the area under his command; included in the list were oil trains from Llandarcy and Avonmouth, ammunition trains from Corsham (Thingley Junction) to War Office ammunition sub-depots, and ammunition trains from Chorley, Longtown, Rotherwas and Savernake.

The movement of ammunition and other high explosives was perhaps the most dangerous work carried out by the railway during the war; normal regulations stipulated that no more than five wagons containing explosives should be marshalled into any one train, but in time of war this rule could not be continued, and as a result up to 60 wagons could be run together in trains run for the government. Locomotive crews were under-standably nervous about working such trains, especially during air raids, but undoubtedly the relaxation of the regulations allowed the GWR to carry huge quantities of explosives for the war effort. Much secrecy surrounds the movement of such material, and detailed evidence of trains and their loads is scarce. One survival is a circular concerning the movement of SIP grenades; these extremely dangerous items were made of glass, and if broken, caused a fire. Staff were warned of their danger, and trains carrying such loads were not to exceed 40 mph, and were not to run through the Severn Tunnel, or through any other tunnel when other trains were passing. Staff were also warned that "the contents of this circular are to be regarded as secret".[26]

In all the major military campaigns, and a large number of military exercises and manoeuvres in between, the Great Western played a vital role in the movement of troops and their equipment. As D-Day approached, so the number of special trains run increased dramatically; to date, no detailed schedules of special trains run in 1944 has been discovered by the author, but the following details of the movement of troops in 1940 will give a flavour of what was involved. Records from the District Superintendent's office at Bristol describe the move of the 52nd Heavy Artillery Regiment from Chipping Sodbury to Harwich. Two trains were to be used, and were assembled at the Rodbourne Lane Sidings at Swindon on 28 March 1940. Both trains consisted of engine, brake van, brake composite coach, third, eight 'Rectank' wagons, eight 'Macaw' type wagons, six 12-ton open wagons and another brake van. These vehicles were used to transport various pieces of artillery, including eight 6-inch guns, as well as troops and other supplies. The trains were moved to Chipping Sodbury the following day, and finally left at 6.32am on 1 April. Timed to run at a maximum of 25 mph, the two trains crawled across country, not reaching Harwich until 7am the following morning.

The 'Rectank' vehicle was one of a series of

special vehicles constructed and used for the movement of bulky military equipment such as guns, tanks and aircraft in cases. Over 700 wagons of these types were in use, most owned by the War Department and part of a special pool of vehicles. The 'Rectanks' were owned by individual railways, but the other two main types used were 'Warflats' with a carrying capacity of 50 tons, and 'Warwells' of which there were two types, with 50 and 80 ton capacity. Care was needed when these wagons were loaded, since they were fitted with jacks to enable them to be stable whilst vehicles were loaded on to them; a GWR circular issued in 1942 reminded staff to wind up these jacks after use, since some had been found running with the mechanism wound down, perilously close to the rail surface![27]

Train loads of these armoured fighting vehicles soon became a common site on the railway however, and in his annual report in 1942, R. G. Pole, the District Superintendent at Bristol noted that in the previous year there had been "a large programme of AFV movements".[28] Another special load carried by the railway was that of aircraft propellers and on 23 May 1940, the Chief Mechanical Engineer reported to the Locomotive Committee that 50 wagons of this type were being

Sherman tanks ready for movement to the front. This picture was used in a number of publicity booklets issued by the railways during the war period. (D. J. Hyde Collection)

constructed by the Company at Swindon at a cost not exceeding £6,900 in lieu of 50 of the 1,650 open wagons authorised by the board in early 1939.[29] This arrangement was on the understanding that at the end of the war, the Company was not expected to bear the whole cost of the work. These wagons not surprisingly were also part of the special pool of wagons.

Some mention has already been made of the movement of troops by the Great Western; even allowing for particularly large movements of troops during specific operations such as the Dunkirk evacuation or the movement of troops for the North African campaign, the number moved is still staggering. Statistics kept by the company on a roughly monthly basis show that from 1941 the number of troop trains run did not drop below 250, with a more general average of around 400 per month. The figures are broadly the same in 1942; an example of a typical month for that year might be the period ending 19 April, when in the previous four weeks 452 troop trains were run, in addition to

this 446 trains carrying equipment were also dealt with. During 1943 not surprisingly, the figures show a steady increase, a high point for the year being reached in November when 1,043 troop trains were run.

Written records of such troop train movements seem almost impossible to locate, although some details can be gleaned from diverse sources. The annual report of the District Superintendent at Bristol, does note some of the troop trains run through the Division; in 1942 there were 30 movements of troops from Salisbury Plain to the North of England and Scotland, each consisting of two or three trains. Even at this stage in the war, records were being broken for traffic handled; the Superintendent noted an increase of 94.7 per cent in troop trains from the previous year.

One further vital load carried by the Great Western in the run up to D-Day was petrol; most supplies of this and other similar products were imported through Western docks such as those in South Wales and Bristol, and until the completion

A train load of tanks at Acton ready for movement, possibly to Russia, in 1942.

Another petrol train, hauled by a Collett Goods 0-6-0, leaves an unidentified depot, possibly Ludgershall or Bulford on Salisbury Plain. Workings like these were a key part of the run up to D-Day.

of pipelines running from these ports to eastern and southern counties the Company ran large numbers of special trains each week. By the end of 1943 the four main line railways had run a total of 31,215 trains of this type; such was the volume of traffic in 1942 and 1943 that as many as ten trains each day from Bristol and South Wales were diverted away from the old Bristol to London main line via other routes such as Yarnton and Cambridge, and Princes Risborough and Neasden.

Sir Andrew Agnew, the Head of the Petroleum Board, wrote to the Company in 1942 to thank it for its efforts in the movement of petroleum products by rail. He noted that between October 1941 and February 1942 464,000 tons of fuel had been moved, mostly on the Great Western system; an additional benefit was he added, that by moving so much fuel, loss of life on coastal tanker ships had been much reduced.[30] Swindon records show that to reduce their vulnerability from air attack, the tank wagons used for the movement of petrol

were painted battleship grey from July 1940, a very necessary precaution in the circumstances.[31]

With the completion of the pipeline grid, the pressure on the railways abated somewhat, but this situation was only short lived since in the run up to the invasion of Europe, the Company was once again moving large quantities of fuel. In the weeks before the invasion millions of gallons of aviation spirit were required for allied bombers occupied in the task of 'softening' up of German defences. To illustrate the amounts of fuel used by the allied air forces, it was calculated that one 1,000 bomber strike needed 650 rail tank vehicles of petrol, which was approximately 2,600,000 gallons of fuel.

To enable all the freight traffic already mentioned to run smoothly, improvements to the Company's network and facilities at various locations was necessary; in the past 40 years the Company had not been slow to spend money to remove bottlenecks and to improve its stations and other facilities, but the pressures put on the system

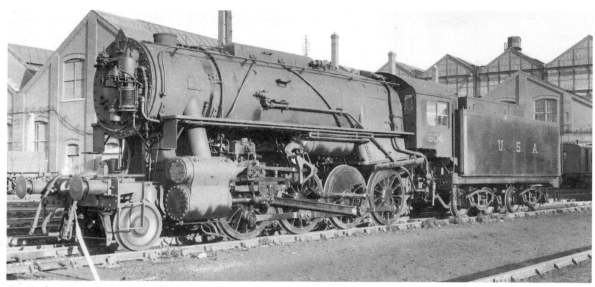

S160 class 2-8-0 No. 1604, built by American Locomotive Company, stands outside the A Shop at Swindon after modification and ready for use on Great Western metals.

both by the vastly increased traffic handled and the threat of air raids meant that further work needed to be done. When the promised invasion of Europe came, it was likely that it would begin in the south of England, and the Great Western, in conjunction with the other railways and the Railway Executive Committee pushed ahead plans to improve certain routes. A large number of plans were introduced, but in a book of this kind, there is not enough space to document all the work done; a number of examples will hopefully give an impression of the type and scale of schemes carried out during the war years.

A number of measures were planned to allow traffic to flow more freely on the companies lines. One measure which was commonplace was the construction of additional loops on double track lines, and the lengthening of some existing loops. Two lines which received a great deal of attention were the Didcot, Newbury & Southampton route, and the old Midland & South Western Junction line from Cheltenham to Andover. In prewar days neither carried particularly heavy traffic, but in the war years both became important North–South routes and thus needed some upgrading to enable them to be worked to their maximum. The Didcot, Newbury & Southampton line was closed to traffic on 4 August 1942, and did not reopen for passenger traffic until 8 March 1943; during this time sections of the single line were doubled and loops were

extended from 300 to 550 yards. Additional crossing places were also added at a number of locations. On the old Midland & South Western Junction route, similar work took place, with doubling of single lines, lengthening of loops and other additional work being done.

The railway also facilitated traffic by either putting in new connections at junctions, or reinstating old connections; an example of the former was the construction of a new connection between the West Drayton to Staines branch and the Southern Railway's Windsor branch, creating an alternative North–South route for freight traffic from the GWR or the LNER avoiding the use of the West London line. An example of the latter, the reinstatement of an old connection could be seen at Thingley Junction, east of Chippenham. Here the restoration of the triangle allowed trains to run directly from the West, and join the West of England main line at Westbury. This connection was particularly important bearing in mind the large amounts of government traffic originating from ammunition and supplies depots in the Corsham and Bath area.

Other important connections were made at such diverse locations as Reading, Oxford Pool Meadow, Launceston and Lydford; all were, as Company paperwork usually noted, "to facilitate the working of wartime traffic". Some also acted as additional routes to be used when main routes were blocked by air raid damage or accident. It should be noted that almost all the work mentioned was paid for by the government and not the railway itself, which could not have afforded the huge expenditure which was entailed in many of these major schemes. The variety of such work was illustrated by the author of a Railway Executive Committee report on preparations for winter traffic in 1942 and 1943 who, as well as listing the improvements to running lines and loops already mentioned, also noted that the railways required new signalling schemes, extensions to goods and marshalling yards, improvements to locomotive depots and better staff accommodation to enable them to cope with the increased demands placed upon them.[32]

Records kept by the Company illustrate the huge amounts of work done, and the enormous cost to the taxpayer of that work; even as early as 1941 the General Manager had estimated that the work required to cope with wartime traffic was likely to cost well over £2 million. Additional siding accommodation was provided at a number of diverse locations including Oxford, Banbury and Exeter; work at the the latter location was agreed by the Great Western board in October 1943, and a breakdown of costs was given. The additional land required was to cost £900 and then expenditure was divided between the major departments of the Company. Civil engineering and tracklaying was to cost £68,983, signalling a further £20,000, work by the Chief Mechanical Engineers Department £6,300, and £80 was allocated to the Stores Department; the total for this project alone was over £95,000.[33]

Smaller but equally vital work was done all over the Great Western network; there are numerous references to the installation of extra water columns, vital to ensure that trains working long distances with munitions or supplies could be

The unloading of one of the American locomotives at Cardiff Docks in November 1942. Note the Union Jack draped over the boiler for publicity purposes.

watered at regular intervals. In June 1943 an additional water column was installed at Stratford Upon Avon costing £790; a similar installation at Exeter (City Basin Junction) cost £818 the same month.[34] Another common occurrence was the introduction of electric lighting at sidings, making shunting and examination of stock much easier; the installation of a system at Aynho for the War Department in 1943 was reported to have cost £351. A new messroom, which included accommodation for female staff, was built at Cardiff General station in July 1943, costing nearly £1,000, less expensive was the provision of cycle storage accommodation at Crudgington and Honeybourne, which cost a total of £251.[35]   Added to the expenditure already mentioned should be further schemes related to the large numbers of government factories, stores and establishments set up immediately before, or during the war. In a report to the board in 1941, the General Manager stated that there were 93 such establishments on the Great Western system. Within this total, 38 belonged to the War Department, seven to the Admiralty, eleven

to the Ministry of Works, 16 to the Air Ministry and the rest to miscellaneous other organisations; the connection of the facilities to the GWR had entailed expenditure of £1,386,000 he reported.[36]

The final element in our description of the build up to the final stages of the war on the Great Western was the involvement of the Company with the United States forces, many of whom arrived at GWR ports, and were moved to their bases by GWR trains. The entry of the United States into the war in December 1941 after the attack on its forces at Pearl Harbor by the Japanese, gave heart to the embattled British population. Churchill articulated the thoughts of many when he argued that the industrial might of the United States would lead to eventual victory; the flow of munitions would "vastly exceed anything that could have been expected on the peacetime basis that has ruled up to the present" he argued.[37] Although United States troops had arrived in Northern Ireland as early as January 1942, the first mention in Great Western Company records appears to have been the arrival of the SS *Uruguay*

A close up view of the motion of USA S160 class 2-8-0 No. 1604.

A petrol train at Kennington Junction being hauled by a USA S160 class 2-8-0 No. 1649 in 1943. (Great Western Trust Collection)

at Swansea on 18 August. All 6,281 troops on board were disembarked and dispersed to various bases within 24 hours, on twelve special trains directly from the docks; a further five special trains also ran from Swansea Victoria, the LMS station in the town. This process was one which was to become a regular occurrence for all the ports in the West and on 18 October 1943 over 10,700 American personnel were disembarked at Newport, Cardiff and Swansea on 28 special trains. In 1942 R. G. Pole, the Divisional Superintendent at Bristol, also reported the movement of US troops from Scotland, the North of England and Avonmouth Docks to bases in the area in ten special movements, each of two or three trains.[38]

The close liaison between the Company and the United States forces was confirmed on 6 November 1942, when Colonel N. Ryan, Chief of Transportation of the United States Army wrote to the General Manager to record that the "support and service received from you exceeds all our expectations and we want to thank you for the efforts that have been made on our behalf".[39] The cordial relations which existed between the railway and the United States forces could be strained slightly at times; the survival of a GWR incident

report reveals that the 'Yanks' could sometimes cause the company some inconvenience. The report gives details of damage done to an overbridge on the line between Wootton Bassett and Badminton on 20 March 1944. A US Army lorry crashed into the bridge dislodging about 40ft of coping stone and badly damaging around the same amount of iron railings; a temporary speed check was instituted at the site, and the company had to employ a flagman on the bridge to control road traffic.[40]

The valuable assistance of American troops in the unloading of shipping in South Wales ports has already been noted, but perhaps the best known assistance given by the United States to the Great Western and the other main line railways was the provision of the S160 class 2-8-0 steam locomotives to alleviate some of the shortages of motive power suffered during the long years of the war. The Railway Executive had been making strong representations to the government since 1940 for the provision of further heavy freight locomotives to assist in the working of additional wartime traffic and in June 1942 the Company was informed that orders had been placed for 400 of these locomotives to be loaned to Britain's railways. Produced by three of the largest American locomotive builders, American Locomotive Company (Alco), Baldwin and Lima, the robust design of the S160 class was intended to be powerful, easy to maintain and with the maximum route availability; as a result, these massive looking engines were able to run in this country, doing valuable work for all the railways, before moving over to the mainland of Europe after the invasion in June 1944.

It was not until 11 December that the first American locomotive was formally handed over at Paddington station, with Lord Leathers, Minister of War Transport, accepting the engine on behalf of Britain. In his speech the minister noted that "We have seen British locomotives leaving these shores for distant theatres of war, and are now seeing American locomotives arriving for service in this country."[41] At the time of the handing over ceremony, only eight engines had actually arrived from the United States; the locomotive handed over had not even been allocated to the Great Western when it arrived at Paddington, having been one of four allocated to St Margarets shed in Edinburgh. Along with a sister engine stabled at nearby Thornton Junction shed, these locomotives had been prepared for service on arrival in this country at Cowlairs Works.

Three of this first batch of engines were transferred to the Great Western in January 1943 and by the end of the year the Company had no less than 174 allocated to no fewer than 28 of its sheds. Some idea of the scale of this allocation may be gained by the fact that its own heavy freight locomotive the 28xx 2-8-0 numbered only 167. Initially Swindon and Wolverhampton were responsible for the commissioning of new locomotives, which involved the fitting of vacuum

Another USA 2-8-0, No. 1639, is seen banking a freight north of Oxford at Port Meadow in 1943. (Great Western Trust Collection)

braking, and a hand brake on the tender; modifications were also done to the tyres, and the ash pan was covered to comply with blackout regulations. After October 1943 however, this work was done at Newport Ebbw Junction, where several hundred further locomotives were stored, ready for export overseas.

Staff soon realised that the American engines were very different to anything ever produced at Swindon; with the spread of engines throughout the system, the Chief Mechanical Engineer instructed divisional superintendents to "impress upon all concerning the various instructions...regarding the maintenance and servicing of the engines".[42] The high sided tenders fitted to the locomotives also caused problems with coaling, and Hawksworth noted that engines could be dealt with at coal stages where lifts were installed.

More important however were problems experienced with boilers; locomotive crews were unfamiliar with the single boiler water gauge used on the footplate, and there were several serious boiler explosions, including one fatal incident on a Great Western train at Honeybourne in November 1943.[43] At a meeting of superintendents in February 1944, it was impressed on staff the "urgent need for care in the maintenance of USA engines".[44] It was reported that severe problems were being experienced by the build up of scale in boiler tubes, with 16 engines out of service for repair to tubes, and another 28 under observation. Pellow, Hawksworth's assistant, went on to say that, "we do not want another case of a fatal injury on the footplate for lack of any steps we can take to obviate such a possibility".[45] Special descaling machines were introduced to combat the problem, and staff were urged to make sure that tubes were 'blown down' regularly to clear them of any scale.

The 174 locomotives loaned to the Great Western were spread throughout the system and used wherever their route availability would allow; by reputation they were powerful and free steaming engines and were used on many of the heavy trains associated with the build up for the invasion of Europe. The *Railway Observer* for March 1943 noted that USA 2-8-0s had been seen at Wolverhampton, Stafford Road and Oxley sheds

and two had been seen on 17 and 24 January at Gresty Lane Crewe, having both worked Great Western goods trains. In October further allocations of the engines were reported, including locomotives moved to sheds including Cardiff, Tyseley, Didcot, Oxford and Banbury.

The last locomotive was not allocated until July 1944, two months before all 174 were handed back to the United States Transportation Corps for use in Europe. To replace these engines, the railways were given 450 of the 'Austerity' 2-8-0 locomotives, and in October 1944 it was reported that the Company had been given only 81 of these engines, which had not helped the motive power shortage. To make matters worse, it was noted that this total might be reduced still further to 63; "All Divisions must do their best to keep...engines in traffic". The Chief Mechanical Engineer told his superintendents.[46] Some of the 'Austerity' locomotives sent to the Great Western were in poor mechanical condition, especially those transferred from the LMS, which had already run up to 49,000 miles; needless to say many of these were in need of overhaul, and 17 of those transferred were already 'stopped' for repairs. The engines sent from the Southern however, were "nine of their youngest".[47]

In December 1943 the *GWR Magazine* printed extracts of a radio broadcast given by Major-General N. G. Holmes, Director of Movements at the War Office, who outlined the methods used to transport munitions, supplies and troops and the contribution made to the war effort by the railways. Touching on many of the topics covered in this chapter, he stated that military movement on the railways had doubled in the previous 18 months, and the trend was still upwards. This was he announced, "the natural outcome of the fighting services going over from the defensive to the offensive".[48] Traffic was likely to be even heavier he considered, and this was a necessary factor he concluded, if "these islands are to be...a base for the liberation of Western Europe".[49] This clear reference to plans for invasion showed that even in the minds of the population, it was now no longer a matter of "if" liberation would take place, but "when" it would take place.

11

To Victory

One further aspect of the Great Western's part in the preparations for the Allied invasion of Europe was the assembly, modification and operation of a special train codenamed 'Alive' for the use of the United States General, Dwight D. Eisenhower. Although the identity of the vehicles used in the 'Alive' train has been known for some considerable time, little else has come to light, mainly due to the intense secrecy which surrounded much of the military work done at Swindon Works during the Second World War.

Although there must have been discussion about the creation of the 'Alive' train by the Railway Executive, there does not appear to be any mention of its formation in Company committee minutes, which presumably would have been accessible to the public. The first mention of the project seems to have been in a letter written by Gilbert Matthews, Superintendent of the Line at Paddington, to the Chief Mechanical Engineer at Swindon, F. W. Hawksworth, in June 1942. The exact contents of this letter are unknown, but it led to a New Work Order being generated which outlined the work to be done on the train by the Carriage Works. The order noted that the work should include "Alterations to Saloon No. 9364, Sleeping Composite No. 9079 and Covered Carriage Truck No. 485"; a handwritten addition to the order further instructed the works to prepare 'Monster' wagons Nos 483 and 485 by the addition of double-hinged end doors and loading ramps.[1] This enabled jeeps and Eisenhower's personal vehicle to be loaded and unloaded easily at each location he visited.

It can only be presumed that at least initially, the train was small or was bolstered by the use of unmodified ordinary coaching stock, since no further references have been found for the train until early 1943; indeed, the work order issued on 23 June 1942 must have been given urgent priority, since the train made its first journey, on a long round trip starting at Waterloo and visiting Salisbury, Bristol, Ashchurch and Birmingham on 8 July. Details of the movement of the train have been gleaned from a diary of the journeys made from 1942 to 1946 kept by the train steward, Frank Brookman and his wife Irene. The keeping of such a document must have been against the rules, not to mention against the Official Secrets Act, but fortunately for us, it survives today, giving a wonderful portrait of both the locations visited and the huge mileages run up by Eisenhower and his staff in the months before the invasion of Europe in 1944.[2]

Once the train was put at the disposal of the United States forces, it was used initially by a variety of staff; General Eisenhower himself did not arrive in England until the autumn of 1942, having been appointed as Commander of US Forces in Europe in June. His first recorded use of the train appears to have been on 18 October 1942, when he travelled from Addison Road to Scotland, to observe combined manoeuvres for the North African campaign, codenamed 'Torch'.

Many of the journeys recorded by Frank Brookman began at Addison Road, (now known as

One of the sleeping coaches from the 'Alive' train. The livery was not brown as many thought, but British 'Army green' according to contemporary sources.

Kensington Olympia) which had been closed for normal passenger traffic because of the war since October 1940, and a large number included a stop at Cheltenham, where the American forces had their headquarters, and intelligence and information gathering centre. General Eisenhower had little time to acquaint himself with the train, leaving for North Africa at the beginning of November. By the time he returned victorious after the successful Allied defeat of Rommel in the desert, the 'Alive' train had been much refurbished.

Further New Work Orders issued in February 1943 show how the train was improved; on 16 February alterations were ordered to additional stock – added to those already mentioned were another sleeping car, No. 9093, and a brake third, No. 1647.[3] Estimated to cost £3,500, the nature of these alterations is not known, but on the same day, a further New Work Order was issued for the conversion of passenger brake van No. 121 to a utility van for the train, which involved the installation of both electrical generating equipment, and steam heating boilers, allowing the train to be lit and heated independently of any locomotive.[4] This was essential when the train made overnight stops at distant locations, where an

engine could not be spared. At the same time the remaining vehicles in the train were adapted to accept power and heat from the utility van.

In the absence of Eisenhower the train was used extensively; in the month after his departure, visits were made to Nottingham, Rudgeley, Liverpool, Savernake, Amesbury, Bristol, Sutton Coldfield, Cambridge, Stranraer and Newbury. In December 1942 it made the Addison Road–Cheltenham round trip at least eleven times, a trend which continued into the early months of the new year. Another American, General Devers, arrived in May 1943, and it appears that he used the train for some months, culminating with a trip on 27 June when he travelled to Largs in Scotland, where he and Lord Mountbatten met for a combined forces conference. The train returned to Scotland almost a month later, travelling to Prestwick to meet a party of US senators who had flown across the Atlantic. On 14 August the GWR, at the request of the Americans, fitted a wine cupboard, two potato bins and shelves and trays for food in brake third No. 1647, and supplied additional wardrobes and a collapsible desk in sleeping car No. 9079.

No doubt the equipment installed was necessary, since a great deal of entertaining must have been

The interior of one of the carriages of General Eisenhower's 'Alive' train, converted for his use by the GWR. (Tony Brookman Collection)

done by the United States staff whilst travelling around the country; on 27 August 1943 the diary records that General Lee, on a journey commencing at Bristol, which included stops at Okehampton, Tavistock, Plymouth, Exeter and Taunton and ending at Cheltenham, had as his lunch guest Lord Astor. In September the train visited Penrith, where General Devers inspected tank manoeuvres and met members of British Army staff. Another General, Knox, only recently arrived in England, used the train between 18 and 21 September 1943 to inspect the fleet at Scapa Flow, travelling from Addison Road to Gourock, and then on to Thurso, before returning to London.

General Eisenhower did not return to England until the middle of January 1944, and from this date onwards, the 'Alive' train was used almost continuously to plan and oversee the preparations for the Allied invasion of Europe. In all, the train was to travel over 95,000 miles in the months before D-Day. In that hectic period, Swindon Works undertook a considerable amount of work on the train; a glimpse of what was to come arrived in the form of instructions on 11 March which

called for the preparation of the 'Alive' Train for use overseas. This included the fitting of Westinghouse braking, the installation of a coal burning cooking range in the dining car, and additional furniture for the conference car. The fact that the train was going into enemy territory was underlined by the fact that the order also included the cost of bulletproof glass to be supplied by Messrs Pilkington.[5]

In the months immediately after D-Day the train was kept very busy, and in August 1944 Eisenhower visited various locations including Guildford, Hungerford and Leicester, the diary recording that he inspected paratroops, who may well have been training for the ill-fated Arnhem raid which took place the following month. It was not until the beginning of November that the train was finally made ready for its trip across the English Channel, and after a trip from Windsor to Addison Road on 7 November, it was taken to Swindon where it remained in the workshops until the 15th, and following final preparations, it was then returned to Windsor, where it was stabled until the 26th. It was then used for the next four days by members of the United States Congress who travelled around England, visiting Liverpool, Coventry, Ashchurch and Cambridge before returning to Windsor.

On 11 December 1944 the 'Alive' train ran its last journey on British metals for a period that would last over six months, departing from Addison Road *en route* to Southampton. Two days later it was shipped across the English Channel on the Southern Railway train ferry the SS *Hampton Ferry*. Its first journey on French rails was from Cherbourg to Paris, where it remained over Christmas, not leaving for Brussels until 27 December. After the Liberation, Eisenhower had made Paris his headquarters whilst overseeing Allied progress in Northern Europe, and in the next six or so weeks the train made numerous trips in Northern France and the Low Countries, mainly supervising the fighting in the Ardennes where the Germans fought a fierce rearguard action resulting in severe losses to both sides.

The train was never far from the front line, and it is significant that on 8 February 1945 Swindon Works issued an order for steel plates to be supplied by Messrs Hadfields to enable movable shutters to be fixed to coach No. 574. The train made a number of dangerous trips near the enemy lines, the most memorable recorded by Frank Brookman being on 29 and 30 April, when it was used to transport the British General, Strong, and a high ranking American officer across German lines to negotiate a truce on the Dutch-German border.

In March the train was used on five occasions, and only twice in April, as the pace of the Allied advance speeded up; on 2 May Eisenhower returned to Paris to record his victory speech, returning to Rheims the next day. It was here five days later that General Alfred Jodl of the German High Command, signed the surrender of the German forces, effectively ending the war in Europe. The 'Alive' train remained at Rheims until 25 May when Eisenhower moved his headquarters to Frankfurt, and it was stabled there out of use

until 30 July when it made a journey to Hanover. Frank Brookman's diary records that the train was then returned to England via the British sector; the train was to return less than six months later, acting as the mobile headquarters for General Robinson, the deputy military governor of Germany. The train ranged far and wide across the country, not finishing its tour of duty until the end of January 1946.

With the end of the war, and the safe return of the 'Alive' train to the Great Western Railway, it only remained for the vehicles to be restored to normal condition, allowing them to be returned to traffic. Charges for the hire of train were then calculated, and as a result, in May 1945, the 'Alive' train was valued by the Chief Mechanical Engineer's Accounts Office for exactly this purpose. Initially Swindon issued four New Work Orders for the refurbishment of various items of

The scene at Swindon for the handing over of the first United States Ambulance Train in 1943. Note the newsreel camera on the roof of the van. Aptly, a USA 2-8-0 has been used to head the train.

American P-47 Thunderbolt aircraft on the dockside at Swansea after being unloaded from the tanker Caydse.

rolling stock on 3 January 1946. The work to be done was estimated to cost £1,300, and it is interesting to note that these orders were then superseded by a further reissued New Work Order on 22 March 1946 where the cost of work was directed to the Ministry of Supply.[6]

The momentum generated by the building up of Allied Forces for the North African campaign in 1942 was the beginning of the process culminating in the invasion of Europe on 6 June 1944. The embarkation of troops in 1942 for Operation 'Torch' showed that the railways and the services still had much to learn about coordination of effort as it was noted that a tremendous number of illogical cross country movements took place, including the embarkation of troops from Taunton at Glasgow, and troops based at Liverpool at Avonmouth.[7] In the ensuing years however, the Great Western participated in an increasing number of exercises and large scale troop movements which helped tighten up procedures for both the railway and the armed services.

The military authorities were well aware of the problems they caused the railways and in late 1941 the Secretary of State for War had written to the General Manager thanking him for assistance in manoeuvres which had taken place in the autumn. He noted, "I realise that military traffic often reacts unfavourably on other traffic and I want you to know that...we endeavour to adjust our demands so as to cause the least possible interference with other aspects of our war effort."[8] Increasingly though, the GWR was called on to make tremendous efforts on behalf of the war effort; during the 1942 Christmas period the Company moved a large number of United States M3 tanks from Tidworth to ships at Liverpool, Birkenhead and Swansea. A letter sent to the Superintendent of the Line on 1 January 1943 from the War Office, congratulated the railway on its efficiency.[9]

A much larger exercise took place in the early part of 1943 codenamed 'Spartan' involving the movement of thousands of troops and their equipment. A Control office to coordinate the

Allied craft ready for D-Day waiting at Swansea Docks in 1944.

movement of trains had been set up at Oxford; this, General Sir Bernard Paget, Commander in Chief Home Forces wrote, had been "worked most efficiently and with marked 'dispatch'."[10] He asked the General Manager to convey his appreciation of the large part played in the success of the operation by the railways, a factor which was to be vitally important in the months to come. A further large exercise took place in West Wales between 13 July and 3 August 1943, for the General Manager reported, "the purpose of trying out the organisation required for maintaining a force on beaches for a considerable period".[11] Once again a foretaste of what was to come was experienced by the Great Western who ran 88 special trains to assist in the operation, which also included extensive use of the Company's docks in South Wales.

By this point, labour shortages were so acute that volunteer labour was being used to help unload wagons; this innovation allowed around 24,000 wagons to be unloaded each weekend. In

January 1944 it was reported that staff shortages were so acute that the Company required an additional 2,100 men and 1,700 women; as a temporary measure the War Department loaned the Company the services of 1,000 men from military Railway Operating Companies. Another measure adopted was the use of Italian prisoners of war, who were employed from 1943 onwards at a number of locations mainly in locomotive sheds and depots; in October 1944 it was reported that Italians employed at Salisbury, Severn Tunnel and Cardiff were doing good work.[12] Problems did occur, complicated by the fact that as Ken Gibbs in his book on Swindon Works noted,[13] Italian prisoners were divided into two groups, 'collaborators' and 'non-collaborators'; in general the former, as might be expected were better workers. A circular issued by the Great Western at Swindon works seems to suggest that working with prisoners was not always a fruitful experience; the circular stated that with regard to the conduct of Italian prisoners, it was felt that "the position

United States troops board the SS Santa Paula *at Cardiff Docks for an unknown destination.*

would be more satisfactory if employees had no contact with them."[14]

As invasion preparations continued, the Company's South Wales docks became busier and busier, not only with the unloading of munitions and stores, but also as places where the invasion forces were to be concentrated. The greater part of the GWR facilities at Penarth Dock were taken over in December 1943 by the United States Army for the accommodation of landing craft, and landing ships which were arriving from America under their own steam. In March 1944 it was reported that US troops had used the docks at Port Talbot for an exercise, although no further details were given.

Secrecy was one of the key elements to the success of the invasion plans; as early as March 1944 a circular had been issued to all staff noting that, "It is common knowledge that we are on the eve of major military operations, and, as with previous campaigns, the element of surprise will be

of vital importance in these new operations."[15] The cooperation of railway staff in previous campaigns had maintained that element of surprise the General Manager noted, urging staff to be "constantly on your guard against any action which might give the slightest assistance to the enemy".[16] Employees when discussing traffic movements or enemy action, were instructed to converse in a manner which if overheard would not give any information to "enemy agents".

Railway officials were given details of military plans for what became operation 'Overlord' some months before General Montgomery gave his now famous speech to railwaymen at Euston in February 1944. Great coordination had been necessary to organise the movement of troops from ports to various centres, and a new scheme was evolved to move troops from these bases to numerous concentration points near the coast. Stabling points were selected for both ordinary coaching stock and ambulance trains; the date chosen for the beginning of the movement of personnel was 26 March 1944, and for the next two months the railways ran 24,459 special trains for the movement of troops, personnel and equipment. Monthly statistics for the GWR show a staggering increase in trains run as D-Day approached.

Special Trains Run January–July 1944

Period Ending	Troops	Munitions, Equipment, etc.
23.1.44	852	1,143
13.2.44	492	592
19.3.44	861	1,251
23.4.44	1,080	1,539
20.5.44	924	1,865
24.6.44	1,161	3,003
22.7.44	1,226	2,620

Source: General Manager's Report to the Board. PRO RAIL 250/776

The movement of most of the heavy equipment and stores needed by the invasion force began as late as 10 May, and was divided into three distinct stages, the first material likely to be carried by landing craft, the second, items being moved by coaster, and the final phase, equipment being moved by larger cargo ships. This movement required a further 800 trains from the railways as a whole, with the Great Western and the Southern contributing the lion's share. With the movement of over 7,000 vehicles including many tanks, the railways were stretched to the limit, especially since a good number of these loads were large and 'out-of-gauge'. With the start of this huge operation, the Home Guard were mobilised to protect railway lines; on the old Midland & South Western Junction route at Collingbourne and Ludgershall, the 10th Battalion, Wiltshire Regiment were called into action, occupying waiting rooms at the stations. "At last we have something to do that is worth doing" was the remark noted in the post war history of the regiment.[17]

Perhaps the most striking aspect of the whole operation was that for the most part the public were mostly unaware of the large scale movement of equipment which was taking place. Although train loads of tanks and other equipment were to be seen, great efforts were made to disguise loads

A plaque given to the captain of HMS St Helier *by Canadian forces who had used the ship during the D-Day landings.*

under sheets or to conceal equipment in unobtrusive box vans, leading the whole operation to be nicknamed the 'tarpaulin armada'.

Great Western Docks also played a vital part in the D-Day landings themselves; for as well as being the first port of call for much of the material arriving from the United States, they were also the departure points for a large proportion of the landing force. In South Wales 159 vessels were loaded with over 90,000 tons of supplies, which included munitions, food, fuel and over 6,000 vehicles. The railway also ran a considerable number of special troop trains which brought over 42,000 soldiers to the dockside, ready for embarkation. After the invasion, both the South Wales ports and Plymouth acted as supply points for the maintenance of the Second Front. By the end of 1944 more than 611 ships had been loaded in South Wales with supplies for the Allied forces in Europe.

Great Western ships, which had already played a vital part in the war effort, were also at work during the Normandy landings; the SS *St Julien* was once again in action as a hospital ship, but on 7 June she struck a mine which blew a 10ft hole, extending from keel to waterline. After a three-week repair, she was back in action, but was once again damaged, this time in a collision with another allied vessel. Two other vessels the *Roebuck* and

Sambur, which had both had a narrow escape at St Valery in 1940, played a very different role in the 'Overlord' operation, assisting in the manoeuvring of the huge prefabricated 'Mulberry' harbour at Arromanches. Once this task was completed, they carried cranes, dredger spares, and other vital supplies "braving bombs, rockets, shellfire, mines and submarines".[18]

One ship not present during the landings was the SS *St David* which, along with the *St Julien* and the *St Andrew,* had done valuable work in the Mediterranean in 1943. All had travelled large distances carrying casualties from the Allied invasion of Italy to safety in Malta or North Africa. The *St David* was bombed 25 miles south of Anzio on 25 July 1943, and sank with the loss of 55 crew. Amongst the casualties was the Master, Captain W. E. Owens, who after giving the order to abandon ship, stayed on board in an effort to rescue patients and medical staff. A further dozen crew were lost, but many of the patients and medical personnel were saved. The *St Andrew* rescued 60 survivors from the incident, and although she continued to do good service in the Mediterranean area, was eventually forced to limp back to Britain in September 1944 after hitting a mine.

When D-Day finally came, further efforts were required, with over 1,000 trains conveying 230,000 troops to embarkation points, and then hundreds more trains carrying equipment, fuel and munitions were also run. The *GWR Magazine*, in its account of the Company's part in 'Operation Overlord', stated that its "arresting success and the achievements of our forces have brought richer rewards than we dared hope for after the last four years hard work and harder waiting".[19] During the two months prior to D-Day it added "our war carrying climbed higher peaks than our traffic graphs had ever shown".[20] If these figures were considered high, then the following months were to cause the statisticians even more trouble; the four weeks after D-Day were the busiest ever recorded in the history of Britain's railways, with over 17,500 special trains run, an increase of 33 per cent on the previous month.

On the GWR a considerable number of these trains carried men, munitions and equipment; the total number of troop trains run for the government in June 1944 was 1,167, an average of 39 per day. In July this total increased to 1,374, with a high point being reached in August, when 1,401 troop trains were operated over Great Western rails, at an average of 46 per day. Similar peaks were reflected in the figures for numbers of stores and supplies trains run by the Company; June saw a total of 2,813 Government Stores Trains run, with 2,831 being operated the following month.[21] A new burden placed on the railways was the carrying of

The nursing staff of one of the casualty vacuation trains converted for use as ambulance trains later in the war (Courtesy Mrs A. Tallboys)

US troops embarking from South Wales Docks in 1942.

mail and parcels to the forces fighting in Europe, and the mail they sent back in return; 113 train loads of mail of this type were carried by the railways in the first month after the invasion.

An important if more regrettable addition to the work carried out by the Great Western after the commencement of the Allied invasion of Europe were the considerable numbers of ambulance trains which were routed over Great Western lines on their way from the battlefields to hospitals all over the country. Very little detail has been available on the composition and use of such trains, but the minutes of a special secret Ambulance Trains Committee, coordinated by the Railway Executive Committee and the Ministry of War Transport do give a good idea of something of the scale of the operation involved. This committee was set up when it became all too apparent the twelve

ambulance trains designed by the LMS and assembled by the various railways in 1939, would not be nearly enough.

In all cases, distinction was made between trains destined for 'home' use and those for 'overseas' use; by the spring of 1940 a total of 25 trains had been made ready, twelve for the former and thirteen for the latter. Once again LMS stock was used, with a total of 344 vehicles being converted. In September 1942 it was stated that a further 27 ambulance trains were required by the armed forces, with 14 to be delivered by 1 June 1943, and the remainder by December 1943.[22] Each train was to include ward coaches of two designs, one holding 36 stretcher cases, the other 30 stretchers, a 'sitting coach' for the 'walking wounded', staff accommodation and kitchen and dining cars.

Considerable work was involved in the

US troops ready to embark from a South Wales port prior to D-Day.

production of these vehicles by each of the railways, and at a meeting in September 1942, the Ambulance Train Committee "expressed their appreciation of the promptitude with which these matters had been dealt with by the railway companies, involving considerable detailed examination and the preparation of detailed plans".[23] The Great Western were to contribute four trains, two by July 1943, and two by the end of the year; in September it was reported that the first batch, Nos 32 and 33 had been completed, but that work on the other two had only just been authorised. No. 34 was finished on schedule, but the last, No. 35, was not ready until the end of January 1944, completion delayed by the

late arrival of a Clarkson heating boiler.

By the beginning of 1944, with preparations for D-Day well in hand, concern was expressed that there might not be enough ambulance trains to cope with the expected number of casualties likely to be sustained, once 'overseas' trains had been moved to the Continent. On 10 January 1944 it was reported that railways would be allocated the use of twelve 'home' ambulance trains. Matters were eased however, by the use of the 21 casualty evacuation trains still in existence. The situation had been made much worse by a late request by the United States Forces for a further ten trains; by early 1943 there was little chance of constructing any new stock, and little other existing rolling stock

British troops waiting to board ship at a South Wales port, in preparation for the D-Day invasion, with landing craft on the side of the ship.

owned by the four main line railways could be spared. As a result, it was decided to make use of ten 'overseas' ambulance trains which were not destined to be shipped to the Continent until D+90.

It is thought that the first of these trains was handed over at a ceremony at Swindon Works on 24 March 1943. The 14-coach train consisted of six ward cars, a carriage for sitting patients, and carriages for medical staff, nurses and attendants, two kitchen cars, a pharmacy with operating theatre, a brake and stores coach and a brake and boiler car. Stock was converted from 57ft third class passenger carriages, of both the corridor and vestibule type; coaches were turned out in a khaki colour, each with a large red cross painted prominently on the roof. Capable of holding over 300 stretcher cases, the train was officially handed over by F. W. Hawksworth on behalf of the GWR,

to Brigadier-General P. R. Hawley, representing the US Army Medical Department. As the event was filmed for the newsreel cameras, one of the USA S160 2-8-0 locomotives was, not surprisingly, chosen to head the train. Special sidings were also provided at Shrivenham, near Swindon, for the unloading of American casualties from ambulance trains before being moved to military hospitals in the surrounding area.

From the beginning of the D-Day landings to the the end of September 1944, 1,026 trains were operated, with Southampton being the main port for the reception of casualties, as had been the case in the Great War. As a result, on the Great Western, many ambulance trains ran up both the Didcot, Newbury & Southampton line, to Reading, Oxford and beyond, and the old Midland & South Western line from Andover to Cheltenham. In a memorandum prepared for the General Manager, it was recorded that in the month of June 1944, the Company ran a total of 142 loaded ambulance trains, with an additional movement of 225 empty ambulance trains. The busiest day recorded was the 12th, when 17 empty and 13 full trains were dealt with, involving the movement of 2,461 injured service personnel. In total, over 36,000 casualties were carried by the GWR in that month.[24]

Few accounts of what conditions were like on wartime ambulance trains exist, but the recollections of a former nurse on the train, Mrs A. Tallboys, illustrate some of the difficulties faced by patients and staff alike. Employed on one of the converted casualty evacuation trains, Mrs Tallboys was based at Reading West, and noted one of the biggest problems for staff was to negotiate the tangle of sidings "desperately trying to locate our set of carriages in the blackout".[25] Days were spent maintaining the high standard of cleanliness

required in a hospital situation, something difficult to achieve in a dirty railway yard! Once under way, journeys were often long and tortuous; "we never knew where we were going or how long we had before receiving our casualties".[26] Carriage doors were always kept locked since, if the train stopped at a station, people would try to board the train and Mrs Tallboys remembers "waking around midnight in Salisbury station and people frantically trying to wrench the doors open".[27] Conditions for the patients were less than satisfactory, since the casualty evacuation trains had only the most basic facilities, with the injured having to lie on stretchers for many hours at a time. Most of those moved were American troops, although British prisoners of war, liberated by the US Army were also carried. Many of the nursing staff were wartime volunteers, being drawn from organisations such as the Red Cross or St John

Paddington station in August 1943, with crowds of passengers cramming the carriages which are in wartime brown livery. (D. J. Hyde Collection)

Ambulance Brigade. On the train described by Mrs Tallboys, there were also a number of male orderlies, who assisted with any heavy lifting required.

As the campaign in Europe progressed, so the flow of ambulance trains bringing casualties from the front line continued, with a total of over 3,270 loaded and empty trains run being registered by January 1945; soon after the invasion, many of the trains destined for overseas use were shipped abroad, and the Great Western and the other railways continued to ready stock for export to the European theatre. As the advance continued, larger numbers of a further new type of passenger were carried, the prisoner of war. Although Italian prisoners had been transported in relatively small numbers, after D-Day, larger numbers of German prisoners and their escorts were moved. Evidence of the first POW trains after the invasion is recorded on 10 June with the running of two specials, carrying nearly 500 prisoners and 59 guards.[28] By the end of 1944, 6,509 prisoners had been carried by the Great Western, a total which was to be swamped in 1945, when a staggering 74,389 were moved.[29]

With all the special traffic being dealt with by the railways through this crucial period, it was inevitable that the ordinary travelling public would suffer some considerable inconvenience due to the operating difficulties experienced by the railways. As early as the summer of 1943, the public, frustrated and exhausted after four years of war, had not heeded the call by the government to stay at home. Over the August holiday period it was calculated that over 172,000 passengers were dispatched on long distance trains from Paddington alone, leading to extremely overcrowded trains. More difficult for the Company to cope with were the huge crowds which gathered at the station long before their trains were due to depart. As in previous years, the Minister of War Transport had ruled that no increase in the number of trains run could be permitted.

At the May 1944 board meeting, the General Manager had noted that the Minister of War Transport had announced that a summer service could be introduced, but "it will be necessary to withdraw without notice many more trains this summer".[30] With the Invasion of Europe in progress, there was an almost palpable feeling of relief amongst the population, particularly since air

raids had not resumed; unfortunately however, this relief was short lived, since the population and the railway companies were faced with a new and deadly hazard, the flying bomb. Less than a week after D-Day the first V1 rockets fell on the Capital, causing extensive damage. Throughout June, July and August 1944 6,725 flying bombs had been spotted over Britain, of which almost half had reached their targets. More than 5,000 people were killed in these attacks, and over 16,000 injured, leading to another voluntary evacuation by people wishing to leave the Capital.

Once again enormous pressure was put on Great Western staff, as Paddington became the departure point for many thousands of women and children wishing to escape the terror raining down from the skies above. In the first week of the flying bomb campaign, 57,038 passengers were dispatched from Paddington, although this was nothing to the week ending 25 June, when the Company moved over 97,000 women and children. Matters continued to worsen, with demand increasing still further in the next two weeks, the numbers moved peaking at 108,167 in the week ending 9 July. In addition to this unofficial evacuation traffic, the GWR also participated in a government evacuation scheme to move nearly 40,000 evacuees from the Capital on 6 July; 50 special trains were run, with another 16,758 passengers also being received by the Company from trains originating from stations on the Southern Railway.

By the end of the month the situation had not improved, and congestion was so bad on the morning of Saturday, 29 July, that management were forced to close Paddington for three hours, the first time in its history such a measure had been necessary. As had been the case earlier in the war, the Ministry of War Transport had resolutely refused to allow the running of any substantial numbers of extra trains, causing extraordinary scenes at the station. Both the approaches to the terminus and the underground stations were choked with passengers, and the situation seemed likely to get out of hand; furthermore, the potential casualties likely to be suffered if a flying bomb had hit the station were extremely high. Repeated requests to the Ministry to run extra trains were to no avail, until the General Manager reported the matter to the Prime Minister's office; finally permission was given to run an extra 63 trains allowing the enormous backlog of passengers to be dealt with.[31] The *Railway Gazette* reported that "not

United States stores vessels at anchor at Newport Docks in July 1944, with equipment bound for the Allied Forces in Europe.

withstanding its competence in other directions, the Ministry of War Transport has not shone in its dealings with passenger rail travel."[32]

It was reported that 25 locations on the Great Western had been hit by V1 flying bombs, but none had sustained serious damage; Paddington seems to have escaped relatively lightly, even though it had been the subject of attack by both incendiary and high explosive bombs in February and March the previous year. As 1944 continued however, and the threat of "Doodlebugs" receded, tension reduced considerably; holiday traffic was increased by the relaxation of restrictions on the visiting of coastal areas such as Devon and Cornwall. A much more visible sign of the easing of the war situation was the standing down of Great Western Railway Home Guard Units; the December 1944 issue of the Company magazine gave accounts of farewell

United States invasion craft moored in Penarth Docks, awaiting the beginning of 'Operation Overlord' in June 1944.

parades held by units from all parts of the system. The General Manager, Sir James Milne, sent a personal message to all those who had volunteered for service stating that every man "may well feel proud that in the time of need he was not found wanting".[33]

The end of the blackout at Great Western stations and depots was yet another milestone on the road to full recovery after the exertions of the war period; reporting the news, the *GWR Magazine* noted that no one would welcome the end of this wartime measure more than the railway worker, whether they were shunter, footplatemen or station staff. There was it reported "a special gaiety in the way certain artisans at Paddington were officiating as undertakers to the dim-out."[34]

Within a month however, there was more momentous and consequential news to celebrate, that of victory in Europe; to mark the occasion, the hooter at Swindon Works was blown for a full minute at the beginning of the public holiday called on 8 May 1945. The General Manager, in a message to staff, said that "During the past five and a half years

the Great Western Railway has played a very important part in maintaining the flow of essential war materials on behalf of the Government."[35] This had only been possible he stated, by the loyal cooperation of the staff; he also mentioned the fact that over 15,000 employees were still serving with the forces, and, he added "we also recall with a deep sense of gratitude the names of those who have sacrificed their lives".[36] Figures released at the end of the war show that 573 staff were known to have lost their lives in action, with another 130 being reported as missing; 274 were taken prisoner. At home, 68 staff were killed in air raids, with a further 241 being injured; off duty, another 88 were killed, and 255 were injured.

VE Day was followed in September by victory over Japan and VJ Day. The *GWR Magazine* reported that the complete end of the war should have been the occasion for even more celebration than the end of hostilities in Europe, but that any festivities were "tempered by the intrusion of certain graver intrusions...prompted by the awe-inspiring colourings which heralded the dawn of

The stand-down parade of the Swindon Works Home Guard Battalion, with a pannier tank in the background, whistling as the salute is taken.

The busy scene at Paddington in August 1944 with enormous queues of passengers waiting to enter the station.

the atomic age".[37] Although the end of the war led to a sharp decrease in the number of special trains run by the Company for the government, traffic was still heavy. Yet another new strain on the system was the handling of special trains carrying 'demobbed' service personnel home; in October and November 1945 a total of 134,993 such passengers were carried in 163 special trains. Peace also brought additional business generated by increased numbers of military staff being granted more leave, leading to large numbers of personnel returning to their depots on Sunday evenings.

In the first post-war annual general meeting of the Great Western Railway, held on 6 March 1946, the Chairman, Viscount Portal, conceded that the Company had much work to do to restore prewar standards; the renewal of locomotive and carriages curtailed during the war would occupy the works for some years to come, and the restoration and acceleration of train services was to be introduced as quickly as was possible. Two years after the end of the war it was noted that in 1939 the reputation of the railway "stood higher than ever before. To restore that high standard has been the Railway's first and greatest objective...since the war ended."[38]

The years following the war were to see many changes, not least proposals to nationalise the Big Four railways, an idea which was not universally welcomed by the fiercely independent Great Western; our story is not concerned with the fighting of that particular battle, but has hopefully chronicled some of the achievements of those thousands of men and women who remained behind to carry on. Their bravery, determination and sheer hard work in the most difficult of conditions helped the Great Western Railway play its part in the final victory won by the Allies in 1945.

References

Introduction

1 *It Can Now Be Revealed* British Railways Press
   Office. 1945
2 *GWR Magazine*. March 1938. p91
3 *GWR Docks*. GWR Paddington. p330
4 Ibid. p99
5 *GWR Magazine* March 1939. p105

The Exodus

 1 *GWR Magazine* 1940 p79
 2 *GWR Magazine* 1939 p393
 3 Statutory Rules & Orders 1939 No.1197
 4 Bell, R. *History of the British Railways During the War*.
    1946 p9
 5 *GWR Magazine* October 1939 p393
 6 GWR Circular London Evacuation Scheme No.2 also
    Altered Working of Through Passenger Trains
    August 1939
 7 Quoted in: Knox, C. *The Unbeaten Track* 1944 p20
 8 *GWR Magazine* November 1938 p458
 9 Knox. Ibid p22
10 Knox. Ibid p25
11 Harrisson, T. *Living Through the Blitz*. 1990 p34.
12 *Railway Gazette* 15 Sept. 1939 p366
13 GWR CME Dept. Swindon, Circular No. 5969
    25 Oct. 1939
14 *GWR Magazine* October 1939 p432
15 Recollections of Mrs J. H. Newell, August 1939.
    (GWR Museum Collection)
16 *GWR Magazine* April 1940 p122
17 Ibid p122
18 GWR Circular August 1939 Ibid. p161
19 *GWR Magazine* November 1939 p459
20 GWR National Emergency Timetables commencing
    25 September 1939
21 Ibid
22 *Railway Magazine* December 1939 p431
23 Minutes of REC Passenger Superintendents Committee
    2 October 1939 p7
24 Ibid p8
25 REC Passenger Superintendents Committee
    19 September 1939 p2
26 Ibid p2
27 Ibid p2
28 Ibid p3
29 *GWR Magazine* January 1940 p27
30 Statutory Rules & Orders 1939 No. 1085
31 GWR Circular: 4 September 1939
32 Ibid
33 *GWR Magazine* March 1940 p83
34 *GWR Magazine* March 1940 p84
35 Ibid p84
36 Ibid p84
37 GWR Circular No. 59500 Swindon 12 September 1939
38 Ibid p88

Air Raid Precautions

 1 *GWR Magazine* January 1940 p19
 2 *GWR Magazine* February 1940 p64
 3 Ibid p64
 4 GWR Timetable: London Evacuation Scheme No. 4
    February 1940. (D. J. Hyde Collection)
 5 For Further Detail see: "Wartime Storage of Pictures from
    the National Gallery" Transactions of Hon. Society of
    Cymmorodorion. 1946
 6 Harrisson p21.
 7 Harrisson p25
 8 Ibid. p25
 9 GWR Board Minutes 20 January 1939
10 Ibid
11 *GWR Magazine* July 1939 p292
12 GWR Board Minutes 5 October 1939
13 GWR Board Minutes 20 January 1939
14 GWR Circular No. 3451. GMO Paddington 28 July 1937
15 Ibid
16 Swindon Communist Party Handbill, 4 August 1937.
    (GWR Museum Collection)
17 Harrisson Ibid p24
18 *GWR Magazine* June 1938 p242
19 Ibid
20 Ibid p243

21 ARP: Notes of Lectures on Anti-Gas Training. GWR pamphlet.1938 p4
22 Ibid p4.
23 *GWR Magazine* February 1939 p114
24 *GWR Magazine* March 1940 p92
25 GWR Circular: CME Dept. *Examiners Handlamps*: Swindon 21 September 1939
26 GWR Circular: Paddington 26 September 1939
27 Ibid
28 GWR Circular CMM Dept. Swindon 26 September 1939
29 *Railway Gazette* 6 October 1939 p451
30 *GWR Magazine* November 1939 p453
31 *Railway Gazette* 17 November 1939
32 GWR Circular No. 5977 CME Dept. Swindon 20 November 1939
33 GWR Circular No. 5150/ARP SOTL Paddington 27 November 1939
34 GWR Circular No. 5968 CME Dept. Swindon 20 October 1939
35 *Railway Gazette*, 17 November 1939 p651
36 GWR Circular No. 3508 GMO Paddington *Air Raid Precautions* 26 September 1939
37 GWR Circular: No.3508 GMO Paddington *Air Raid Precautions* 16 October 1939 p2
38 Ibid p3
39 GWR Circular No.5956 CME Dept. & SOTL Office *Air Raid Warning Arrangements*: October 1939
40 Ibid
41 *Notice to Passengers Following Air Raid Warnings* Undated Handbill. (GWR Museum Collection)
42 *GWR Magazine* November 1939. p453
43 GWR Circular No.5956. Ibid
44 GWR Circular CME Dept. *Anti Glare Screens for Locomotives* Swindon 28 August 1939
45 GWR Circular; CME Dept. *Anti Glare Screens on Locomotives* Swindon 7 September 1939
46 *GWR Magazine* March 1940. p94
47 *Swindon Evening Advertiser:* 29 January 1940
48 Hosegood, J. *'Wartime' Great Western Echo* Winter 1991 p22
49 *Railway Gazette* 2 February 1940 p165

Operation Dynamo

1 *Railway Gazette* November 24 1939 p676
2 *Railway Gazette* 24 November 1939 p677
3 *GWR Magazine* April 1940 p127
4 Ibid.
5 GWR Locomotive Committee Minutes 14 December 1939
6 GWR Locomotive Committee Minutes 5 October 1939
7 *Railway Gazette* December 6 1939 p735
8 *GWR Magazine* April 1940 p128
9 *Railway Gazette* November 3 1939
10 *Chronicle of the Second World War* p75
11 *Dunkirk & The Great Western*. GWR Paddington, 1946.
12 Quoted in: Plummer. R. *The Ships that Saved an Army* PSL 1990. p14
13 *Dunkirk & The Great Western*. GWR 1946 p.14
14 *Dunkirk & The Great Western*. Ibid p10
15 Quoted in: Knox, C. *The Unbeaten Track*. Cassell. 1944 p45
16 Ibid. p39
17 Copy of letter from Minister of Shipping dated 17 June 1940. (GWR Museum Collection)
18 *Dunkirk & The Great Western*. Ibid p23
19 *Dunkirk & The Great Western* Ibid. p31
20 GWR Circular: SOTL Paddington: 26 May 1940 (D. J. Hyde Collection)
21 *GWR Magazine* July 1940 p207
22 *Dunkirk & the Great Western* Ibid p35
23 *GWR Magazine* July 1940 p203
24 General Manager's Report to the Board 28 June 1940 PRO RAIL 250/776
25 For further detail see: *GWR Magazine* August 1940 p232-3
26 See Lucking, J. *The GWR at Weymouth*. P154-155
27 General Manager's Report to the Board: 28 June 1940 PRO RAIL 250/776
28 *GWR Magazine* August 1940 p.235
29 General Manager's Report to the Board 28 July 1940 PRO RAIL 250/776
30 Ibid. p236

Under Siege

1 Quoted in: *Chronicle of the Second World War* p97
2 *GWR Magazine* July 1940. p211
3 Mackay. E. A. *The History of the Wiltshire Home Guard*. Wilts. County Terr. Association.1946 p7
4 GWR Circular No.284 *Local Defence Volunteer Corps* Paddington: GMO 22 May 1940
5 Correspondence File: GWR *Protection of Railways in Time of War* (GWR Museum Collection)
6 GWR Circular No.3600. *Home Guard* GMO Paddington, 14 September 1940
7 Macka. E. A. *The History of the Wiltshire Home Guard*. Wilts County Terr. Assn. 1946. p77
8 Ibid
9 *GWR Magazine* September 1940 p257
10 Ibid
11 GWR Correspondence File: *Home Guard: Units & Categories Q.E. 30th June 1943*. (GWR Museum Collection)
12 *Railway Gazette* 21 June 1940 p873
13 *GWR Magazine* July 1940 p218
14 GWR Circular No.6047a *Removal of Direction Signs* CME Dept. Swindon 10 July 1940
15 Ibid
16 *Railway Gazette* 4 October 1940 p346
17 *GWR Magazine* November 1940 p317
18 Quoted in: *Railway Gazette* 28 June 1940 p902
19 Ibid
20 Ministry of Home Security: ARP Training Pamphlet No.3 *Advising the Public in the Event of Invasion* HMSO 1941. p2
21 Railway Executive Committee: Notice. *Duty of Staff in the Event of Invasion. N.D*
22 Ibid
23 GWR Circular *Warning* CME Office Swindon. 28 October 1940
24 GWR Circular *Railway Service* Identification Badges. GMO Paddington July 1940
25 Ibid
26 Letter: CME Swindon to Divisional Superintendents. 26 August 1940
27 Letter: CME Swindon to Divisional Superintendents. 3 Jan 1941
28 John, E. *Timetable For Victory*. British Railways. 1946. p95
29 GWR Circular. CME Swindon *Immobilisation of Cranes: Civil Defence* 24 February 1941

30 GWR New Work Order 6023/13/82 15 June 1940. (GWR Museum Collection)
31 GWR New Work Order 6043/6/85 26 June 1940
32 Letter: GWR CME Office Swindon: *Immobilisation of Railway Workshops* 15 July 1942
33 Letter: GWR SOTL to F. W. Hawksworth. Swindon, 22 August 1941
34 Ibid
35 Quoted in *Chronicle of the Second World War* p113
36 Album of photographs: Newton Abbot 20.8.40. (GW Trust Collection)
37 See: Kingdom. A. R. *The Newton Abbot Blitz* OPC 1978. p6-7
38 GWR Circular: *Gift of Aircraft to the Royal Air Force* GMO 21 August 1940
39 *GWR Magazine* September 1940 p265
40 *GWR Magazine* October 1940 p286
41 *GWR Magazine* June 1941 p145

Under Attack: Part 1

1 *GWR Magazine* January 1941 p3
2 Ibid
3 John, E. *Timetable to Victory British Railways*, 1946.   p106
4 *General Analysis of Reports of Damage & Delay* REC Correspondence: 16 July 1943. p2
5 Ibid. p1
6 GWR Circular No.3601: GMO ARP: *Action to be taken by staff on receipt of warnings* 7 October 1940
7 GWR Circular No.5142: GMO SOTL *Air Raid Warning Arrangements: Instructions to Drivers...etc.* 12 October 1939
8 General Manager's Report to the Board 28 June 1940 PRO RAIL 250/776
9 GWR Circular: CME Swindon *Notice to Enginemen* 8 March 1940
10 GWR Circular: CME Swindon *Maximum Speed* 14 March 1941
11 General Manager's Report to the Board: 28 June 1940 PRO RAIL 250/776
12 General Manager's Report to the Board: 16 February 1940 PRO RAIL 250/776
13 Ibid. 4 Oct. 1940
14 GWR Circular: CME Dept. *ARP Train Lighting: Blinds* 17 May 1940
15 GWR Circular: CME Dept. *Train Lighting etc.*
16 GWR Circular: CME Dept. *Glare from Locomotive Fireboxes* 11 July 1940
17 GWR Circular: CME Dept. *Application and Maintenance of Detector Paint of Locomotives* 13 August 1940
18 GWR Circular GMO *ARP Anti-Gas Measures* 9 April 1941
19 Ibid
20 Awards to Railwaymen for Gallantry: Railway Executive. (GWR Museum Collection)
21 General Manager's Report to the Board 4 October 1940 PRO RAIL 250/776
22 Ibid
23 GWR Letter: CME Dept. *Air Raid Precautions . . . Continuance of Work during Air Raids* 9 October 1940
24 Minutes of Meeting: Paddington 20 November 1940: Re *Roof Spotting Arrangements*. (GWR Museum Collection)
25 Letter to Divisional Superintendents 14 November 1940

26 General manager's Report to the Board 29 November 1940 PRO RAIL 250/776
27 Glover, M. *Invasion Scare 1940* Leo Cooper. 1990 p168
28 See. Harrison. D. *Salute to Snow Hill* Barbyn Press. 1982 p51
29 For further details see: Underdown. H. J. *The Bristol Blitz* Bristol City Council. 1942.
30 Calder A. *The Peoples War* Pimlico Press. 1992. p172
31 *GWR Magazine* May 1941. p128
32 Letter: From F. R. Potter SOTL Paddington 26 December 1940. (GWR Museum Collection)
33 Ibid
34 GWR Circular: Store Supdt. Swindon. *Sandbags* 28 August 1941
35 GWR Circular No.6104: CME Dept. Swindon: *Maintenance of Stirrup Pumps* January 1941
36 Calder. A. Ibid. p165
37 GWR *Report of Collision, Derailment, Fire, Flood, etc.* 10 January 1941 (Ian Coulson Collection)
38 Ministry of Transport Report: *Great Western Railway* 7 December 1940
39 *Railway Gazette*: 29 November 1940
40 *Railway Gazette*: 20 December 1940

Under Attack: Part 2

1 General Manager's Report to the Board: 31 January 1941. PRO RAIL 250/776
2 *Railway Gazette*: 3 January 1941 p1
3 Ibid. p23
4 See: Winstone R. *Bristol in the 1940s*. Burleigh Press. 1961 p22
5 *GWR Magazine*: September 1939. p380
6 GWR *Report of Collision, Derailment, Fire, Flood, etc.* 10 March 1941. (Ian Coulson Collection)
7 GWR *Report of Collision, Derailment, Fire, Flood, etc.* 1 April 1941. (Ian Coulson Collection)
8 *GWR Magazine*: May 1941 p.130
9 General Manager's Report to the Board: 21 March 1941. PRO RAIL 250/776
10 *Railway Gazette* 8 November 1940
11 Ibid
12 Harrison. D. *Return to Snow Hill*. Barbyn Press 1982 p51-53
13 *GWR Magazine* December 1940. p343
14 *GWR Magazine* February 1941. p43
15 Ibid
16 General Manager's Report to the Board: 25 April 1941
17 John, E. *Timetable for Victory: British Railways*. 1946. p121
18 Information of incidents during this period supplied from material kindly loaned by Mr Ian Coulson
19 General Manager's Report to the Board: 27 June 1941. PRO RAIL 250/776
20 *GWR Magazine* October 1940. p293
21 Awards to Railwaymen for Gallantry. (GWR Museum Collection)
22 General Manager's Report to the Board: 27 June 1941. PRO RAIL 250/776
23 *GWR Magazine* July 1941 p175
24 General Manager's Report to the Board: 25 July 1941. PRO RAIL 250/776
25 *Facts about British Railways* British Railways. 1941

Is Your Journey Really Necessary?

1   See: Lewis. P. *The Peoples War.* Methuen. 1986. p186
2   *GWR Magazine.* November 1941. p277
3   Ibid
4   Ibid
5   *Facts About British Railways in Wartime*: British Railways Press Office. 1943 p21
6   See: Various General Manager's Reports to the Board: PRO RAIL 250/776
7   *Railway Gazette* 21 March 1941. p340
8   Ibid
9   Reproduced in *Railway Gazette* 5 December 1941
10 Ibid
11 *GWR Magazine* September 1941. p232
12 General Manager's Report to the Board: 3 October 1941
13 General Manager's Report to the Board: 28 November 1941
14 Quoted in: General Manager's Report to the Board: 19 December 1941
15 General Manager's Report to the Board: 27 March 1942. PRO RAIL 250/776
16 General Manager's Report to the Board: 31 January 1941. PRO RAIL 250/776
17 Ibid 3 October 1941
18 Ibid
19 Ibid 24 October 1941
20 Ibid
21 *Railway Gazette*; 8 May 1941. p542
22 Bell. R, 'History of British Railways During the War'. *Railway Gazette.* 1946. p65
23 GWR Circular: CME Dept. Swindon *Antimacassars...* 5 February 1941
24 GWR Circular No.6290: CME E. Dept. Swindon *Provision of Non-Smoking Accommodation* 11 July 1942
25 Bell. R. Ibid p65
26 General Manager's Report to the Board: 29 May 1942. PRO RAIL 250/776
27 *Railway Gazette* 24 April 1942 p498
28 Ibid. 22 May 1942. p600
29 General Manager's Report to the Board 30 January 1942. PRO RAIL 250/776
30 *Report to the Minister of War Transport on Preparations Made by Railways to Cope with Traffic Winter 1942-3 and further Assistance Required.*: Railway Executive Committee. June 1942
31 General Manager's Report to the Board: 2 October 1942. PRO RAIL 250/776
32 *GWR Magazine* November 1942. p186
33 GWR Circular: CME Dept. Swindon: 12 May 1941. *Train Lavatory Equipment*
34 *Railway Gazette*: 2 January 1942. p35
35 General Manager's Report to the Board. 19 December 1941. PRO RAIL 250/776
36 *Railway Gazette*: 2 January 1942. p34
37 *GWR Magazine* September 1942. p160
38 *GWR Magazine* October 1942. p169
39 GWR Circular: CME Dept. Swindon. *Anti-Gossip Notices* 25 August 1941
40 General Manager's Report to the Board 29 October 1943. PRO RAIL 250/776
41 Ibid
42 *Facts about Railways in Wartime* British Railways. 1943. p39
43 Report of Derailment of 1.30pm Workpeoples Train at Margam Moors. 3.12.41. GWR CME Dept. Swindon. 15 December 1941
44 General Manager's Report to the Board 27 June 1941. PRO RAIL 250/776
45 Ibid 24 October 1941
46 Calder A. *The Peoples War.* Pimlico Press. 1992. p286
47 GWR Report of Divisional Superintendnent Bristol. 3 September 1942 (D. J. Hyde Collection)

Salvage and Staff

1   *Join The GWR Salvage Corps*: GWR Paddington. August 1940
2   Ibid
3   *GWR Magazine.* December 1940. p342
4   GWR Circular No. 5971: CME Department. *Iron & Steel Scrap* 30 October 1939
5   General Manager's Report to the Board. 26 January 1940. PRO RAIL 250/776
6   GWR Circular No. 6039. CME Dept. Swindon *Demand for Scrap Metal* 25 June 1940
7   GWR Circular No. 6039a CME Dept. Swindon *Demand for Scrap Metal* 6 August 1941
8   Letter: From Chief Engineer, Aldermaston. To CME Swindon. 17 April 1942
9   *GWR Magazine* January 1942. p8
10 GWR Circular. No.5992a Stores Superintendent. Swindon. *Salvage: GWR Campaign* 30 June 1941
11 *GWR Magazine* February 1942. p39
12 GWR Circular: CME Dept. Swindon. *Supplies of Timber.* 7 February 1940
13 Circular: RCH PO/CL 82. *Timber for Railway Wagons* 8 April 1940
14 GWR Circular: CME Dept. *Washing of Towels.* 21 May 1941
15 GWR Circular: CME Dept. Swindon *Recovery of Oily and Greasy Rags.* 23 June 1942
16 GWR Circular: Chief Goods Manager. Paddington *Shortage of Ropes* 23 September 1939
17 *GWR Magazine* January 1942. p8
18 *GWR Magazine* February 1942. p39
19 Ibid March 1942 p53
20 GWR Circular: CME Department. Swindon. *Economy in the Use of Stationery.* 25 October 1939
21 General Manager's Report to the Board. 28 January 1944. PRO RAIL 250/776
22 GWR Circular: CME Dept. Swindon. *Waste of Fuel Order 1942* 22 July 1942
23 GWR Circular: GMO Paddington. *Economy in the Use of Fuel* October 1942
24 *GWR Magazine* November 1943. p165
25 Ibid December 1943. p182
26 Letter: From F. W. Hawksworth: To Divisional Superintendents: Swindon 12 November 1942
27 Report to Minister of War Transport on Preparations made by Railways to Cope with Traffic, Winter 1942–3. Railway Executive Committee. June 1942
28 Calder. Ibid p267
29 GWR Circular: CME Swindon: *National Service Act 1939.* 20 November 1939

30 *GWR Magazine* January 1942. p9
31 GWR *Staff Serving With The Forces or Civilian Defence Services* Form 4901-4 (GWR Museum Collection)
32 *GWR Magazine* February 1942. p31
33 GWR Circular: CME Dept. *Retirement of Staff 60 years of Age.* 20 December 1940
34 GWR Circular No. 6132: CME Swindon. *Footplate Staff Position* 2 May 1941
35 Letter: GWR CME Department Swindon. *Recruitment of Engine Cleaners.* 11 August 1942
36 GWR Circular. CME Dept. Swindon. *Employment of Young Persons...* 10 December 1942
37 GWR Circular. CME Dept. Swindon. *Manpower Requirements* 25 March 1941
38 *GWR Magazine* March 1941. p73
39 Ibid
40 General Manager's Report to the Board: 21 March 1941. PRO RAIL 250/776
41 Leaflet: *Heavy Parcels Cause Delay* British Railways. N.D. (GWR Museum Collection)
42 *GWR Magazine* June 1941. p146
43 *Railway Gazette* 15 August 1941. p173
44 *GWR Magazine* August 1941. p233
45 *GWR Magazine* July 1941. p183
46 Letter: GWR Staff Office Aldermaston. 30 June 1942
47 GWR Circular: CME Dept. Swindon. *Recruitment of Female Engine Cleaners* 17 July 1942
48 GWR Letter: F. W. Hawksworth to Divisional Superintendents *Operating Staff Requirements* 17 July 1942
49 GWR Letter: F. W. Hawksworth to Divisional Superintendents. 6 August 1942
50 GWR Circular: SOTL *Cleaning of Carriages* 10 March 1942
51 GWR New Work Order No.1452/13/82 16 July 1943
52 Minutes of GWR Staff Committee 6 December 1943
53 GWR Circular: CME Dept. Swindon. *Position for Engine Power* 22 August 1941
54 Memorandum of Meetings held 29/30 December 1941. To Discuss Position for Locomotive Power
55 GWR Circular: CME Dept. Swindon: *Use of Green Arrow...* 21 January 1942

Swindon Works at War

1 Cook. K. J. *Swindon Steam 1921–1951* Ian Allan. 1974 p130. Also Peck. A. The Great Western at Swindon Works OPC 1983 p227
2 Cook. K.J. Ibid. p130
3 Pratt. E. *British Railways and the Great War.* Selwyn & Blunt. 1921 p600
4 N.W.O. 5164/13/82 18 May 1939
5 N.W.O. 5379/13/82/82
6 N.W.O. 5952/13/82 1 July 1940
7 N.W.O. 5116/13/82 5 May 1939
8 N.W.O. 5362/13/82 1 September 1939
9 N.W.O. 6058/13/82 2 July 1940
10 *GWR Magazine* May 1943. p70
11 GWR Circular: CME Dept. Swindon. *Fire Hydrant Covers* 24 June 1942
12 *Swindon Evening Advertiser* 8 May 1945. p3
13 General Manager's Report to the Board: 2 October 1942
14 *Swindon Evening Advertiser* 29 April 1986.: Letter by A. L. Skeates
15 *It Can Now Be Revealed* British Railways 1945 p13
16 N.W.O. 8395/96/01 26 May 1942
17 N.W.O. 8364/96/01 5 March 1942
18 N.W.O. 8131/96/01 7 March 1942
19 N.W.O. 8327/97/21 18 February 1942
20 N.W.O. 8369/96/01 20 May 1942
21 N.W.O. 8107/96/01 20 December 1941
22 N.W.O. 835/96/01 24 February 1942
23 N.W.O. 9396/96/01 13 February 1942
24 N.W.O. 2061/94/86 11 December 1943
25 N.W.O. 1927/94/86 18 November 1943
26 *It Can Now be Revealed* Ibid. p15
27 GWR Locomotive Committee Minutes. 23 May 1940
28 Ministry of Supply: Letter 11 December 1942
29 Ibid
30 GWR Circular: CME Dept. Swindon. 17 December 1940
31 GWR Circular CME Dept. *Smoking in Offices & Workshops* 18 March 1941
32 GWR Circular. CME Dept. *Office Messengers* 20 May 1942
33 GWR Circular No. 3619. GMO Paddington *Sale of Coal to the Company's Staff* 26 May 1941.
34 GWR Staff Office, Swindon: *Staff Receiving Company's Coal* 24 May 1941. (GWR Museum Collection)
35 Memorandum of a meeting of Superintendents: Friday, 2 July 1942. Swindon
36 GWR Circular: CME Dept. *Engines Overdue...* 24 August 1943
37 Memorandum of a meeting of Superintendents: Thursday, 1 June 1944. Swindon
38 *GWR Magazine* October 1940. p295
39 *Railway Gazette* 4 July 1941. p16
40 General Manager's Report to the Board 1 October 1941 PRO RAIL 250/776
41 GWR Locomotive Committee Minutes 5 October 1939
42 For Further Detail see: *Locomotives of the GWR Part 14.* Railway and Correspondence Society. 1994
43 Railway Correspondence and Travel Society: *Stock Book* June 1946. p75
44 Ibid. p59–60
45 Information kindly supplied by Mr Bill Peto, Great Western Society
46 GWR Circular No. 6251: CME Dept. Swindon. *Painting of Locomotives* 3 April 1942.
47 GWR Circular. No.6259: CMM Dept. Swindon. *Painting of Carriage Stock* 20 April 1942
48 GWR Swindon: Drawing Office *New Diesel Rail Cars* 8 April 1940
49 Ibid
50 Letter: C. B. Collett to Chief Goods Manager Paddington 10 December 1940
51 Ibid
52 GWR Circular: CME Dept. Swindon. *Wagons awaiting or under Repair* 11 September 1942
53 GWR Circular: CMM Dept. Swindon. *Painting of Wagon Stock* 30 May 1942

Prelude to D-Day

1 Quoted in: *It Can Now Be Revealed* British Railways. 1945 p38
2 *GWR Docks* GWR Paddington. 1938. p7

3 *GWR Magazine* January 1940. p7
4 General Manager's Report to the Board: 26 January 1940. PRO RAIL 250/776
5 Ibid 30 October 1942
6 Knox C. *The Unbeaten Track*. Cassell. 1944. p131
7 Ibid 25 April 1941
8 Ibid 17 December 1943
9 GWR New Work Order: 8368/6/92. 30 March 1942
10 Knox. C. Ibid. p129-130
11 General Manager's Report to the Board: 20 February 1943. PRO RAIL 250/776
12 Bell. *'History of British Railways During the War'* Railway Gazette. 1946. p152
13 Knox. Ibid. p135
14 McGivern C. *Junction X* Baynard Press. November 1944. p29
15 *Railway Gazette* 19 June 1942. p672
16 General Manager's Report to the Board: 21 February 1941. PRO RAIL 250/776
17 GWR Circular: CME Dept. *Distribution of Brake Vans* 12 August 1943
18 GWR Circular No. 6340: CME Dept. Swindon *Banana Vans* 26 November 1942
19 GWR N.W.O. No. 5845. 14 March 1940
20 GWR N.W.O. No. 5849 16 April 1940
21 GWR Circular: CME Dept. Swindon. *Control of Brake Vans* 20 October 1942
22 GWR Circular: CME Dept. Swindon. 6 January 1941
23 GWR Circular: CME Dept. Swindon. *Examination of Wagons* 14 January 1941
24 Ibid
25 GWR Circular: District Superintendents Office Bristol 31 July 1940. (D. J. Hyde Collection)
26 GWR Circular: SOTL Paddington. *Movement of SIP Grenades* 28 October 1941
27 GWR Circular: CME Dept. Swindon: *Damage to Warflats* 20 April 1942
28 GWR DSO Bristol: Annual Report for 1942. 22 January 1943. (D. J. Hyde Collection)
29 GWR Locomotive Committee Minutes 23 May 1940
30 General Manager's Report to the Board: 27 March 1942. PRO RAIL 250/776
31 GWR Circular: CME Dept. Swindon. *Painting of Inflammable Liquid Tank Wagons* 8 July 1940
32 Report to the Minister of War Transport on Preparations made by Railways to Cope with Traffic Winter 1942/3: Railway Executive Committee. June 1942
33 Minutes of GWR Board 1 October 1943
34 Ibid 25 June 1943
35 Ibid 28 May 1943
36 General Manager's Report to the Board: 21 March 1941 PRO RAIL 250/776
37 Quoted in: *Chronicle of the Second World War*. Longman. 1990. p251
38 DSO Bristol: Annual Departmental Report for 1942. 22 January 1943. (D. J. Hyde Collection)
39 General Manager's Report to the Board: 27 November 1942 PRO RAIL 250/776
40 GWR Report of Collision, Derailment, Fire, Flood, etc. 1 April 1944. (Ian Coulson Collection)
41 *GWR Magazine* January 1943. p2
42 Minutes of a Meeting of Superintendents at Swindon: 2 July 1943
43 For further details see: Higgins. R. N. *Over Here The Story of*

the S160 Big Jim Publishing. 1980
44 Minutes of a Meeting of Superintendents at Swindon. 3 February 1944
45 Ibid
46 Minutes of a Meeting of Superintendents held at Swindon. 12 October 1944
47 Ibid
48 *GWR Magazine* December 1943. p182
49 Ibid

To Victory

1 GWR N.W.O. 8820/82/89 23 June 1942
2 Information supplied courtesy of Mr Tony Brookman
3 GWR N.W.O. 8820/82/89 16 February 1943
4 GWR N.W.O. 9779/82/89 16 February 1943
5 GWR N.W.O. 2500/82/89 11 March 1944
6 GWR N.W.O. 4726/82/89 22 March 1946
7 Quoted in: Carter E. F. *Railways in Wartime* Muller. 1964 p.173
8 General Manager's Report to the Board: 28 November 1941. PRO RAIL 250/776
9 Ibid 29 January 1943
10 Ibid 26 March 1943
11 Ibid 1 October 1943
12 Minutes of a Meeting of Superintendents held at Swindon 12 October 1944
13 Gibbs K. *Great Western Apprentice in Steam* OPC 1988
14 GWR Circular: Swindon Works. *Italian Prisoners* 28 October 1944
15 GWR Circular: GMO Paddington: *Security* 10 March 1944
16 Ibid
17 Mackay E. A. *The History of the Wiltshire Home Guard* Wiltshire Regiment. 1946 p128
18 *GWR Magazine* January 1946. p10
19 *GWR Magazine* July 1944. p101
20 Ibid
21 Statistics courtesy: D. J. Hyde Collection
22 Minutes of Ambulance Trains Committee. 3 September 1942
23 Ibid. 17 September 1942
24 Memorandum to the General Manager: *Military (Personnel) Special Trains* 3 July 1944. (D. J. Hyde Collection)
25 Recollections courtesy of Mrs A. Tallboys
26 Ibid
27 Ibid
28 GWR Statistics: *Prisoner of War Special Trains* June 1944 (D. J. Hyde Collection)
29 GWR Statistics: Comparison 1944–1945 (D. J. Hyde Collection)
30 General Manager's Report to the Board: 26 May 1944 PRO RAIL 250/776
31 General Manager's Report to the Board: 28 July 1944. PRO RAIL 250/776
32 *Railway Gazette* 4 August 1944. p101
33 *GWR Magazine* December 1944. p187
34 Ibid May 1945. p73
35 Ibid June 1945 p89
36 Ibid
37 Ibid September 1945. p137
38 Barman C. *Next Station* Allen & Unwin. 1947. p6

Sources and Bibliography

A variety of sources have been consulted in the research for this book, an important record was the monthly reports of the General Manager to the GWR board, which revealed much information not previously published. This source, and other important archive material, are housed at the Public Record Office at Kew. Much material has also been drawn from official company sources such as handbills, circulars, reports and timetables, although the secret nature of much of the work done by railways during the war has left a somewhat patchy record; I am grateful to those institutions and individuals who allowed access to their collections of such items.

An useful source of information as always has been the *GWR Magazine*, although as the war continued, articles grew shorter and less specific due to the the sensitive nature of the subject matter. Surprisingly, the *Railway Gazette* often gave more information on Great Western matters than the company's own journal, and also provided valuable details of the work done by the railways during this period. The *Railway Magazine* and the *Railway Observer* (RCTS) were also consulted.

Unless otherwise indicated, all photographs are from the collection of the GWR Museum, Swindon. Specific items are noted in the references for each chapter, but listed here are some of the general publications consulted during the research for this book:

Bell, R. H*istory of British Railways During the War 1939–1945*. (Railway Gazette 1946)

Belsey, J. & Reid, H. *West at War* (Redcliffe Press 1990)

Bryant, A. *The Turn of the Tide* (Collins 1958)

British War Production (The Times 1945)

Calder, A. *The Peoples War* (Pimlico 1992)

Green, B. *Britain at War* (Coombe Books 1993)

Harrisson, T. *Living Through the Blitz* (Penguin 1990)

John, E. *Timetable For Victory* (British Railways 1946)

Knox, C. *The Unbeaten Track* (Cassell 1944)

Nock, O. S. *History of the Great Western Railway Vol. III* (Ian Allan 1967)

Peck, A. S. *The Great Western at Swindon Works* (OPC 1983 & 1994)

Railway Correspondence & Travel Society: *The Locomotives of the Great Western Railway*: (Various volumes)

Semmens, P. H*istory of the Great Western Railway: 3* (Allen & Unwin 1985)

Waller, J. & Vaughan, M. *Blitz: the Civilian War 1940–45* (Optima 1990)

Wicks, B. *No Time to Wave Goodbye* (Bloomsbury Books, 1989)

Wildish, G. N. *Engines of War* (Ian Allan 1946)

Index